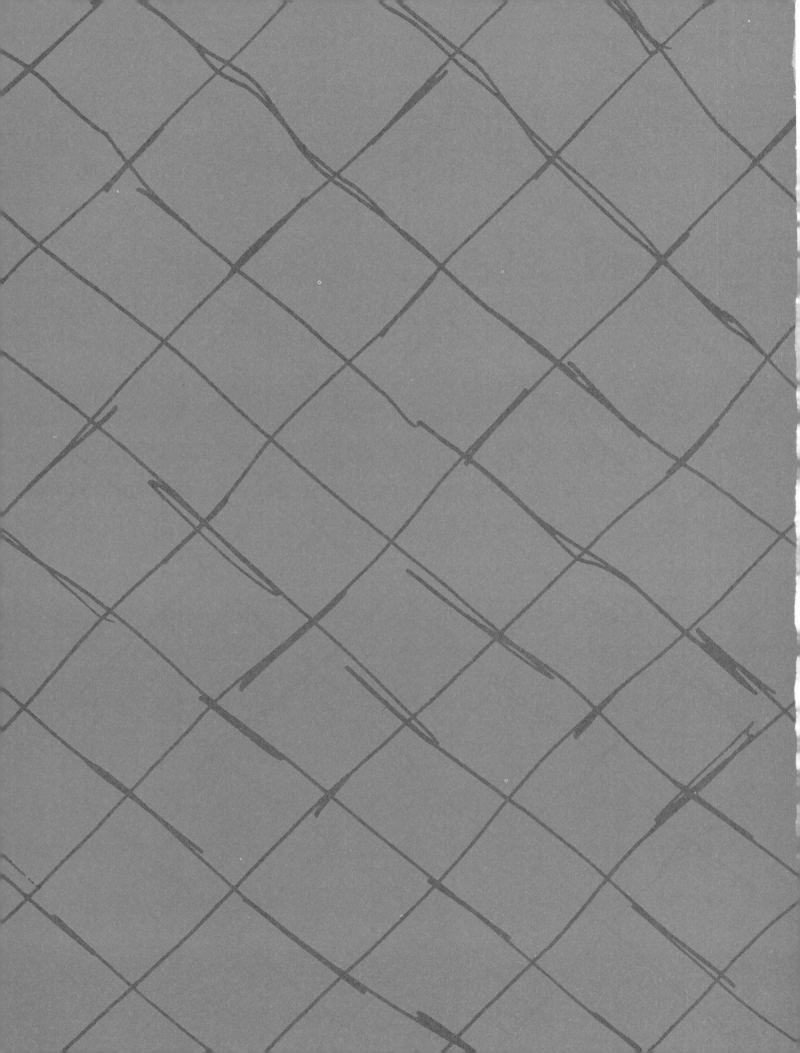

ARATA ISOZAKI

ARCHITECTURE 1960–1990

ARATA ISOZAKI
ARCHITECTURE 1960–1990

Preface by Richard Koshalek

Essays by David B. Stewart and Hajime Yatsuka

THE MUSEUM OF CONTEMPORARY ART, LOS ANGELES

RIZZOLI
NEW YORK

First published in the United States of America in 1991 by
RIZZOLI INTERNATIONAL PUBLICATIONS, INC.
300 Park Avenue South, New York, NY 10010

Arata Isozaki: Architecture 1960–1990 is published on the occasion of
the exhibition organized by The Museum of Contemporary Art
(MOCA), Los Angeles, the Centre de Création Industrielle,
Centre Georges Pompidou, Paris, and the Asahi Shimbun, Tokyo.
Following its presentation at MOCA (March 17–June 30, 1991),
the exhibition will travel from mid-1991 through late 1992 to
museums in Japan and Europe and to others in the United States.

Generous support for the exhibition and the book has been
provided by the East Japan Railway Company and the Fukuoka
Culture Foundation/Fukuoka City Group in collaboration with
Matsushita Electric Industrial Co., Ltd.

Library of Congress Cataloging-in-Publication Data
Stewart, David B., 1942–
Arata Isozaki: architecture 1960–1990 / preface by Richard
Koshalek: essays by David B. Stewart and Hajime Yatsuka.
p.   cm.
Catalogue of a travelling exhibition to the Museum of
Contemporary Art, Los Angeles, et al.
Includes bibliographical references.
ISBN 0-8478-1318-5 — ISBN 0-8478-1319-3 (pbk.)
1. Isozaki, Arata — Exhibitions.   I. Yatsuka, Hajime.
II. Isozaki, Arata.   III. Museum of Contemporary Art (Los
Angeles, Calif.)
NA1559.I79A4   1991   90-50795
720'.92—dc20   CIP

Designed by Abigail Sturges
Edited by Kate Norment
Project descriptions translated by John Lamb

Printed and bound in Japan

For information about our audio products, write us at:
Newbridge Book Clubs, 3000 Cindel Drive, Delran, NJ 08370

Front cover: Art Tower Mito, Ibaragi, Japan, 1990. Detail of the
gallery exterior.
Back cover: Drawing by Arata Isozaki of The Museum of
Contemporary Art, Los Angeles.

Contents

Preface

Arata Isozaki is one of the most innovative and influential architects working today. Over the last thirty years, he has designed an extraordinary series of projects and buildings that have made a significant contribution to the evolution of contemporary architecture. His highly original approach replaces the purely rationalist precept underlying modern architecture with a more personal, even idiosyncratic, aesthetic—one that is a synthesis of historical symbolism and the most advanced developments in technology and communication. His architecture neither blatantly quotes from a romantic past nor wholly embraces the hyper-technology of the present, but rather creates a delicate balance between these forces in a specific contemporary context.

In the summer of 1980, Isozaki began to work with The Museum of Contemporary Art, Los Angeles, on the design of its California Plaza structure. The museum was Isozaki's first major commission in the United States and, as such, marked a particularly crucial point in his career. Since its completion in 1986, MOCA has received resounding acclaim throughout the world, bringing well-deserved attention to an architect of exceptional sensibilities and supreme talent.

With the celebrated inaugural exhibition of the museum in 1986, the MOCA staff was again privileged to collaborate with Isozaki on the California Plaza installation design of "Individuals: A Selected History of Contemporary Art, 1945–1986." Since that time, we have worked with the architect on additional designs for two more recent exhibitions: the Louis I. Kahn retrospective organized by MOCA for an international tour that commences at the Philadelphia Museum of Art in October 1991, and the current exhibition examining Isozaki's own remarkable career to date.

The museum is profoundly honored and pleased to present this retrospective, timed to coincide with Arata Isozaki's sixtieth birthday, an occasion that has special significance in the Japanese culture. According to Japanese legend, by age sixty an individual has accumulated sufficient experience to have achieved the essential wisdom and knowledge necessary to make significant contributions in the future. "Arata Isozaki: Architecture 1960–1990" is a thorough examination spanning thirty years of the architect's impressive oeuvre, from the early visionary proposals of the 1960s to the large-scale urban projects of the present time. The exhibition both illuminates the complex, multifaceted nature of Isozaki's past work and provides insights into directions that the architect may pursue in the future. Documenting more than thirty projects and buildings, the exhibition includes one full-scale "folly" reconstruction, roughly forty scale models, 250 original drawings, and a series of three high-definition-television presentations, each focusing on a different phase in Isozaki's career.

The architect's work is organized into five thematic groups. "Theme I: Genesis of Imagination" features conceptual proposals for Tokyo from the 1960s, including such schemes as Clusters in the Air and the Marunouchi Project, along with such high-tech environmental designs as the Computer-Aided City. These projects demonstrate Isozaki's early interest in merging technology with urban design and show an already rich imagination working to address the challenges of contemporary urban existence.

The evolution of Isozaki's work over the following decades is explored in three successive phases, beginning with "Theme II: Birth of an Architect." This section, which focuses on the early concrete buildings and those public structures of bold geometric form realized primarily on Isozaki's home island of Kyushu, examines his emergence as a rising architect. These designs include the Fukuoka City Bank Head Office; the Fujimi Country Clubhouse; the Kitakyushu City Museum of Art; the Kitakyushu Central Library; and the West Japan General Exhibition Center. "Theme III: Catastrophe Japan" explores Isozaki's search for a more individual architectural expression, one that also incorporates references to past historic styles. Among the buildings included in this period (to which the term "schizophrenic eclecticism" has been applied) are the Gunma Prefectural Museum of Fine Arts; the Kamioka Town Hall; the Tsukuba Center Building; and the Art Tower Mito. "Theme IV: Architect as World Citizen" includes the Phoenix Municipal Government Center; The Museum of Contemporary Art, Los Angeles; the Brooklyn Museum; the Sant Jordi Sports Hall; and several other international projects that have occupied Isozaki in the latter part of the 1980s.

The exhibition concludes with "Theme V: Hyper-Technology," which includes Isozaki's most recent proposals for the Tokyo City Hall, Ueno Station, and the NTV Plaza redevelopment plan. These projects present his most recent, mature thoughts for a greatly changed Tokyo in the 1990s, three decades after the initial proposals shown in "Theme I" of the exhibition. In a deliberate way, then, the exhibition comes full circle through the fascinating terrain of the architect's brilliant and highly charged imagination.

The exhibition and this accompanying book have resulted from the exceptional cooperation and dedication of Arata Isozaki and his wife, Aiko Miyawaki. They have devoted an enormous amount of time, energy, and creativity to this collaboration, for which we are exceedingly grateful. Their inspiring work has been a vital and compelling force abetting us throughout our endeavors. The supremely committed and efficient staff of Arata Isozaki and Associates, including Hiroshi Aoki, Yoshiko Amiya, David Gauld, Ko Ono, Tomoko Mizukami, and Shuichi Fujie, has contributed immeasurably to the realization of this exhibition, and we would like to express our special appreciation to them for their extraordinary care and assistance. I would also like to recognize and thank my co-curators, François Burkhardt, Director of the Centre de Création Industrielle, Centre Georges Pompidou, and Akira Asada, Associate Professor, University of Kyoto, for their invaluable participation in this project.

I am deeply grateful to the Board of Trustees of The Museum of Contemporary Art and its Program Committee for their recognition of the importance of architecture and design as an essential component of a balanced museum program that reflects the reality of contemporary culture. Our special gratitude goes to Frederick M. Nicholas, Chairman of the Board of Trustees, Douglas S. Cramer, President, and Daisy Belin, Chairman of the Program Committee, for their leadership, encouragement, and keen sensitivity to the museum's programming concerns and their ongoing encouragement of the curatorial staff.

I would also like to thank those staff members of The Museum of Contemporary Art who have worked closely with me on this project. Special recognition is due to Associate Director Sherri Geldin, who played an integral role at every phase of this project, from the early conceptual stage through the many creative and logistical planning sessions that occurred over several years. She and my superb executive assistant, Bonnie Born, traveled with me to Japan at the invitation of Arata Isozaki and Asahi Shimbun to help organize the exhibition and arrange for its premiere in Los Angeles. During this trip, we had the opportunity to view firsthand many of the buildings designed by Arata Isozaki, from the early works on the island of Kyushu to the most recent, the Art Tower in Mito and the Hara Museum ARC in Gunma Prefecture. An important contribution was also made by MOCA Exhibitions Coordinator Alma Ruiz, who became involved in the project at an important stage in its organization and presentation in Los Angeles.

8 Particular thanks go to other members of the staff as well, among them, Editor Catherine Gudis, who worked closely with Rizzoli International Publications to produce this book; Director of Development Erica Clark, who provided the leadership necessary to obtain appropriate funding for this project's presentation in Los Angeles; Director of Education Vas Prabhu, for her development of special educational programs associated with the architecture of Arata Isozaki; and Public Information Officer Anna L. Graham, for her distribution of press material on the exhibition. We are also most grateful to Exhibition Production Manager John Bowsher and his outstanding staff for their work on the installation and, particularly, for their fabrication of the full-scale "folly"; to Registrar Mo Shannon, who assisted our colleagues in Japan with all shipping and registration; and to Controller Jack Wiant, who provided financial and administrative assistance.

This book was co-published by MOCA and Rizzoli International Publications, Inc. Our sincere appreciation to Rizzoli President Gianfranco Monacelli, Vice-President Solveig Williams, and Senior Editor David A. Morton, who, in cooperation with MOCA, worked closely with both the architect and the authors through every phase of this book's realization. In addition, our deep gratitude to Kate Norment, who sensitively and incisively edited the texts for this publication, and to Abigail Sturges, who provided its elegant design. My profound thanks to Yasuhiro Ishimoto for his superb photography, and especially to the authors of this book, whose special insights into Isozaki's work are of inestimable value: David Stewart, architectural historian and Visiting Foreign Professor at Tokyo Institute of Technology; and Hajime Yatsuka, architect.

The exhibition was organized by The Museum of Contemporary Art, Los Angeles; the Centre de Création Industrielle, Centre Georges Pompidou, Paris; and the Asahi Shimbun, Tokyo. Generous support has been provided by the East Japan Railway Company and the Fukuoka Culture Foundation/Fukuoka City Group in collaboration with Matsushita Electric Industrial Co., Ltd. These institutions have our deepest gratitude for their essential collaboration and their magnificent encouragement of this endeavor from its inception.

Following its opening in Los Angeles, the exhibition will travel from mid-1991 to mid-1992 to museums throughout Japan. It will then travel on to the Centre Georges Pompidou in Paris and the Brooklyn Museum in New York.

On the occasion of his sixtieth birthday, we wish Arata Isozaki continued success in his remarkable career and, more importantly, a long and healthy life in which to experiment with the same confidence, sensitivity, and originality that have distinguished his first three decades of work. We look forward to following his future work, knowing that his intellectual, spiritual, and creative energies will greatly enhance and enliven the critical international dialogue within the world of architecture and urban design.

Richard Koshalek
Director
The Museum of Contemporary Art, Los Angeles

Gods and Men
David B. Stewart

The palace of the kings is shut now, the tribunals have abandoned the gates of the cities and secluded themselves in inner rooms, writing has thrust aside the living word, and the people itself, the worldly and sensuous masses, if it forgoes the violence of the mob, becomes the State, and thus an abstract concept; the gods have sought refuge in the bosoms of men.
—Schiller, preface to *The Bride of Messina*, 1803

For the first twenty years of my career as a professional architect, I believed that architecture could only be accomplished by irony.

It could allude to treason.
It made it possible to create architecture as criticism.
It could admire the vulgar against the noble, the secular against the sacred, without shame.
. . .
It was an unfulfilled wish, a mourning for what was lost—
Hiroshima, holocaust.
To bridge over the gap—
A style of wit, a sense of humor and paradox were adopted.
. . .
After twenty years of practical experience, I am now going to find a method to create architecture without irony.
—Isozaki, "Architecture With or Without Irony," 1985

When compared with Arata Isozaki's entry for the 1980 Tegel Harbor competition in Berlin, the splendid copperplate engravings commissioned between 1819 and 1840 by the Prussian neoclassical architect Karl Friedrich Schinkel after his own works seem rather inadequate. This is partly because the Tegel area redevelopment comprised, within a single project, housing, a cultural center, and sports and other recreational facilities. It is also because, according to Isozaki, the low-rise housing in his scheme was set off by precast-concrete panels that were to have been "exact replicas of facade motifs" designed by Schinkel. In the panoramic restaurant overlooking the Tegeler See, Isozaki seized the rationale for a "dummy facade" replicating the Humboldt-Schloss in Tegel, the house that Schinkel remodeled and extended from 1820 to 1824 for his friend the philologist and diplomat Wilhelm von Humboldt, former Prussian ambassador to Rome. The perspective view of Isozaki's submission for the harbor complex was freely adapted from Plate 115 of Schinkel's *Collection of Architectural Designs*, which depicts the Berlin Building Academy, finished by Schinkel in 1836. The engraving by Mandel, after Schinkel, published in 1833—a year after the Building Academy was begun—is the last of the great architect's much-loved topographical views drawn from the banks of the River Spree. Like the Tegel Harbor Complex, the

Building Academy project was conceived in a spirit of urban improvement, and Schinkel actually lists the advantages that "will come about as a natural consequence of this project." The school itself occupies the former site of a customs depot, and its planning suggests various street widenings, the provision of new amenities, and the disengagement of urban vistas, none of which Schinkel wishes to have escape public notice.

Still, despite the fact that the ensemble of Schinkel's works, such as were built, profoundly changed the face of Berlin in the course of the architect's lifetime, he was never allowed free rein of his instinct as an urban planner, in the full sense that term has taken on in the last hundred years. Instead of being called upon by his sovereign to redesign whole districts of Berlin, the Prussian capital—or even isolated spatial tracts—Schinkel was, even as state architect, obliged to live by his wits. Fortunately, he built widely enough within the city that his works do, to a certain extent, coalesce, leaving Berlin, inevitably almost, with his stamp— just as Isozaki's three major buildings in Kitakyushu City would endow it with an architectural character rare among the urban environments of modern-day Japan.

Isozaki's Tegel project, however, remains unbuilt, like so many of Schinkel's refinements, not to mention the Berlin master plan he submitted in 1817. The waterfront design Isozaki elaborated in 1980 transforms the footprint of the Building Academy, rendered strikingly in balanced perspective by Schinkel in his drawing of 1831, into a skewed open plaza. This is partially colonnaded and presided over at its center by the Humboldt facade, with steps leading away obliquely in the corner opposite, down the embankment to the water. Clearly, the plaza is the central feature of the design, yet 150 years later there is so much more to be taken into account.

Even so, the more crowded arrangement forced upon Isozaki and other entrants by the multifunction program of the Tegel Harbor Complex competition was not unknown to Schinkel. While the shoulder-to-shoulder jostling of built forms is consciously absent from the austere engravings, it may be seen in other media. As is well known, these engraved drawings appear stripped to a bare formal minimum. In fact, for us today this constitutes the essence of Schinkelian neoclassicism, though its pristine quality may have been obscured in the rush of attention to Schinkel's work since the celebration of the bicentennial of his birth in 1981. Thus, too, the famous Berlin monuments—the museum, the theater, and the Building Academy itself (each

Karl Friedrich Schinkel. Project for a Royal Palace on the Acropolis, Athens, 1834.

of which has now been restored or rebuilt)—are models of architectural clarity and restraint. Yet these works were created when Schinkel was at the pinnacle of fame and favor, while as a young man after the return from his Italian tour in 1805, and during the years of Napoleon's threat to the nation, Schinkel's employment as an architect was sporadic. Hoping in vain to publish his Italian sketches, he turned instead to the elaboration of panoramas, a new, light-based medium that first appeared in Berlin in 1800. Schinkel's initial essay in the technique was an 1808 view of Palermo, of which only an engraving survives but which must have been exhibited fully in the round, with no side edges—the beginning connected to the end—and illuminated by means of a high, hidden light source. Palermo was succeeded the following year by St. Mark's Square, Venice, and three views of the Milan Cathedral (one by moonlight), shown in a performance with musical accompaniment, which was attended by the royal family.

Consistent with the public aim of early-nineteenth-century works of panoramic art, it is clear from the surviving miniature Palermo torus that there were few lapses of scenographic interest in designs of this sort. The same was true of Schinkel's work for the stage, which continued well into the 1820s, and, in particular, his Egyptianized sets of 1815–16 for Mozart's *Magic Flute*, a production that opened in Berlin half a year to the day after Waterloo. Motifs of an extremely complex romanticism, both functional and ideological, surface continually in Schinkel's work, especially in his numerous unbuilt palace designs of the 1830s. These seem to take their inspiration from Pliny's villa, a reconstruction of which was intended at Charlottenhof for the Crown Prince Friedrich Wilhelm. Schinkel's *Collection of Architectural Designs* ends somewhat anticlimactically, given the radical simplicity and even austerity of so many of its plates, with a later version of this scheme. More to the point, and perhaps closer to Schinkel's own inner romantic inclinations, were plans for a Crimean palace overlooking the sea near Yalta, to be inhabited by the Czarina, Friedrich Wilhelm's sister. While the elevations, apart from the siting of the palace itself, are unremarkable, the polychrome interiors in an "Asiatic-Scythian" style and the hanging gardens would have been the most elaborate of Schinkel's career. In terms of sheer complexity of organization and massing, the so-called Ideal Capital City (or Residence of a Prince) is Schinkel's most ambitious design. Although of a purely hypothetical nature, it was, significantly, intended for inclusion in a projected architectural textbook.

Most striking of all these late schemes, as a combination of iconic elements with buildings of pure invention, was Schinkel's redevelopment of the Acropolis at Athens as a royal palace for Otto of Greece, nephew of Friedrich Wilhelm's wife. This is again a coloristic exercise, under the influence of then current research into the materials and appearance of classical architecture. The palace itself would have been discreetly sited to the rear of the existing remains, such as the Parthenon and Erechtheion, obscuring the considerable extent and complexity of Schinkel's new construction. In the magnificent colored lithographs of these two projects, for Athens and the Crimea, published toward the end of Schinkel's life and posthumously, the picturesque is raised to a new level and scale. Notably, in the Royal Palace on the Acropolis, much is made of the physical contours of the rocky acropolitan mount itself and the buttressing of the new palace as seen from below on the southeast. Conversely, on the narrow elevation of the hill, the western approach is dramatically cast by Schinkel into deep shadow, with the Periclean monuments picked out above. In both views, a landscaping of palms and cypresses is shown in profile, and towering over all is the colossal bronze Athena Promachos, made to dwarf even the Parthenon. The temple, as one modern commentator remarks, is thus reduced by Schinkel to a virtual garden ornament.

In this eventual pilgrimage to the Acropolis we have come a long way from the Tegel Harbor Complex entry of 1980, as well as from the built oeuvre of Schinkel himself, who in reality never made a building farther afield than modern-day Poland. Yet, just one year before his death in 1841, Schinkel is recorded as discussing the re-exhibition of the Palermo panorama with W. E. Gropius, its original promoter. Moreover, Schinkel raised with him a new idea for the public exhibition of a panoramic display of monuments, from ancient Egypt and Greece down to medieval Germany. Together with the last projects described above, the trend of this grandiose historicizing is as clear as it seems to us today inevitable. The issue, then, is not that Isozaki developed his Tegel scheme of 1980 in the very year following James Stirling's *Shinkenchiku* Residential Design Competition, whose given theme was "A House for Karl Friedrich Schinkel" (*Japan Architect*, no. 262, February 1979). It is, rather, that by the time the machinery for the preparation of his bicentennial had begun to turn, including Stirling's genial notion of a "house" for the architect, K. F. Schinkel stood revealed as the man of the hour. There was in all this, of course, a trap ready-set in aid of the notion of so-called postmodern classicism. And it will not be clear for some

Arata Isozaki. Competition entry for the Tegel Harbor Complex, Berlin, 1980.

time yet to come who among contemporary architects has stumbled into it—or, more delectably, who, having so stepped, has gotten out. For, as is well known to historians, this was the second rediscovery of Schinkel, the first having helped to create modernism: that is, Loos, Behrens, and, as beginner, Mies. Then, about one generation later, came that old Berliner Philip Johnson, who has also had a hand in the current round.

Yet, as I have attempted to suggest, if there was a trap, it is not too much to say that Schinkel, not merely as a "neoclassicist" but as a modern, was the first man in.

What, then, of Arata Isozaki? What were the conditions of genius, and historical inevitability, that led him to the present exhibition, held initially in a museum designed by him that might be the counterpart in contemporary West Coast terms of the Royal Palace on the Acropolis? (N.B.: There are at least two potential rivals to that title, but the fact only reinforces the generalizability of the argument.)

It goes without saying that these "conditions" were as unique to the Japan of the Showa emperor as those governing the meteoric ascent of Schinkel were to the Prussia of Friedrich Wilhelm III. We have sought to recall some of the ways in which the Prussian architect became a prototype of the modern-day architectural practitioner, but we must also note that in the late spring and early summer of 1804, Friedrich von Schiller visited Berlin and Potsdam and contemplated a permanent move there from Weimar. Schinkel had already left Rome and spent the summer traveling in Sicily, considering the landscape and temples and sketching, to be sure. By March 1805, Schinkel was back in Berlin; by May of the same year, Schiller, having remained at Weimar, was dead.

Culturally, Schiller's disappearance marks a watershed, one that, together with the French Revolution and Napoleon's ascent, helped define the romantic classicism of the period, of which Schinkel was such a persuasive, if somewhat late, representative.

But whereas neoclassicism as a "style" engendered innumerable instances of artistic devaluation, not least in the years of the Empire—a time when heroic themes were frequently translated into drawing-room bric-a-brac—Schiller's seminal role, in his partnership with Goethe, and the brevity of his career as well, precluded triviality. He had, certainly, little if anything to do with architecture and was concerned even less than Goethe with any form of antique

revival in stylistic terms. His importance lies in the fact that in the Germany of his time, which then had barely emerged from its feudal past into the modern era, Schiller's access to meaning was, as one authority has succinctly stated, altogether through history. And this meant universal, or world, history, for Schiller discovered his models in Gibbon, Herder, and Kant. From the beginning his dramas and essays aimed at nothing less than a historical understanding of the revolutionary present. It was, moreover, one significant feature of Weimar classicism that this comprehension had to be of an aesthetic nature, but equally of the sort that provided guideposts for a future society. In terms of architecture and art in general, the modern movement was the grateful inheritor of these notions, and Schinkel, who was fifty-one at the time of Goethe's death, was instrumental in transmitting much of this ethos in built form to the early twentieth century.

It would be a truism to state that the example of Weimar classicism—as propounded by Schinkel in a built version at a truly civic scale, for this was his particular genius—entered Japan through that country's own experience of modern architecture and, more especially, of the International Style. In any case, following the Meiji Restoration of 1868 the Japanese were widely receptive to Prussian innovations of their own day, including the bombastic architecture of the Bismarckian German Renaissance style. But the latter, a fairly rapid degeneration from Schinkel's standards of restraint and purity, had offered the raison d'être for the first "rediscovery" of Schinkel's style. Therefore, as a safeguard, the suave Loos-Behrens-Mies connection of the early twentieth century saw to it that the Schinkelian example, as canon, be absorbed and reiterated in the "modern" version as radically dehistoricized (no Royal Palace on the Acropolis, for example). Such was the condition in which it reached America, not to mention Japan and elsewhere. Nevertheless, there has always remained a species of tacit doubt as to whether, perhaps, if Schinkel's classicism, with its historical allusions intact, was right for a young nation like Prussia at its inception, the same might not be true for others, such as Japan or even the United States. America, in fact, possessed its own serviceable version of classicism in the Federal, then the Greek Revival, style, which has surely remained an *architecture parlante* up to the present day. In other words, the question can still be asked whether the cold and beautiful abstract formalist architecture of European modernism was (is) susceptible of a blanket application.

In this respect, we need to remember that not until 1868 did Japan become a modern political entity, and the story

12 begins, from scratch, yet again in 1945. By the latter date, Japan had received the flame of modern architecture, though by that time most of her not inconsiderable examples were literally in flames—or in ruins. Tokyo, and many other cities, most infamously Hiroshima and Nagasaki, were not even that. So the question of architecture, of building, was posed in most critical terms. In the capital, some buildings, mostly large and well built, did not succumb: the Imperial Diet Building, the Tokyo Central Post Office, Wright's Imperial Hotel, the Marunouchi office building, Dai-Ichi Insurance (later to be the American G.H.Q.), much of the Imperial University, the Bank of Japan, Meiji Insurance, various schools and hospitals, the prime minister's official residence, some public housing, Honganji Temple, and others. Mostly they were works of the 1920s and 1930s, including occasional masterpieces, such as Tetsuro Yoshida's post office; some iconic but ideologically sullied monuments, such as the Imperial Diet; and other beloved landmarks in Western revival styles, like Tokyo Station and the Bank of Japan.

Evidently, some thought had been given to reconstruction of damaged cities, and the young Kenzo Tange had already begun to ruminate on a notion he himself called "three-dimensional urban design." In practical terms, this consisted of survey work of potentially high-risk areas likely to be bombed, research in the university library into the themes of the Greek agora and Roman forum, and participation in actual designs for government-sponsored competitions, such as the Japanese Cultural Center in Bangkok (1943) and the Greater East Asia Coprosperity Sphere Memorial near Mt. Fuji (1942). Tange won both competitions, though neither was built. Both designs involved large-scale historicizing layouts, under the influence of roughly twelfth-century Japanese models, with lively ideological associations—and not the least dehistoricized. His later postwar planning work, notably at Hiroshima, is widely known, as are a large number of major public buildings, such as the striking and iconic Olympic Stadia at Yoyogi, Tokyo (1964). This is not the place to rehearse that career; suffice it to say that Arata Isozaki joined Tange's studio at Tokyo University in 1953 as a fourth-year undergraduate and remained under the older architect's tutelage for approximately a decade, eventually founding his own firm in 1963.

Within these formative years, Isozaki crossed the straits of Metabolism (1960), about which more will have to be said. However, even though it is simple to fit together the pieces—formally or formalistically—of this early period in the architect's work, tracing the reciprocity of influence between Isozaki and Tange, it has not been altogether easy to gather what was in the younger man's mind during his twenties. Still, if we find Isozaki at fifty years of age somewhat under the spell of Schinkel and his neoclassicism, at thirty-five, when Isozaki's first mature work, the Oita Prefectural Library, was completed, his attitudes, I would like to submit, have more in common with the aesthetic theories of Schiller. An initial condition was that, for all the sophistication of the architecture of the Japan Style during the 1950s as practiced by Maekawa, Sakakura, Tange, and others, the advisability of applying modern Western architectural solutions in the Japanese case had not been seriously questioned since before the imposition of fascist architectural guidelines in the early years of Showa. The stylistic about-face Tange executed between the winning competition entries in the "traditional" style of the late war years and his premiated Hiroshima Atomic Memorial Museum (1949–55) is the most important indication that, even in architectural terms, something momentous yet unspoken had occurred.

Not since the profound self-interrogation on matters of architectural style in the early 1930s, conducted by Sutemi Horiguchi and a few others—amounting to a full generational gap—had the topic been aired in terms of its basic, underlying assumptions. At its most acclaimed, Japanese postwar modernism proposed an inspirational cocktail of Western steel and steel-reinforced-concrete structures with the lightest of ethnic formal and material embellishments. This was an emotionally freighted mix that sent foreign journalists and magazine editors, as well as heads of schools of architecture and other Western colleagues, head over heels in aesthetic ecstasy. That was the 1950s and early 1960s, and some of the work—like Tange's Olympic Stadia—was very good, and still looks great. But it was not what Isozaki had in mind, and he wanted both to show his work and have the world hear his reasons.

In his long poem "The Artist" (1789), Schiller traces the development of artistic sensibility from a condition of unreflective happiness to a state in which a divided consciousness discovers a rupture between the beauty of phenomena and abstract truth and, finally, reconciles these poles through a process of acculturation and a deeper understanding of the arts. Isozaki's programmatic attempt to refound the principles of modern architecture beyond the reach of conventional Japanizing impulses, and notably the sensuous appeal of tea-garden aestheticism, if *sukiya* ramifications may be thus characterized, was in some sense

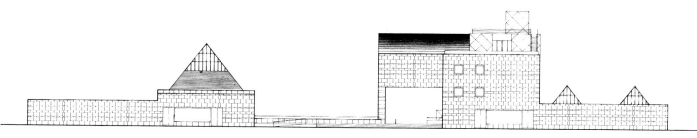

The Museum of Contemporary Art, Los Angeles, 1986. Rear elevation.

a latter-day equivalent. It is true that earlier Tange had attempted to formulate the basis for a new critical self-consciousness, but always in terms that now seem either downright bizarre (witness the early proposal to explicate Le Corbusier via Michelangelo), or overtly political (like the antithesis he designated between the archaeologically descriptive Jomon and Yayoi styles of ancient Japanese art). His intention to re-create in the Yoyogi stadia for the Tokyo Olympics a vision of the ruins of the Colisseum at Rome was more apposite, but the strategy succeeds largely in proportion to the extent to which it remains unintelligible to the average viewer.

Both Tange and his disciple stand in a direct line of artistic confrontation between Western prototypes and, so to speak, the reality of an inherited Japanese design aesthetic that, however skilled, was regarded as constrictive or even demeaning. In such designs as those for his own home, the Kurashiki Town Hall, or Yoyogi, Tange was widely regarded as having struck a wise balance. Yet Metabolism was proof—and, indeed, carried out under Tange's own sponsorship—that for a younger generation at least the issues that had plagued Japanese architects since Meiji had not yet been laid to rest. Here, technology had ostensibly raised the ante, and the simple metaphorical response—metabolism itself as an aspect of biological process—appeared to furnish a universalizing theme. After all, Kikutake, one of the prime formal and ideological contributors, had started as a medical student before turning to architecture. Yet in the Metabolist program, aspects of which Isozaki visibly retained, what reads as unsatisfactory is the injection of a factor so alien to the canons of general artistic production, whether Eastern or Western, familiar since the beginnings of building. By equating art with sheer biological inevitability, the element of personal taste, which is the essence of *sukiya* and would be enshrined by Isozaki in the guise of *maniera,* was disposed of with the bathwater of tradition. The megastructure, that principal leitmotif of Metabolism, seems to have ridden the crest of this particular wave, in analogy with a feudal typology, namely the medieval castle. But that in itself was a regression to a fortresslike ideal, from which *sukiya* architecture, inspired originally by the tea cult, had provided a magnificent and truly liberating escape.

In the course of his subsequent career, the notion of *maniera* (deriving as impeccably from the sixteenth century in Europe as does that of *sukiya* in Japan) freed Isozaki from the ritual impasse of Metabolism. It offered him retreat from a stultifying professionalism in a nation-state where social-engineering skills have never been wanting. Yet, it was not an escape into that ivory tower of what has sometimes been described in questionable art-historical terms as "mannerism" any more than the art of the 1500s, whether in Japan or in Italy, need be thus viewed. To be sure, the early style of Isozaki's independent works—especially those around his hometown of Oita, in Kyushu, such as the Oita Medical Hall (1959–60), the library already mentioned, the Nakayama House (1964), and the Iwata Girls' High School of the same date—is very much a neoformalist idiom. But *form* in this sense was precisely the quality that tradition, in all but a few exceptional cases, had not provided for in Japanese architecture.

Whereas previously Tange and the Metabolists had willed something of the kind in the Tokyo Plan (1960), for example, or the "future dwelling" exhibition of 1962, Isozaki's Joint-Core System or his Clusters in the Air project of the same year, which were cruder and less poetic, nevertheless engaged with *forms* in a way that was totally uncompromising. How, or why, this should have been so will probably remain a mystery. But the issue at stake was that the Western category of "beauty" was unattainable without a commitment to form, which had never been solidly undertaken in the history of Japanese architecture, although subsequently Isozaki saw or pretended to see this step in such monuments to a doubtful past as the Imperial Diet Building or the Dai-Ichi Insurance Company, which stand on opposite sides of the Imperial Palace enclosure in central Tokyo. Without wanting to agree with him, though the doubt may seem prudish, one certainly understands what he was getting at. That aside, whether this be selling an artistic birthright for a mess of pottage is a very different question, but the fact is that Isozaki stepped over the line in the mid-1960s at the latest, and he has not looked back.

The decisive works in this new tradition, or anti-tradition, date from the 1970s and, in terms of a simplified grandeur, come to a close most probably with the Kamioka Town Hall, completed in 1978, finding a definite reverberation in the scheme for MOCA (1981–86), wherein a new level of complexity has already been attained. The Tsukuba Center Building begins even earlier (1979) and, like the Los Angeles museum, is clearly of a different order, but the museum is simpler in program and massing; it seems, therefore, more closely tied to the work of the 1970s. And, in psychological terms, it represents by definition a sea change in the architect's stance; it represents Isozaki, having gained distance, looking back at his heroic and mature period.

13

14 Schiller's essay of 1793 entitled "Anmut und Würde," which continues to reflect the deep Kantian influence on the dramatist, now also turned theorist, dwells on the twin notions of a "state of grace" and a certain "dignity" that are achieved in the resolution of artistic conflict and are prefigured in Shaftesbury. If one considers too much Japaneseness as a baroque perversion, as apparently Tange did at times—although, clearly, the comparison is not altogether safe—Schiller's poetic ideal and its relevance here can be better grasped. It follows that neither Tange nor Isozaki have been exactly destroyers of beauty, though the "destruction" (or the deconstruction) of architecture has been a slogan often on Isozaki's lips since 1975, when he published a tract on that theme, aimed at the canon(s) of modernism. What Schiller does say is that beauty is the manifest achievement of freedom, that is, "freedom in appearance." Without quite destroying sensuality, its patterns are unfolded, so to speak, and its range displayed and explored. A further point, however, is that beauty in the realm of moral deliberation is a public function; thus, in order to be effective, art must be so experienced and represented. With its open-ended relation between the individual and collectivity, this thesis—whatever its remarkable aspects for the twentieth-century West—cannot but appear an extreme and difficult doctrine for the tenets of a neo-Confucianist Japanese aesthetic, even though the radical, liberating aesthetic of "tea" is in its own way a match for what Schiller has proposed. For Schiller, as for Rikyu, it is "through Beauty that man makes his way to Freedom," even if, eventually, the two approaches would have only their inspired radicality in common.

The teamaster Rikyu was, in the end, unsuccessful as a political strategist, paying in 1591 with his life, at the instigation of his disciple-patron Hideyoshi. Nor were further artistic perspectives opened in Japan in 1968 by the attempted student political movement, a checkmated situation that Isozaki and others have never forgotten. Thus, the most perfect of all works of art in Schiller's terms—the construction of true political freedom—was denied, or so it was perceived. And, in Isozaki's case, this provided a narrower—more poignant—interpretation of the retreat into *maniera*. This dates from the late 1960s and early 1970s, the time of his works for the Fukuoka City Bank, which overlap with the official planning undertaken in collaboration with Tange's office for Expo '70 at Osaka, including Isozaki's realization of a robot-activated "cybernetic environment" for the Festival Plaza there. Although the interiors of the various bank branches and the head office were public or semipublic, they were introverted

and lyrical, sometimes to the point of hermeticism, a fact emphasized by dramatic, even jarring, effects of color and lighting. By contrast, the Osaka Expo was, of course, a quasi-official manifestation of Japan, Inc., and the Festival Plaza was a supermechanized, stagelike development of Tange's earliest ideas on the uses of public space in the Greek agora. The implications of a near schizophrenic separation of roles for Isozaki needs no emphasis.

On the other hand, the work for Tange and the nation at Expo '70 provided what seems to have been an essential and formative experience in a certain kind of "play," for the robots, as has often been pointed out, were something like a giant erector set. Once more, Schiller, in his seminal letters "On the Aesthetic Education of Mankind" of 1794, which constitute the schema for a latter-day German classicism, offers a ready-made description of the various kinetic forces Isozaki loosed, straddling the threshold in Japan's debut as a world economic power just two decades ago. Using the term Fichte had employed in his Jena lectures the same year, Schiller characterized human transformational energy as the product of two *drives*—one toward the realization of form, the other toward that of sensation. He then postulates a third "play drive," reconciling the necessary conditions of identity and change. According to Schiller, mankind rediscovers his wholeness within a framework of aesthetic play, and it is this "aesthetic mode of perception [that] makes him whole." As famous as this doctrine was for the following generation and the eventual formation of European romanticism, it bears reiteration here for the simple reason that Isozaki was the first Japanese artist to evolve a rational and conscious program putting such notions into effect. In so doing, he squared his intentions fully with the European tradition of post-baroque theory.

Isozaki, born in 1931, was old enough to have remembered something of the upheaval of World War II; and, coming from West Japan, as did Tange, he was perhaps more closely exposed to the trauma deriving from the atomic destruction of Nagasaki and Hiroshima. Indeed, these were immortalized in the Electric Labyrinth, exhibited by Isozaki at the 1968 Triennale in Milan. Similarly, the notion of the destruction of architecture relates, in one of its possible interpretations, to this strain of thinking. Yet the traumas of the war in the context of the Showa Era have generally been played down; without necessarily being repressed they were integrated into the cultural narrative of Japan's entry, over the space of four generations, into the modern world. In literature, the cycle of this transformation was more or less adequately dealt with from the beginning, while in

"Electric Labyrinth," Milan Triennale, 1968.

architecture—perhaps not surprisingly—there had never been a Japanese Wren or Schinkel or Viollet-le-Duc, at the level of what could be spoken of as national, as opposed to nationalistic, aspirations. Or, rather, it was necessary to pursue the semiprogrammatic aims of Japanese modern architecture of the 1950s and early 1960s, which, however, after 1968 seemed to lead precisely nowhere.

Though Schiller's theorizing took place in the face of the French Revolution and Schinkel's important buildings were erected in the aftermath of the Napoleonic Wars in an era of material hardships, German philosophy was nevertheless in full flower and, for literary and aesthetic theorists, the archaic battling between ancients and moderns afforded an implied European context. In the Japanese case, there was the immeasurable native architectural contribution, since approximately the 1850s, to the formation of a European modernism (one later to become internationalized), so that in a sense the ball has been in Japan's court all along. In another sense, the exercise of modernism in Japan has been foiled by just this substratum of paternity. In what is the keystone of his critical and theoretical enterprise, Schiller ("On the Naive and Sentimental in Literature," 1795–96) depicts the contemporary mind as a consciousness alienated by its own experience, suspended in a state between the simplicity of its original nature and the reflective impulses that are the contribution of culture. When Japan's unique stratification of bicultural attitudes and artifacts is added to this endemic condition or plight of "modernism," the problems of constructing a "reflective" art of self-awareness (apparent in Europe two centuries before) become astonishing. There is also the less obvious Oedipal strain contained within the Japanese relationship to modernism and, finally, the shock troops of postmodernism at the gates.

It is no wonder, then, that an artist and theoretician with antennae as sensitive as Arata Isozaki's had, by the time of his own coming of age (in Japan, something like thirty years), taken up a stand that was not only "reflective" in the Schillerian sense but also committed to romantic irony. In spite of Schinkel's known familiarity with the writings of Friedrich and August Wilhelm Schlegel—and, indeed, despite his romanticism in general—irony was apparently not one of the means of expression open to him. However, irony in the new romantic usage at the turn of the eighteenth century derives in part from Schiller's play-concept of art, and for Friedrich Schlegel the term is closely related to paradox, as Isozaki shows himself aware in the epigraph I have chosen.

Among the elements that have bred paradox and wit in architecture, the foremost is certainly the advent of an industrial technology, in the creation of an industrial landscape and an industrial architecture, as well as in the application of industrially produced building materials to architecture itself. In the history of the profession, Schinkel stands at the threshold of future developments in this connection, as does the entire city of Berlin. But it was not until historicism had proliferated that the exaggeration of contrasts could be held up to ridicule and exploited as ironic. So, even at the end of the nineteenth century the great Viennese architect Otto Wagner was still designing works at the very limit of the means Schinkel had devised—now enriched and empowered by technological gadgetry and vocabulary—but quite without concessions to irony. Adolf Loos, working a few years later in the same city, was a master of the biting, satirical essay on matters of building, yet even his most rhetorical built statements are without humor. Isozaki absorbed much from both these Europeans. It has been advanced that Sir Edwin Lutyens was the first architect consciously to build with tongue in cheek, and he, too, is no stranger to Isozaki.

However, on the whole, it seems to me that Isozakian irony is a native product, and it may even be that "irony" in architecture was originally made possible by the *sukiya* mode. The Romans were, nonetheless, capable of working in the equivalent of Schiller's "sentimental" vein. In other words, at least in retrospect some of their buildings do appear reflective or self-referential, as does certain earlier Hellenistic production. In the case of our architect, the key essay is Isozaki's early City of Ruins (1962), where fragments of some giant classical order have been recycled as a megastructural design, anchored by a strip of urban freeway. The Triennale's Electric Labyrinth (1968), already referred to, takes up where this conceit leaves off, transposing the vision of urban desecration to a metropolitan scale, collaged over an image of Hiroshima. The City of Ruins has affinities with Schinkel's Royal Palace on the Acropolis, but instead of being given a regal and improving tableau with landscaping added, one is confronted intentionally with a patch job—and, in the Electric Labyrinth, we are terrorized.

By the time of Isozaki's projects and works of the 1980s, things have calmed down, so that realizations such as the nevertheless controversial Tsukuba Center Building of 1983 or, in Tokyo, the renovation now known as Ochanomizu Square of 1987 do, actually, in their serenity and complexity—and, above all, in their neoclassicism—

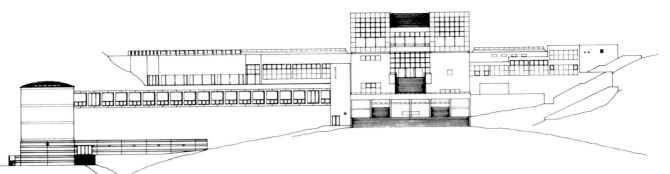

Kitakyushu City Museum of Art, Fukuoka, Japan, 1974/86. Front elevation.

16 resemble the late work of Schinkel, such as the Ideal Capital City or the palaces near Yalta and in Athens. Of the early works by Isozaki, the last to retain traces of the apocalyptic mode initiated in the 1962 composition of ruins *al capriccio* or the *veduta ideata* of Hiroshima of 1968 was the Kitakyushu City Museum of Art of 1974. This was also the first of six large public buildings coming after the Oita works, all of which added up to Isozaki's being the first of the post-1950s generation to complete a substantial corpus of work at a national scale, thus comparable with, say, the oeuvre of Maekawa or Tange. The Oita sequence, from the medical hall of 1960 through the branch there of the Fukuoka City Bank (1967), was executed in form-faced reinforced concrete and aggressively delineated in thrusting or trabeated forms, although the bank branch adds smooth precast panels to this idiom. In 1971 the bank's head office at Hakata (Fukuoka) was the first of Isozaki's works to be faced in red Indian sandstone, a material that reappears in 1986 in The Museum of Contemporary Art, Los Angeles.

The Kitakyushu City Museum of Art, which added an annex in 1986, is a building atop a hill or ridge destined to be reappropriated by the fast-growing local vegetation except for the two massive caissons, square in section, that are aimed like a pair of binoculars at a distant landscape. Kitakyushu was prewar Japan's prime industrial city, formerly an amalgam of townships that went to make up a heavy industrial complex, targeted by the U.S. for atomic destruction at the war's conclusion, in place of which, by miscalculation, Nagasaki was struck. Within the art museum much play is made with black-and-white marble paving and cascading staircases, while the twin oversize flying beams are clad in gridded cast aluminum in order to heighten the powerful sense of abstraction; they render the form a kind of giant toy in the city's landscape. The remnants of the city's industrial monuments (after most were left obsolete following the defeat) make an interesting contrast with the nonutilitarian play of the museum, in repose, as pure cultural infrastructure—and artifact.

Completed in the same year, 1974, is the Kitakyushu Central Library, located closer to the center of the municipality, facing its high-rise town hall. The library, like the museum, is a longitudinal form, but here it is volute and vaulted. Taken together, library and art museum fully exploit the circle and the square, or rather the sphere and the cube, which constitute Isozaki's main formal repertoire during the mid-1970s. Instead of opposing the site, as the museum does, the big volumes of the library are sculpturally integrated and set off by means of a meandering

formal staircase, which affords the principal landscaping element. Inside, the library functions are cleverly planned, joined by a restaurant and a museum of civic history housed under the same roof. In The Museum of Contemporary Art in Los Angeles, twelve years later, the architect created the same kind of milieu—half podium, half burrow, so to speak—and, with its lozenges and pyramids, MOCA might be said to establish a third member, or type, in the geometrically based sequence.

Meanwhile, also in Kyushu, near Oita but farther to the south and east, another vaulted work by Isozaki shows how different the effect of cylindrical form could be made to feel. The Fujimi Country Clubhouse (1974) was derived from Palladio's front for the Villa Poiana, itself descended from Roman architecture through Bramante, and there are additional intimations of Palladio's "Malcontenta" and Frank Lloyd Wright's Dana House at Springfield, Illinois, in various details. However, here the tunnel vault is given precedence and combined with continuous plate glazing in the apse, which forms the dining room of the clubhouse. The overall mood of the work is one of repose allied with the kind of resourcefulness in adapting geometric prototypes to new functions that is the hallmark of Schinkel's mature phase and probably also the distinguishing characteristic of that architect's considerable influence, through drawings, on Frank Lloyd Wright.

In 1977 Isozaki completed a third major building in Kitakyushu City, possibly a record in the brief history of the modern Japanese townscape and its development. This was the West Japan General Exhibition Center, near the Kokura terminal of the Shinkansen railway and in proximity to the port. Here, too, is a large work—by far the biggest of the six under discussion—of great inventiveness. The building consists of virtually a single expanse of support-free exhibition space protected by a roof suspended from cable-anchored masts. Without actually appearing as a predominantly high-tech engineering structure, the work has little pretension to form, since it is a slablike mass with planar sides and a linear support system. This merges with the atmosphere of masts and cranes in the surrounding landscape; however, there is now an annex presenting a true facade, though it makes use of further illusionistic and contextual devices.

Three years earlier, in 1974, Isozaki completed the Gunma Prefectural Museum of Fine Arts in Takasaki, eastern Japan, incidentally his first major work in the close vicinity of Tokyo. Once again, the notion of a building in a dramatic

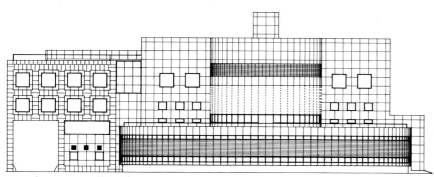

Kamioka Town Hall, Gifu, Japan, 1978. Elevation.

landscape setting presented itself, this time with something of the nature of an English park. As there are no rises or hills, the museum must fabricate its own architectural podium. Enclosing volumetric systems have been abandoned, in an obsessionist frenzy of cubical framing elements and gridded surfaces, used by Isozaki as early as the Nakayama House of 1964. Unlike the exhibition center in Kitakyushu, the Gunma building imposes a true architectural presence, but without taking responsibility for its own rhetoric of enclosure. This quality is minimized by a shiny cladding (it has since acquired a muted patina) of square-cut aluminum paneling that totally conceals the structure, except for window-walls likewise gridded.

The museum strongly evokes Aalto's library of the mid-1930s at Viipuri (now a town in the Soviet Union). However, the Gunma museum is a more abstract exercise, a fact accentuated by the building's being set on flat lawn, with one wing—a double windowless cube—raised over a reflecting pool. This echoes the west (studio) wing of the original Taliesin, Wright's Wisconsin home, where the studio, canted at an angle, joins the otherwise rectilinear massing and adjoins the swimming pool. The angling of the small gallery wing at Gunma, according to the architect, preserves the building from the devastating effect of too much symmetry. Gunma is perhaps Isozaki's major statement about the nature and effects of architectural language—in Schiller's dichotomy, the rereduction (of a building) to a naive, i.e., nonreferential, language. In the sculptural arrangement of giant cubical frames, which *appear* to make up the framing of the museum (actually, as has been said, concealing the structure), Isozaki arguably comes closer than elsewhere to the resonant new neoclassicism of Schinkel's mature phase and the *neo*-neoclassicism of Loos. The building fully embraces paradox at an experiential level while avoiding irony, although that was later supplied by a very straightforward history-museum wing commissioned from another architect and now realized, no less, in a contemporary civic idiom of brick and mortar.

In the sixth and final major project of the 1970s Isozaki had the chance to fight City Hall—or redesign it—in the mining community of Kamioka, near the Japan Sea. This offered a truly acropolitan setting, and by applying certain of the methods evolved at Gunma and crossing these with a few ordinary classical devices, Isozaki produced a work that is both a commentary on a standard typological ploy (in the design of town halls in general) and a return of architectural language from the wilder shores of abstraction, as exemplified in Gunma. The resulting Kamioka Town Hall

(1978) was profoundly schizophrenic, but without a doubt it more than answered the program; and for the sixth time in less than half a decade Isozaki produced an architectural work that had the force of a public utterance.

Unlike Wright (who, at Taliesin, sited his palatial home and studio upon the "shining brow" of a hilltop in rural Wisconsin, thus naming the place), Isozaki inveigled the remote, local township of Kamioka out of its vernacular darkness and isolation. As is perfectly clear even in photographs, Kamioka's "shining brow" was Isozaki's creation, though both architects had fine, dramatic sites to manipulate. For, as Schiller recites in "On the Naive and Sentimental in Literature":

"Poets everywhere are by definition the *preservers* of nature. Where they can no longer be so completely and already experience in themselves the destructive influence of arbitrary and artificial forms or have even had to fight against them, then they appear as the *witnesses* and *avengers* of nature."

And further on, summing up: "The poet either *is* nature . . . or he will *seek* it." Wright, paradoxically, did just that: he sought, or reconstructed, the nature of a mythical Nippon in his realization of the Imperial Hotel during the 1920s in Tokyo. But that is another story.

As was the theater for Schiller (and for Goethe), for Wright and Isozaki architecture is, above everything, an "institution of morality"; and the more so, finally, in light of the fact that *all* these men are fully acquainted with the sensuality of art. Yet, despite this attitude of engagement, which, in Schiller's case, had he lived, would probably have precipitated a move to Berlin, where his tragedies were spectacularly produced and received by an avid public, Wright felt hounded by civil society, which he came to consider in its mobocratic aspect. For Isozaki, Kamioka Town Hall is a pronouncement of the end of irony and marks the beginning of a new phase of activity in which irony and paradox are appropriately, and duly, transmuted and transformed.

Arata Isozaki after 1980:
From Mannerism to the Picturesque
Hajime Yatsuka

The Tsukuba Center Building, designed and constructed between 1979 and 1983, was a major turning point in the career of Arata Isozaki. For some it indicated the end of his mannerist period; for others, the beginning of his postmodernist phase. In fact, this huge complex perpetuated the manneristic handling of themes and forms that had characterized most of Isozaki's works in the 1970s, but it also contained quotations of Western classical, or neoclassical, idioms never before introduced by the architect in such an overt and literal way.

Yet, just how sudden was this "classicist shift"? To be sure, "hidden" classical dimensions show even in the works of the modernist architects who set the tone during Isozaki's formative years. Thus, in Isozaki's early oeuvre references to the works of the Russian avant-garde, Le Corbusier, Mies van der Rohe, and Adolf Loos appeared along with allusions to Palladio and Ledoux. This kind of exchange between the classical and the modern had been examined by Colin Rowe and others as early as the 1940s. Rowe's investigation—inspired by Rudolf Wittkower's study of Renaissance Neoplatonic architecture—proved to be a decisive influence on Peter Eisenman, who was to become a close friend of Isozaki's in the course of the 1980s. However, while Eisenman unearthed similarities between the works of Palladio and those of Terragni in terms of syntax, Isozaki's development was largely without theoretical background. It seems, rather, that the modernist-classicist paradigm formed an unconscious base for his work.

It is not without interest to discover a related paradigm in the works of Isozaki's teacher Kenzo Tange. Tange's earliest works, winning competition projects of the war period, were widely regarded as among the most ambitious attempts to offer a new synthesis of modern and nationalist languages. His projects displayed sophisticated Shinto imagery grafted onto a prototypical Corbusian urban compositional scheme, such as the Mundaneum project of 1929. But Le Corbusier's project revealed his classicist nature, and it was this quality that provoked attacks by more rigorous modernists such as El Lissitzky. Tange's success opposed the direction of Lissitzky's Constructivist paradigm.

Immediately after the war, Tange won a major competition, for the Hiroshima Peace Center. The subject here reversed that of the two earlier competitions, dedicated as they were to the glory of Japan's Pan-Asian empire. However, in spite of this substantial difference, the Hiroshima Peace Center project revealed a similar Corbusian composition. There is

reason to believe that this time the "contradiction" was based on more than simple opportunism. Even before the earlier competitions, the young Tange had written a well-known ode to Michelangelo that he described as an introduction to Le Corbusier. In both style and content the article showed the influence of the so-called Japanese Romantic School, whose literature would later have a strong effect on Yukio Mishima. It was characterized by a combination of German Romantic spirit and the aesthetic adoration of ancient Japanese art. In the same way that classical art of both Japan and the West could be the dual object of modern aestheticism for Japanese Romantics, so could the interaction of Shinto idiom and Greek typology (the Acropolis for Hiroshima) with a Corbusian composition be seen as justifiable and consistent for Tange.

A comparison of Tange's Hiroshima Peace Center and Isozaki's Tsukuba Center Building uncovers common characteristics—as well as major differences—between the two architects. As an architect of the symbolic public building, Isozaki was to some extent a successor to the modernist-classicist legacy of his former teacher. Compared with authentic modernists, Tange, like Le Corbusier, was a mannerist in his tendency toward the dramatic. He transgressed the modernist sense of discipline, and was never afraid of his buildings appearing symbolic beyond the dictates of program. Rather, his intention was to appeal to the collective imagination. Tange's position could be thought of as modernist-mannerist. What made it modernist was not the fact that he now eschewed Shinto (or other overtly traditional) formal devices but the fact that he believed so strongly in the possibility of the grand narrative of society.

This was no longer the case with Isozaki, whose position we could call postmodernist-mannerist. For Isozaki, the commission for the Tsukuba Center Building was rather puzzling: although his earlier works had exhibited monumental qualities without reservation, that monumentalism had always been the distillate of a personal and often ironic statement. The most characteristic is the Kitakyushu City Museum of Art, which obviously borrowed its primary motif from El Lissitzky's 1924 Wolkenbügel project but remained without any social statement, such as the Russian's "Architecture for World Revolution."

The Tsukuba Center Building was designated as the central element of the new town called Tsukuba Science City, one of the most pointed attempts on the part of the Japanese

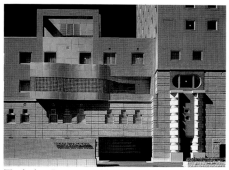

Tsukuba Center Building, Ibaragi, Japan, 1983.

government to restructure the country's postwar society. The program was such that the building, if monumentally designed, would appear as an authoritative representation of the "will of the nation," independent of stylistic aspirations on the part of the architect himself. At the same time, since it would be the only major public space in the new town, the building nevertheless needed to take the form of a symbolic center. Responding to this "double-bind" had become something of an automatic reflex for the Japanese intelligentsia of the period, most of whom still nurtured a leftist view of society. By contrast, in designing the Hiroshima Peace Center, Tange was able to be far more straightforward and optimistic about the relationship between architecture as symbolic form and society, its symbolic content.

Isozaki's strategy for the Tsukuba Center Building was to try to bridge the contradictory, half-hidden gap in the nature of modern architecture. Just as modernism had wanted its buildings to appear free of imposing symmetry and authoritarian character, Isozaki, though adopting a more literal classical vocabulary, tried to avoid an excessively hierarchical ordering of the composition. He did this by presenting a void—a sunken plaza—in the center, where one would expect the most monumental element of the composition. Although perhaps not by intention, this refusal of the monumental seems to have fulfilled Hans Sedlmeyer's apocalyptic view of modernism as "loss of the center." The Tsukuba building demonstrates the impossibility of any "center" for architecture in contemporary society. But despite the intellectual underpinnings, because it uses classical language and *is* simply monumental, the complex offers an easier reading, and we are left with two ways of interpreting it: we can see it as a manifestation of the architect's uncertainty, or as a successful attempt to inspire a plurality of readings, depending on the observer's own preoccupations and interests.

Whatever the interpretation, Tsukuba creates a sort of maze from which even the architect himself cannot escape. Isozaki made it clear that although he may not have followed the path of his former teacher, Tange, he could not be indifferent to the social responsibility that goes with the profession of architect. The "suspended monumentality" of Tsukuba represents the suspended (but never absent) public consciousness of the designer.

Isozaki's work in Tsukuba would generate two types of reactions. The first was from such younger architects as

had been much influenced by Isozaki during the 1970s. For them, the undeniable monumentality of the Tsukuba Center Building signaled blatant commitment to the idea of the public realm, a notion that in their minds had lost all validity. From this viewpoint the building seemed to be a gesture of compromise with the prevailing establishment and its ideals. The attacks from Osamu Ishiyama and Toyo Ito, to name only two architects ten years Isozaki's junior, were typical reactions from those who had been active in the period after 1968. But eventually this radical "opposition" revealed itself as a product of the political and social climate of the time. It was nullified by a shift of perspective concerning the nature of society, which formed the basis for the second reaction—in fact, more an *absence of* reaction to Isozaki's bitter gesture at Tsukuba against the "shadow of the State." In a highly developed consumer society where distinctions between ruler and ruled have virtually ceased to exist, the State is no longer a consolidated identity requiring the support of strong visual imagery. Isozaki, who had been turning out ironic statements about society for quite some time, must have realized that the ultimate irony resided in eliminating the form (and, with it, the shadow) of the State. Was this not, perhaps, prefigured earlier, when he proposed the notion of the "city invisible" more than fifteen years before? At any rate, after Tsukuba, Isozaki ceased to be an "architect of irony."

II

By the 1980s definitive norms for architecture had disappeared. This absence seemed to raise the same issues for architects in Japan, the United States, and Western Europe—that is, in all highly developed capitalist societies— and was especially vexing for architects of Isozaki's generation, most of whom are at the peak of their careers. This period also marked the beginning of a new international phase in architecture. Major architects, both Japanese and Western, began receiving many more overseas commissions than they had in preceding decades. They now spend more time on airplanes than ever before; they have become regular participants in invitational competitions throughout the world, and not infrequently find themselves sharing first prizes. They thus form, in Isozaki's words, an architectural "mafia." Architects such as James Stirling, Michael Graves, Peter Eisenman, Richard Meier, Hans Hollein, and Frank Gehry, as well as other prominent members of this group, had all been close friends of Isozaki's since before this period. But unlike the architects of CIAM and Team X, who held common ideals, these are individual designers with very different concepts and working

Tsukuba Center Building. View from hotel.

methods, and there is no close ideological bond between them. As seems fitting for a consumer culture, these architects have become brand names, so to speak. They are obliged, consciously or unconsciously, to make changes in stance as shifts occur in the social context.

Isozaki's eventual disinvolvement with the "architecture of irony," as explained above, is an example of this process. We need to bear in mind, of course, that the "postmodern" itself is somehow the product of social conditions. Whether we call the whole phenomenon (including the works of Isozaki) "postmodern" or something else, only one thing is certain: that nothing—even a gesture of refusal—is assured or absolute in this empire of the "ephemeral," as Gilles Lipovetsky put it. Before the 1980s, avant-garde architects (or philosophers) could depend at least on that ultimate strategy of the historical avant-gardes, negation. This is exemplified by the works of Peter Eisenman (or Jacques Derrida, to whom Eisenman owes much of the theoretical background of his deconstructive methodology). However, this kind of apocalyptic approach to zero degree ideological status is in the end condemned to eternal return because any ultimate center—or final goal—has been abolished from the start, as if by mutual agreement. Thus, architecture can never hope to free itself from the spiral of eternal return inherent in the consumer circuit. If repeated often enough, even negation and irony will become prosaic, outdated, and ineffective.

For those who took a less conceptual stance, the relativistic tendency was more apparent. In the work of Michael Graves, for instance, the overt and almost superficially hedonistic gesture; the rarefied mixture of mid-Corbusian vocabulary (denominated *objets à réaction poétique*) and revisionist Art Deco; and his virtually unconditional commitment to the collective lifestyle of capitalist society have placed him in the company of the late Edward Durell Stone. This kind of hedonism reflects the essential nature of our times and is one of the predominant characteristics of the empire of the ephemeral, which now rules beyond national boundaries, as confirmed by the fluctuating cycles of capitalism and its international conquests. There is today a general desire, accelerated and condensed in the melting pot of the contemporary metropolis, that obliterates the distinctions between individual architects. Stylistic differences that might once have provided clues to authorial ideology, whether modern or postmodern, rationalist or historicist, have become relative at best.

Architects have not, however, surrendered their national or regional identities. James Stirling became increasingly British in character during the 1980s, and Frank Gehry remained archetypically West Coast, just as Aldo Rossi is undoubtedly Italian. Nevertheless, their respective contexts have changed. Their works, which had sprung from local soil, are now being transplanted to other terrains. Seeing Stirling's new building in Berlin, aligned between Mies van der Rohe's National Gallery and Emil Fahrenkampf's Shell Building, both of which are strongly Teutonic, or seeing Rossi's hotel in Fukuoka among vernacular and distinctly *un*-European town houses, evokes a very strange sense of something "out of place." The advocates of critical regionalism would perhaps object to this kind of decontextualization; but, in fact, decontextualization could be a more serious and significant phenomenon than deconstruction.

Compared with Stirling, Gehry, or Rossi, Isozaki has never been an architect with a local bias. Even with his extensive general knowledge of traditional Japanese art, he has rarely used the vocabulary of traditional Japanese architecture. (An exception would be his teahouse "folly" for the 1983 exhibition at the Leo Castelli gallery.) This seems to have puzzled most Westerners, including Michael Graves, who, in an article on the Tsukuba Center Building, found it strange that nothing Japanese could be distinguished from the multitude of Western formal components there. During the 1980s, when Isozaki became one of the central figures of the international architectural "mafia," he was often referred to as an architect "from Japan," rather than an architect "*of* Japan." In this sense, Isozaki has been perceived as out of place wherever he has worked, in Japan or in the West.

Other architects, like Kisho Kurokawa or, more recently, Kazuhiro Ishii, deliberately adopted a Japanese vocabulary in their works. For Kurokawa, Japanese art and culture were, and still are, free from Western dualism—in this respect, the Japanese sensibility prefers "gray" to black and white. Such practitioners therefore appear to present an alternative to modernism. Whether or not Japan is a culture of *pre*-realized postmodernism is an issue that can be left for discussion elsewhere. It is clear, however, that the mere inclusion of Japanese references is not enough, that such an approach is nothing but simple eclecticism. Except for the superficial play of associations it would provide, adopting an indigenous vocabulary will never work, because distinctions between specific vocabularies, stripped of all essential context, are now becoming almost negligible. In fact, this was exactly what Isozaki had been saying since the 1970s, reiterating how everything in the entire historical

New Tokyo City Hall Project, 1986. Model.

corpus was now within reach of all contemporary architects. But in spite of this belief, his own preferences were evident: Western modernism and classicism (without Gothic overtones) as discussed above, and virtually no Japanese, or other Asian, elements.

On the subject of the Gothic, we find two typical but contrasting forms of adaptation in contemporary structures. The clearest example of explicit and intentional adaptive behavior is Tange's premiated project for the new Tokyo City Hall. The other approach, less literal and deliberate, is seen in the headquarters for Lloyd's of London by Richard Rogers. Both represent very different approaches from Isozaki's. Among the invited participants in the Tokyo City Hall competition, Isozaki submitted the best and perhaps the only truly ambitious design. In contrast to several entries that proposed high-rise solutions—including Tange's—Isozaki's scheme was for a vast horizontal block, a simple rectilinear body with a gigantic antenna, a sphere, and a pyramid on top. The scheme has a strong affinity with projects of the Russian Constructivists, like the Vesnins' 1923 scheme for the Palace of Labor or certain designs of Leonidov (place, for instance, his Palace of Culture for the Proletarsky district of Moscow of 1930 atop his entry for the Centrosoyus building). After the competition, Isozaki attacked the winning scheme by his former teacher because he saw its borrowing of Gothic decorative motifs as superfluous. This critique illustrates Isozaki's dislike of the Gothic and his contempt for decoration. (It also suggests a shift on Tange's part away from the modernist-classicist paradigm.)

But what of Richard Rogers and his Gothicizing? Although Rogers has never adopted the Gothic in any conscious way—in appearance or obliquely—he is, I believe, a Gothic architect by temperament. I have two things in mind: the obsessive use of contemporary technology in his work, regardless of historical implications, and the absence of any intellectually and abstractly conceived hierarchical order. In other words, in the work of Rogers everything is direct, literal, and unmediated. If we could argue very approximately for a moment, the architect was a product of the Renaissance, of a new abstract consciousness of historical process. Renaissance architects, furthermore, maintained a symbiotic relationship with the philosophical discourse of the Neoplatonists. Rogers is a builder in the true sense of the word. Isozaki, in contrast, has never been one of these, though he does not hesitate to use the most advanced technology for construction. In Isozaki's works, technological elements usually function as stylistic

components laden with historical, metaphorical, and other indirect associations. While Rogers is trying to present an "object," Isozaki is presenting instead an "idea" or a "model." In this sense he remains fundamentally a modernist-classicist architect.

III

In the 1980s, the word "disjunction" made its appearance as one of Isozaki's preferred terms. Bernard Tschumi often referred to this notion in his *Manhattan Transcripts,* as did the French philosophers Deleuze and Guattari (the concept of *disjunctive synthesis*), notably in their *Anti-Oedipus.* Disjunction means, essentially, the abandonment or rejection of hierarchical organization. As will be recalled, such negation was operative in the Tsukuba Center Building design, but there it was a temporary device for avoiding possible political implications, an attempt that turned out to be futile. So why did Isozaki use disjunction after Tsukuba, especially if it were not to function ironically? Simply, I believe, because he found it difficult to return to the hierarchical world; it was after the dissolution of hierarchy that irony, by means of anti-hierarchical devices, lost its political force, not vice versa. Thus the disjunctive state already existed in the order of things. One of the most interesting aspects of developed capitalist societies is the fact that they manage to function successfully within this irregular state of affairs, which diverges sharply from traditional utopias, including the socialist one, where harmony depends on a hierarchically determined order. What we have, therefore, is a post-ideal society, not a post-ideological one, as some ideologues too naively put it.

The disjunctive condition is present in various dimensions. For Tschumi, who developed his theories from an analysis of Manhattan, disjunction acts to tie urban phenomena to human activities. (This later led to another set of ideas in the "Dis-, Cross-, Trans-" program.) But for Isozaki, who is more of a formalist than Tschumi, disjunction has to do with physical forms and objects. And Isozaki's approach to forms and their manipulation has not changed significantly since the 1970s; the tendency is deeply rooted in his modernist-classicist spirit. It can best be understood by contrasting it with the approach of Deleuze and Guattari, the anti-classicists.

By developing their idea of "disjunctive synthesis," which spawned other concepts like *Rhizome* and *corps sans organs* [body without organs], Deleuze and Guattari have been trying to abolish the idea of organization itself. In the

The Museum of Contemporary Art, Los Angeles, 1986.

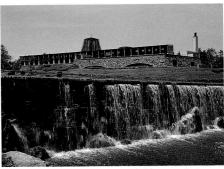

Musashi-kyuryo Country Clubhouse, Saitama, Japan, 1987.

22 Rhizome model, no distinction is made between the whole and its parts. To illustrate this anti-organization they refer to the Gothic, contrasting it with the classical articulation of parts within the whole. While most of Isozaki's works are handled in the latter manner, this may not be true of some of his works in the 1970s—for instance, those with barrel vaults crowning the building, such as the Kitakyushu Central Library and the Fujimi Country Clubhouse. Although the clubhouse, with its distinctive frontality and Palladian flavor, was undoubtedly more classicist than the library, the continuous curved vaults of these buildings tend to nullify the impact of the elevations, thus obscuring any sense of classical unity. But since that time, such barrel vaults themselves have become "components." This seems to be confirmed by the fact that vaults with a perfect semicircular section—which, if used in a low building, tend to dissolve everything below into a single unarticulated (*sans organs*) space—have been replaced by yet shallower ones, which act only as sections of roof.

Typical examples include The Museum of Contemporary Art in Los Angeles and the much smaller Okanoyama Graphic Arts Museum. In MOCA, the vault is still semicylindrical and constitutes the tallest part of the building, yet it is not powerful enough to rule the whole. The shallow vault of the Okanoyama museum also crowns the main part of the building, but without sufficient power to rule the detached wings. The mode by which the individual parts are connected is "disjunctive," but never in a shocking way. They form, as it were, passive collages—a description that might be applied to nearly all of Isozaki's works in the 1980s. As with the barrel vaults, he continued to use geometric elements such as cubes, cones, and pyramids—a tendency inspired by the works of Enlightenment architects like Boullé and Ledoux. But these forms act as episodes in the loosely composed whole; and they are treated not as stark geometrical objects deprived of meaning but as elements with rich associations. A typical example of this is the steep-stepped and truncated pyramid of the Musashi-kyuryo Country Clubhouse, which is made of timber and seems somehow reminiscent of the pagodas that appear in English landscape gardens of the eighteenth century. Although the pyramid is the tallest and most conspicuous element, it is still not indispensable to the whole and could be replaced by something else. The Aristotelian idea of the ideal composition, which cannot be added to or taken from without fatally damaging the ensemble, does not apply here. Regardless of which of Isozaki's buildings from this period are considered the best, the clubhouse seems to be the most characteristic, not only because of its nonhierarchical structure, but also because of its use of varied, mostly natural, materials, which had been rather restricted in his earlier works. It is simply picturesque.

This drift away from mannerism to the picturesque also reflects the fact that many works of this period were designed for sites in the country or with abundant natural surroundings, which tends to inspire the use of picturesque devices. Even Isozaki's proposal for the new Tokyo City Hall, involving a site that is the most urban of all of his recent projects and incorporates two bare geometric forms as a roofscape, serves to illustrate the new tendency. But even given the relative rigor of an urban picturesque scheme, it seems undeniable that Isozaki took a more relaxed approach after the Tsukuba Center Building. This reflects changes in society—and, more generally, the birth of the empire of the ephemeral. The implication is that our social and cultural circumstances echo the atmosphere of hedonism that prepared the way for the picturesque style in eighteenth-century Britain.

All this does not, however, suggest that architecture in a suspended context cannot be political or ideological in import. Depending on the political situation, hedonism does not necessarily exclude a critical position, even if it is deprived of the idealistic overtones of a truly heroic period. It simply means that sometimes the same gesture can be simultaneously affirmative—even optimistic—and negative, which is a natural result of the dissolution of absolute norms. Dogmatic approaches based on such norms are now destined to appear irrelevant or cliché-ridden, even if they still have significant impact. It seems the practice of confronting one orthodoxy or ideal with another belongs to the old order of things.

Isozaki was faced with this problem in competitions for the Phoenix Municipal Government Building in Arizona and the Paternoster Square Urban Design Project in London. Their distinct programs reflect differences between the milieus of these two places: the Phoenix building was conceived to give focus to urban activities in that loosely structured southwestern city, while the London project was aimed at redeveloping the area around St. Paul's Cathedral, one of the most important historical monuments in the British capital.

In Phoenix, Isozaki confronted themes that were both timely (the end of the Cold War) and outdated ("Architecture for Democracy"). Other entries, like those of

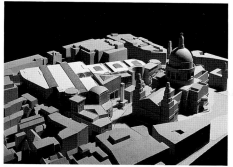

Paternoster Square Urban Design Project, London, 1987. Model.

Art Tower Mito, Ibaragi, Japan, 1990.

Barton Myers, Ricardo Legorreta, and Michael Graves, represented the idea of a classical civic plaza in front of the city hall; none of these included any hint to the effect that, despite local differences, the word "democracy" is becoming a cliché throughout the world. This unexciting scenario is typical of post-ideal society. Isozaki's scheme was based on a modification of the basic idea of the Tsukuba Center Building, which was to inscribe a void in the center of the complex. But at Phoenix the void is intended not as a negative or positive statement about the political situation but as a way of evoking the image of the prototypical spaces found among the early desert dwellers of the area, the Pueblo Indians. His clustering of buildings around a central void was an act of embracing what Isozaki referred to as the "desert landscape." Buildings surrounding this "desert" were loosely connected groups with precise articulations, forming picturesque complexes.

The basic vocabulary—classicism freely arranged—is no different from that of Isozaki's other works, but it now also incorporates the Pueblo typology of the indigenous inhabitants, which is, in a certain sense, a rather orthodox strategy whereby the picturesque is invoked. It is not a superficial adoption of a vernacular idiom, like the approach taken by the tourism industry, for there must also be a hedonistic play of imagery and icons within the picturesque. But Isozaki's provocative gesture—adopting a space of Pueblo origin instead of the classical Western cliché of the European civic plaza—may have been interpreted by local authorities as unnecessarily critical of the significant Anglo establishment. That an urban form originating in ancient Greece was judged more appropriate to Phoenix than that of an indigenous culture is curious. But it is also a paradoxical conclusion for Isozaki, who chose to eschew Japanese forms in the Tsukuba Center Building.

The London project reflected political issues more critically, owing to the intervention of HRH Prince Charles. Historically, Paternoster Square was the legacy of the modernists' failure to restructure the old cathedral precinct around St. Paul's. Redevelopment gave the antimodernist camp an opportunity to redress the incompetence of modern town planners. For authentic modernists, the ensuing reactionary attempt to reassert revivalist principles had to be resisted at all costs. Just as in Phoenix, this was an exclusively local political debate, in which invited foreign architects could hope to play only a somewhat obscure role. Isozaki's St. Paul's solution was one of his most eclectic designs. He gave a homogeneous modern expression to the rear, while the facade giving onto the cathedral and square

comprises picturesque juxtapositions of several different-shaped volumes presenting various fronts—some abstract and homogeneous, others figurative and heterogeneous. As collage, it proclaims a suspended judgment—not just revivalist, not wholeheartedly modern. In any case, both sides were too dogmatic to accept Isozaki's sophisticated compromise.

The strategy of the suspended narrative of the picturesque is in danger of becoming conformist. In the age of the "empire of the ephemeral," only the subtlest distinction exists between criticism and conformism. For the general public, the mutually exclusive intentions communicated by the architecture of Isozaki and of Graves are barely discernible. In this respect, Isozaki's most recently completed work, the Art Tower Mito, is informative. This is a cultural complex (the name applies to both the 330-foot-high tower and the complex as a whole) consisting of a theater, a concert hall, an art museum, and other facilities. The huge triangulated tower covered in silver titanium panels dominates the whole complex, an exceptional condition in Isozaki's recent projects. It appears, however, not as the summit in a proposed hierarchical order but a sudden protrusion above the low volumes of the other masses, which are moderate, restrained, and classicizing.

At Mito, the astonishing contrast between the tower and the agglomerate structures at its foot—not quite loosely dispersed enough to be characteristically picturesque, but connected only in their tightly regulated uniformity—provides the main theme. Lacking any kind of harmony with its surroundings, the tower is distinctly "out of place." Being too disproportionately large for a mere episode, it is a *tour*-de-force, at once distracting and disorienting. It would be premature to say whether this huge tower, an abrupt departure, will initiate a new phase of Isozaki's work, or even whether it will be convincingly successful. One thing does seem certain, however: to be effective, the urban monument in the post-ideal society *must* be out of place, because architecture is now deprived of all native context and conventions. Being simply out of place, though, is not enough—the work might be irresponsible. Being out of place and *extra*ordinary at the same time is what is required. And if the architecture is more than just extraordinary, which needs true intelligence and imagination, it might supersede the picturesque. Only time will tell whether this will lead to a period of the sublime, as in the eighteenth-century post-picturesque period—and whether the gigantic "folly" in Mito will endure.

23

BUILDINGS AND PROJECTS 1960–1990

Oita Medical Hall and Annex

Oita, Japan, 1959–60 and 1970–72 (annex)

1

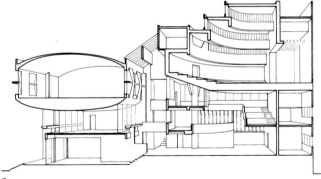

2

The idea of floating a truncated cylinder in the air, the impetus for the medical hall scheme, originated in a competition proposal that was completed just before work began on this project. The earlier proposal was a grotesque design—an elliptical caged frame curved into a crescent moon shape floating in space—and had little chance of being accepted. It drew on one of the basic themes with which Isozaki was obsessed at the time: the mechanical expression of urban-scale megastructures.

The initial system of materials, construction techniques, structural composition, and functional distribution established for the medical hall was later abandoned. In developing the final design, Isozaki reworked the entire structure, using a fundamentally different formal concept. This process of revision became typical of his working methods in subsequent designs.

The architecture of the medical hall appears unprocessed and primitive: slabs of exposed concrete; shapes that seem both unstable and animalistic; an unorthodox, antitechnological relationship between construction and form; a discontinuity with the building's surroundings. The outstanding feature of the design is a truncated oval raised high on sturdy legs. Doctors' offices and conference rooms are contained within this form and in the spaces below; entry is through doors on the ground level, beneath one of the long sides of the elevated structure.

Twelve years after the hall was built, an adjacent annex was completed. The principal space here is the semicircular conference hall on the fourth level, lit by tiers of curved skylights. The lower levels hold lecture, lounge, and office areas, all visually and spatially interconnected by bridges, balconies, and stairways. Annex and medical hall are linked by an interior courtyard, which is bounded on one side by the original rear facade of the earlier structure.

1. *Axonometric (silk screen).*
2. *Section perspective of the medical hall (left) and the annex (right).*
3. *View of the entrance, with the annex in the background.*

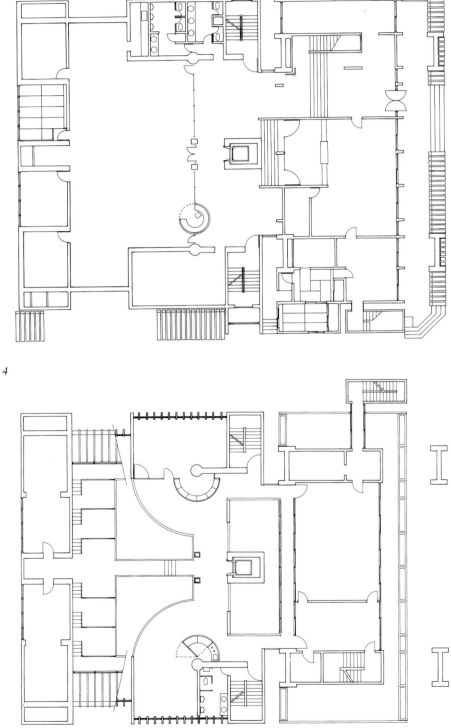

28

4

5

4. First-floor plan.
5. Second-floor plan.
6. Third-floor plan (mezzanine level).
7. Fourth-floor plan (conference hall level).

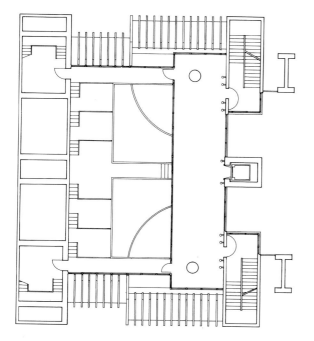

6

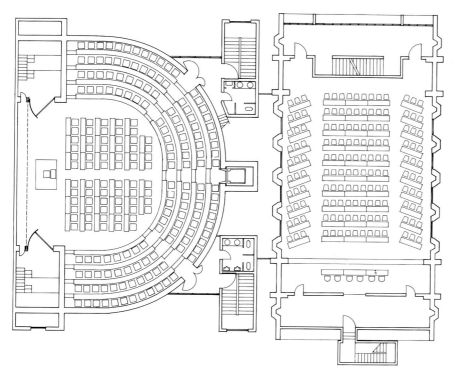

7

30

8

9

8. The semicircular conference hall.
9. The tiered skylights of the conference hall.
10. The annex office space.
11. The bridge over the office space.

10

11

City in the Air

Shinjuku Project

Shinjuku, Tokyo, 1960–61

32

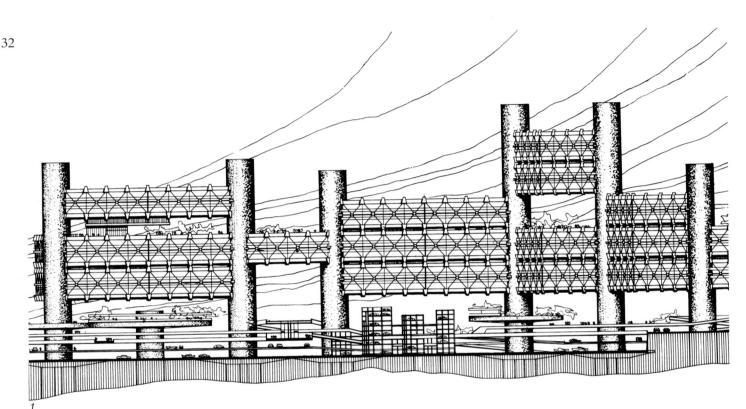

1

2

Created as a counterproposal to the planning that was under way for the skyscrapers that now dominate the Tokyo skyline in Shinjuku, this concept took issue with the prevailing notion of dividing the district into horizontally limited rectangular sections and erecting sheer vertical structures on them. Instead, the proposal suggested that the urgent need for new metropolitan architectural types could be met only by growing forms linked with each other horizontally in the air.

In this project, cylindrical shafts (the "joint cores") containing elevators and other infrastructure rise high and are interconnected by a flexible system of long-span truss structures housing offices and other business spaces. The Joint-Core System was the starting point for the series of sketches and models entitled City in the Air, which set out to revamp the typology of massive architecture by stretching built form to an urban scale and, conversely, introducing urban infrastructure components into the architecture itself. The concept was used in the Central Business District project, part of "Tokyo Plan: 1960," led by Kenzo Tange at Tokyo University.

1. One of the cylindrical shafts that form the
   basis of the Joint-Core System.
2, 3. Elevations.
4. Plan.

Peugeot Building
Argentina, 1961

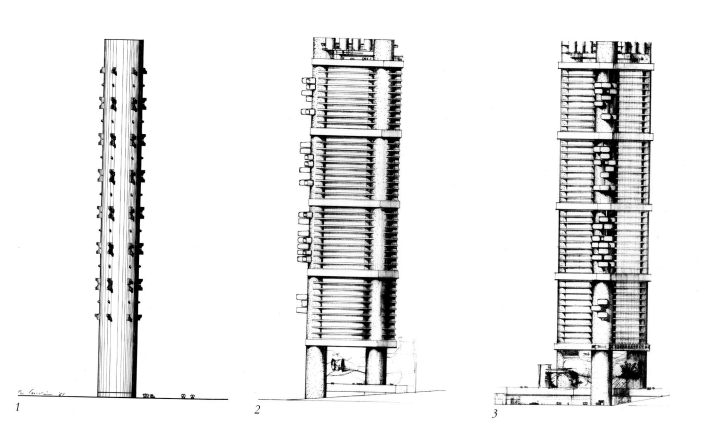

1

2

3

4

In this competition entry for the Peugeot Building in
Argentina, the joint-core concept is applied directly. The
vertical cores swell into great cylinders housing the
infrastructure, while the horizontal elements contract into
components in various forms determined by the program
that are either "plugged into" or "stuck onto" the surface.

Although the concept is fully delineated here, the
competition entry was not completed or submitted.
However, a similar principle was used for the Skopje City
Center Redevelopment Plan competition by the team in the
Kenzo Tange Laboratory, Tokyo University, of which
Isozaki was a member. Their proposal won the competition,
but in the process of realization it was completely
transformed.

Clusters in the Air
Tokyo, 1960–62

34

1

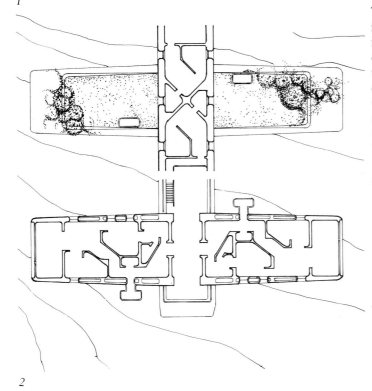

2

The Joint-Core System was initially conceived as a proposal for urban residential architecture, a radically new principle for structuring housing clusters in the sky over existing city districts. Continuity between the existing urban fabric on the ground and the new "district in the air" would be established by the balanced urban scale of the joint cores. Construction would proceed by selecting the desired empty site in the district and then erecting the vertical cores so that they do not impede traffic or pedestrian circulation routes. "Branches" (horizontal energy-flow lines) and "leaves" (housing units) grow on the "trunks" of these "trees" in the sky, all of which are interconnected. As the trees grow and proliferate, they form a "forest," where the branches touch and start to intertwine. In plan this forest would look like a net laid over the existing street layout.

A botanical metaphor, the system also refers to structural elements—such as the horizontal, beamlike *sashihijiki* and the elaborate capitals called *tokyo*—found in traditional Japanese wooden architecture like the Todaiji and Nandaimon in Nara.

1. Aerial perspective.
2. Section.

Marunouchi Project
Marunouchi, Tokyo, 1963

1

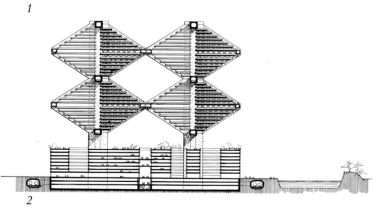

2

The City in the Air series set out to explore the possibilities of new space above existing urban areas to expand the life of the communities on the ground. This project applies the concept to Tokyo's main business and financial district, Marunouchi. Here, business space in the sky is organized around vertical infrastructure cores on a square plan in tetrahedral skeletons. The slanting surfaces feed external light into the elevated clusters and on down to ground level.

Oita Prefectural Library

Oita, Japan, 1962–66

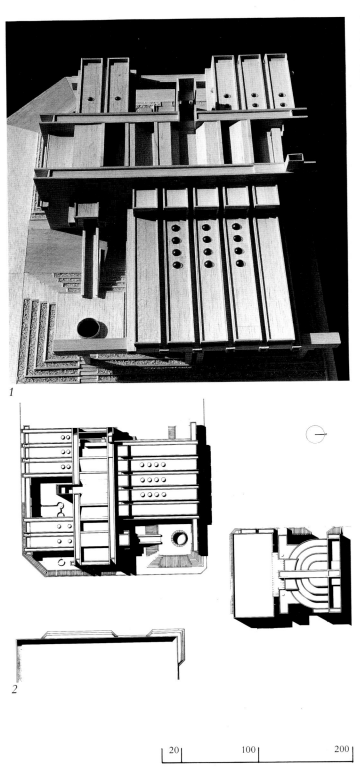

1

2

The site for this public library is very close to the Oita Medical Hall, completed six years earlier. The medical hall was Isozaki's first building of a public nature, designed independently while he was still working with Kenzo Tange. But the library was the first official public commission, and it was substantial enough to enable him to set up his own design firm, Arata Isozaki Atelier.

Still showing the influence of Metabolism, this design was initially conceived as "growing architecture," and the preliminary proposal was published together with an essay exploring the notion of "process planning." The elements were classified by program into several types with different dimensions, and the basic structural system was designed to allow for extensions of floor area according to these dimensions. The interconnecting sections between parts became the primary image for the design, in which the appearance of the whole was secondary to growth patterns developed through these nodes.

The initial proposal had principal component structures formed into prefabricated units, which were stacked on top of each other. However, financial constraints forced the substitution of the original finish with cast-in-place concrete. At the time, this was the most readily available material in Japan to provide a good-quality finish at a reasonable cost. The design of the interiors also had to be considerably simplified.

The reinforced-concrete building frame is divided into a core section, delimited by paired walls, and subsidiary units composed around protuberant, box-shaped beams containing both air-conditioning ducts and circulation spaces. What is seen from the exterior is the repetition of room units enclosed in the wall pairs and distributed around the exposed box beams. Extending out from the central zone—the core of the functional system—are the units containing reading rooms, stacks, and service areas, as well as administration offices and other ancillary facilities. These extensions are supported by box frames with thicker sides.

The original inspiration for the design was an analogy with the human body's skeletal system (concrete skeleton), circulatory system (ducts), and musculature (interior spatial composition)—with obvious affinities to the interconnected trunk, branches, and leaves underlying the Joint-Core System. Although traces of these origins remain in the structure as built, exposed concrete is the overwhelming force in the finished expression.

20 100 200

1. View of the model.
2. Site plan, showing the library in relation to the Oita Medical Hall on the right.
3. View of the entrance.

3

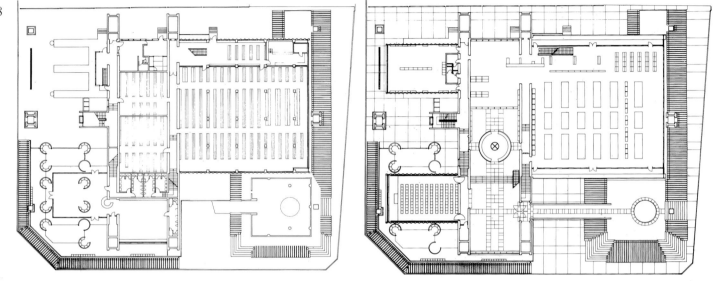

4

5

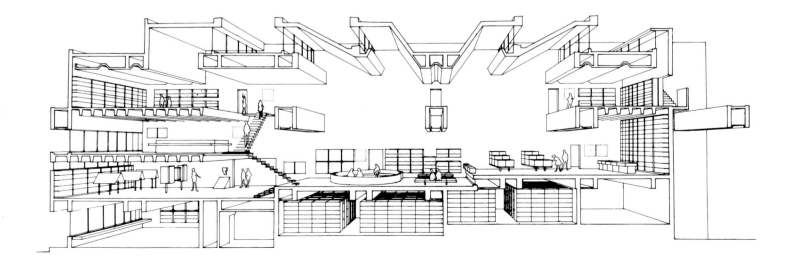

6

4. First-floor plan.
5. Second-floor plan (entrance level).
6. Section perspective.
7. Front elevation.
8. Section.

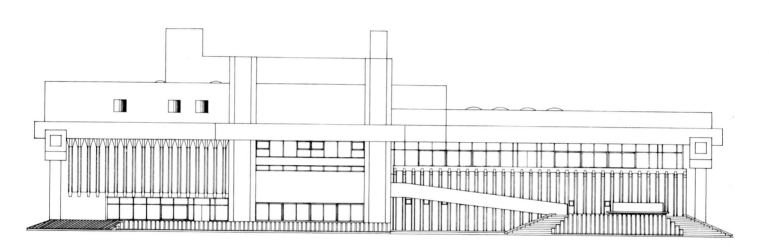

7

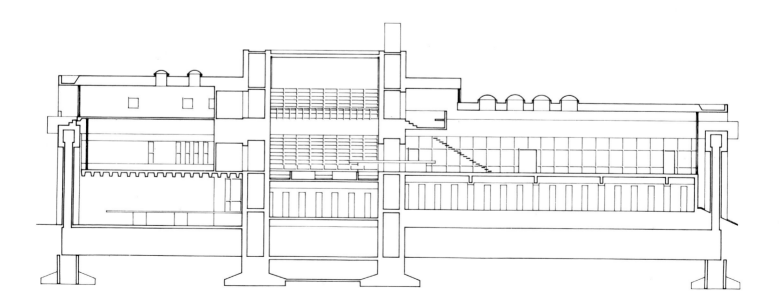

8

$\overline{}\underset{10}{|}\underset{25}{|}\underset{50}{|}$

9. *The entrance hall.*
10. *Third-floor corridor.*
11. *The central open space.*

40

9

10

The Festival Plaza, Expo '70

Osaka, Japan, 1967–70

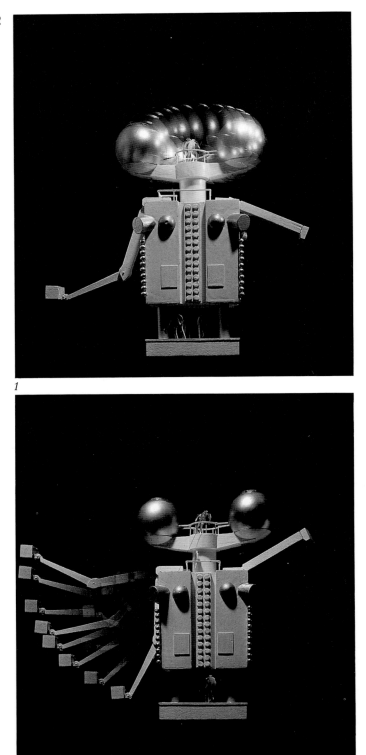

1

2

Expo '70 was conceived as an international event to celebrate Japan's rapid economic growth during the 1960s. Isozaki participated in drawing up the master plan, proposing the concept for the central facility of the exhibition spaces, the Festival Plaza. The intention here was to orchestrate theatrical space that could bring together a large number of performers and visitors, using a variety of new technologies. The variable, computerized components—a roof that could be opened to the sky; robots moving on the ground; sound, lighting, and other equipment hanging from above; movable seating—would make for a truly "cybernetic environment."

The proposal was approved in principle and a team was formed to implement it. Kenzo Tange and URTEC designed the vast roof; Yoshikatsu Tsuboi and Mamoru Kawaguchi were the structural consultants; and Isozaki Atelier organized technological systems and functional programs for using them in festive events.

Two large robots, one for performance (called Deme) and the other for control (called Deku), "performed" in the space, which could accommodate up to 10,000 people. Among the new technologies used in the Festival Plaza were flexible spectator seating and stages whose reconfiguration for different events was controlled by computer; an acoustic system consisting of hundreds of speakers in dynamic three-dimensional matrices of sound sources; and a performance lighting system on gantries hung from the top frame that could be moved both horizontally and vertically. Synthesizers and other equipment not commercially available at the time had to be developed for the plaza to coordinate with the computer system. Although the relatively unsophisticated technology of the time proved to be a serious limitation, this complex ensemble served the purpose for which it was intended: to give people an invigorating, memorable experience of the versatile technology of theatrical and creative environments.

The term "festival plaza" became well established after this design, and the concept was widely used for central facilities in exhibitions and urban development plans. Unfortunately, the same cannot be said for the expression "cybernetic environment," although as large entertainment facilities like discotheques have grown in importance, the concept has finally begun to take on new life.

1. Deme, one of two large robots used in the plaza.
2. Deme's kinetic arm.
3. Section, showing the robots and components hanging from gantries above.
4. Overall view of the Festival Plaza.

3

43

4

Fukuoka City Bank Head Office and Addition

Fukuoka, Japan, 1968–71 (head office) and 1978–83 (addition)

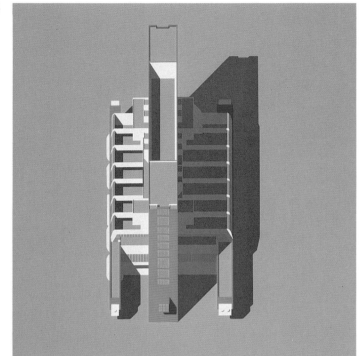

1

Isozaki Atelier, which had designed several branches of the Fukuoka City Bank (formerly the Fukuoka Mutual Bank), was asked to create their new headquarters on a site across from Hakata Station in Fukuoka, Kyushu. Design was initiated in 1968, and construction was completed in 1971. Ten years after the commission for the head office, new designs were required for an addition on a neighboring site.

The Oita Prefectural Library is the prime example of the architectural and structural techniques developed by Isozaki in the 1960s. There the central zone, the core of the architectural system, is bounded by paired walls, and other functional elements are projected out from the core. This design concept is developed on a much larger scale for the Fukuoka City Bank Head Office. During the design process the specifications for floor space and the number of rooms were changed several times, and provisions had to be made for expected fluctuations in floor-space requirements that would continue after the building was finished. The clients also needed a scheme that was open to expansion, as they were planning for extensions every ten years or so. The first of these was designed in 1978.

The overall structure is defined by two large walls running parallel along the full length of the site (260 feet) and rising to 160 feet, the maximum height permitted due to air traffic from the nearby airport. To house the required spaces at high levels, the core section has projections front and back in which rooms are arranged in units. The first floor of the forward section contains the banking hall, and at the back is the parking garage; on the next level are administrative offices, with executive offices on top. Just as in the Oita Prefectural Library, the total image is established by the subordination of the variously shaped elements to the imposing central core with its great walls.

The high-rise section is faced in red Indian sandstone, whose color and surface texture are enhanced by the strong light characteristic of this area in the south of Japan. Sandstone was used again for MOCA, also in a location with strong sunlight (southern California), and in that regard the bank was an important precedent in the design of the art museum.

Sepia-colored cor-ten steel was selected for the protruding units in the lower structure to match the red sandstone, while red granite was used for the surfaces of the huge beams receiving these sections. Wide cylinders containing rooms and stairways stand like circular columns on the exterior of the banking hall, establishing the bank's monumental presence across from the station plaza.

1. *Axonometric (silk screen).*
2. *Exterior wall, faced in red Indian sandstone.*

46

3. View of the bank from Hakata Station.
4-7. Exterior details.

4

6

5

7

48

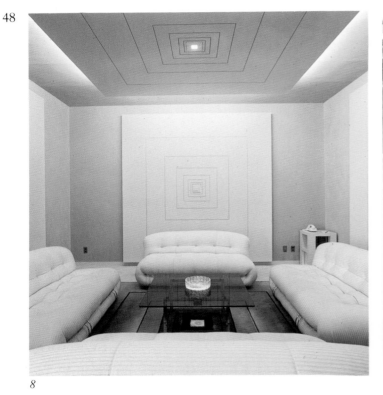

8

9

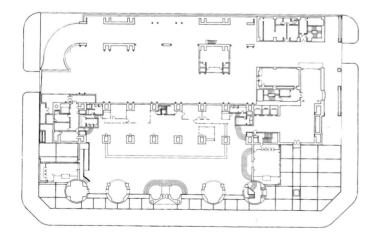

12

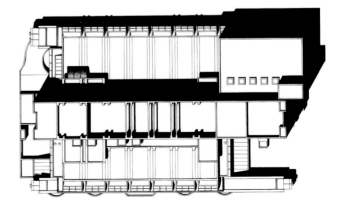

13

```
20     100          200
```

8, 9. *Interior views.*
10, 11. *Meeting rooms.*
12. *First-floor plan.*
13. *Roof plan.*
14. *Front elevation.*

49

10

11

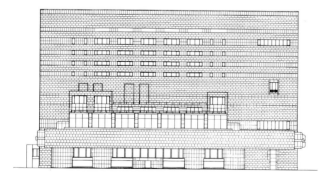

14

50

15

17

16

18

15-18. *Interior views.*
19. *Aiko Miyawaki's screen in front of a*
    meeting room.

19

Computer-Aided City
Makuhari, Chiba, Japan, 1972

1

Combining the concept of computer-supported urban space with that of the "festival plaza" leads to something like a cabled city, animated by information exchanged through coaxial lines. Today data transmission is restricted to the one-way systems of current TV and radio, but coaxial cables can easily handle the transmission of large volumes of data in both directions. With this network in place, a supercomputer for information exchange, processing, and storage could function as the "brains" of the city. Although cities may now be capable of handling the distribution of information, the constant flow of massive quantities of visual and tactile information can only be processed with advanced technology.

53

54

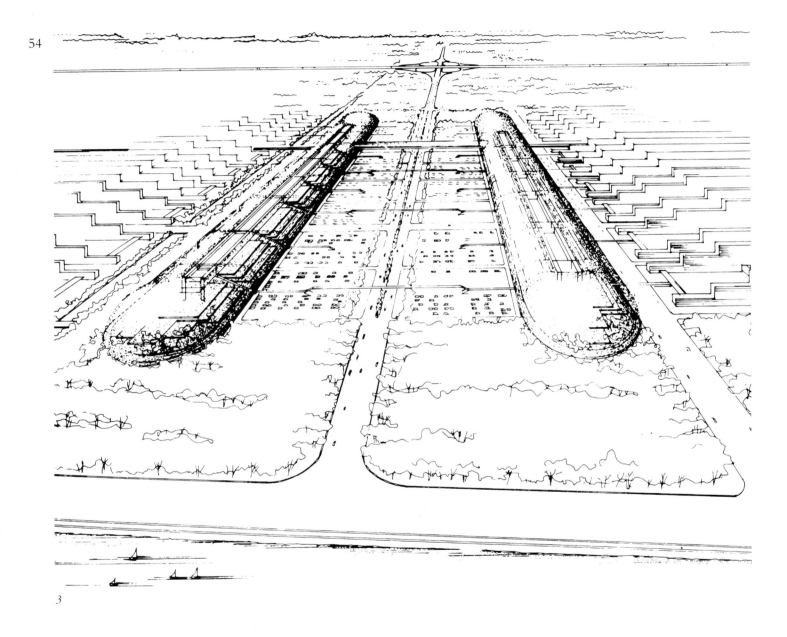

3

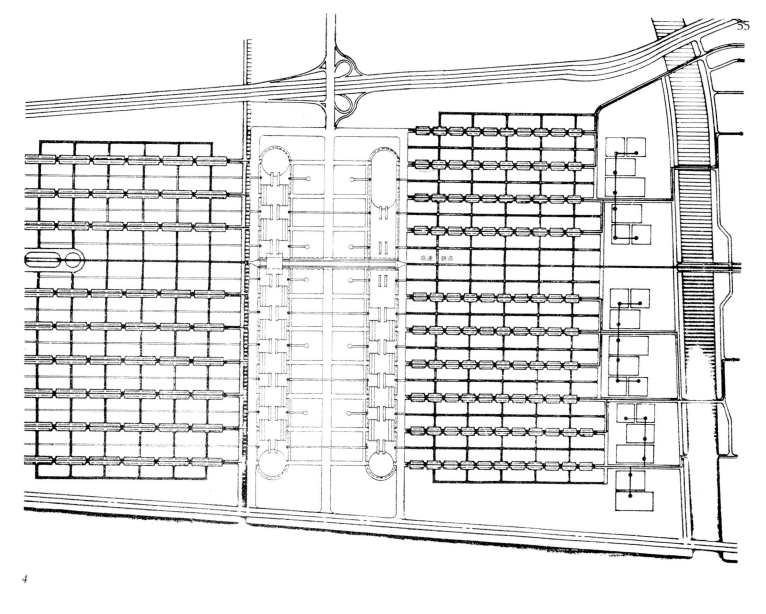

高速 鉄道

4

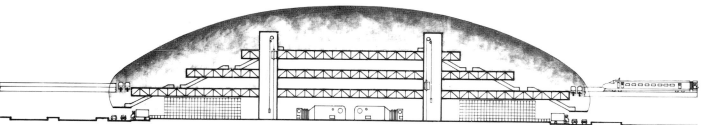

5

Fujimi Country Clubhouse

Oita, Japan, 1973–74

56

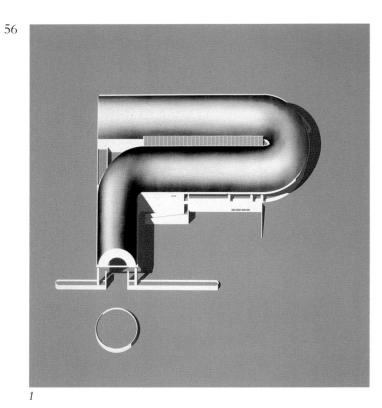

1

2

The question "Why is it that the Japanese love golf so much?"—often asked in Japan as well as elsewhere—is embodied in the plan of this golf clubhouse, which takes the shape of a question mark. The form was arrived at only in the final stage of design; the initial concept simply outlined a continuous barrel-vaulted structure. This was Isozaki's first use of the barrel vault, which appears again in several later designs. In the early 1970s he was working with the purest and most basic geometric forms, like the square, the circle, and the equilateral triangle, creating architecture by developing them into three dimensions. Here the barrel vault is reinterpreted in this spirit.

One reason for choosing a vault form was to secure the view over the golf course from inside the building. In terms of structure, this means that the vault must be supported with transverse tension bars to allow for windows in the walls beneath it. Sections that need to be closed off, like locker rooms, are set partially underground. Located above these are semi-independent spaces for the entrance hall, lounges, restaurant, meeting rooms, and other functions—developed in one almost continuous whole. It is the winding of the barrel vault that makes it possible to create areas of spatial independence. The vault protrudes in front, forming a semicircular entrance canopy. The design of the front elevation includes references to the entrance section of Palladio's Villa Poiana.

Both exterior and interior walls are concrete faced with stucco. Sound-insulation plaster is sprayed onto the interior surface of the vault, while copper covers the roof on a base of thermal insulating material.

10 50 100

1. Axonometric (silk screen).
2. Roof plan.
3. View of the clubhouse within the
   surrounding landscape.

3

58

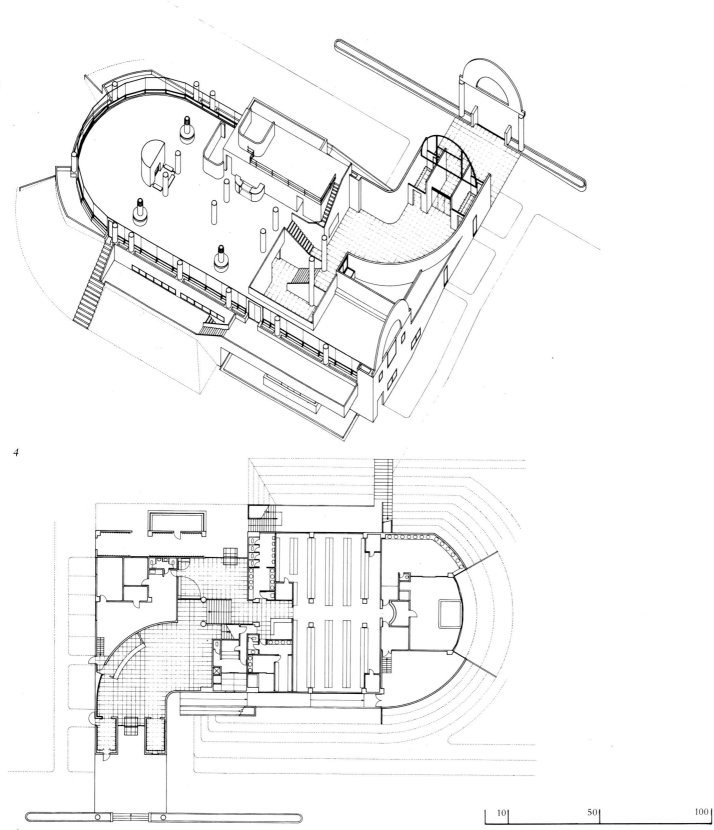

4

6

10   50   100

59

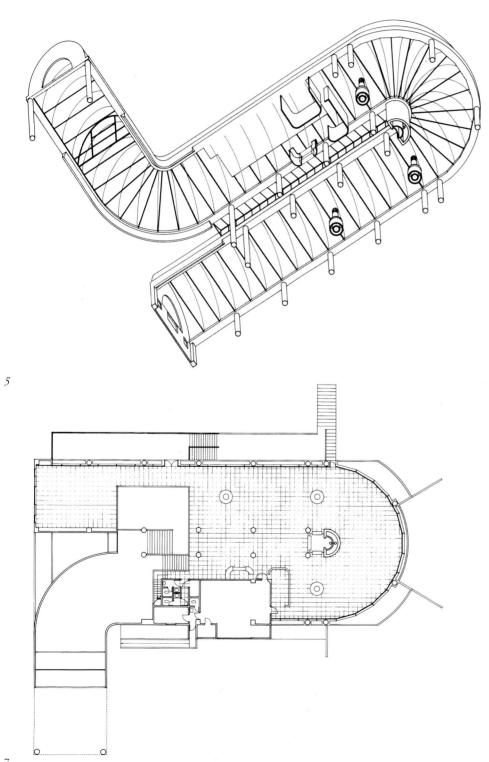

5

7

60

8

9

8, 9. *Exterior views, showing the barrel-vault roof.*
10. *The entrance.*

11. The restaurant and lounge.
12, 13. Interior details.
14. View of the restaurant.

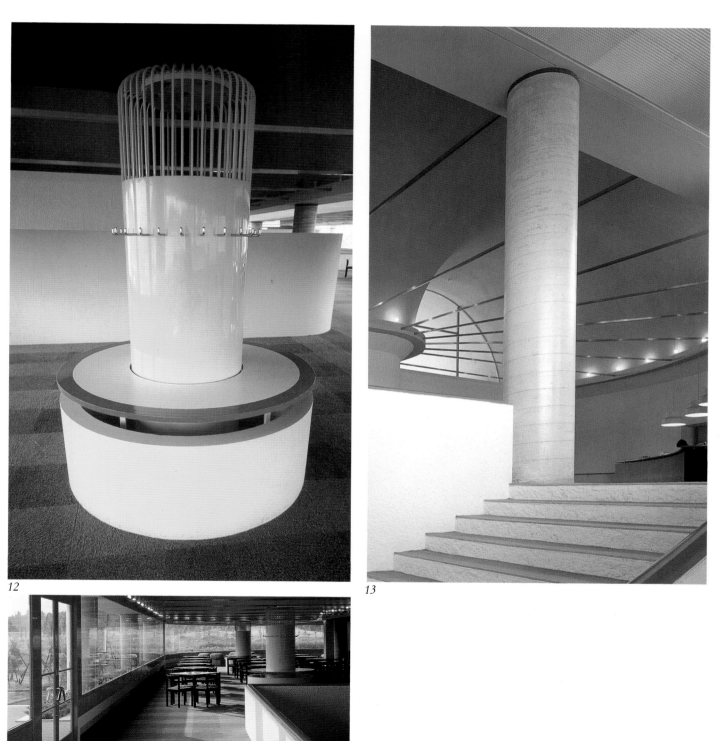

12

13

14

Kitakyushu City Museum of Art and Annex

Kitakyushu, Fukuoka, Japan, 1972–74 and 1985–86 (annex)

The Kitakyushu museum, located on a hilltop in the center of the city, has a commanding view of the surrounding area. One of its main purposes was to foster community pride, and it now stands as a distinctive monument and landmark.

The main gallery, completed in 1974, consists of two elongated cubes, 32 feet square on the face and 200 feet long. The two square faces seem to float out of the building, and the rest of the design has been submerged as much as possible to enhance this effect. Whereas the outer walls of the cubes are covered with four-foot-square die-cast aluminum panels, the lower part of the building, housing the other facilities, has walls of exposed concrete. This is to encourage ivy growth, which will eventually cloak the base of the structure in green, further accentuating the hovering cubes.

Beneath the cubes is the entrance hall, covered in white marble. To the left of the entrance is a naturally lit exhibition wing, and to the right is the office wing. An auditorium, a studio, and a small hall in the basement serve as a "living museum" for the community.

The annex was built to alleviate the space shortage in the main building, especially in the community galleries, and it stands to one side of the entrance court and main approach. The lower portion of the annex is of rusticated concrete; the upper portion is of brick. The first floor is an independent community gallery, and the second floor provides storage space and research areas. On the third-floor level are a sculpture garden, a gallery for woodblock prints, and an atrium that connects directly to the main gallery through an open corridor.

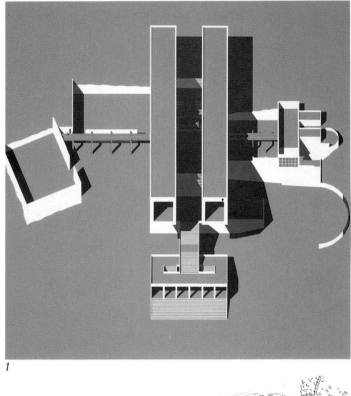

1

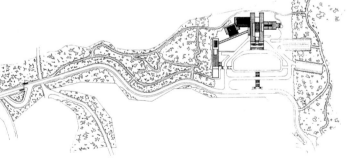

2

500   1000

1. *Axonometric (silk screen)*.
2. *Site plan*.
3. *View of the entrance, with the annex in the background*.

3

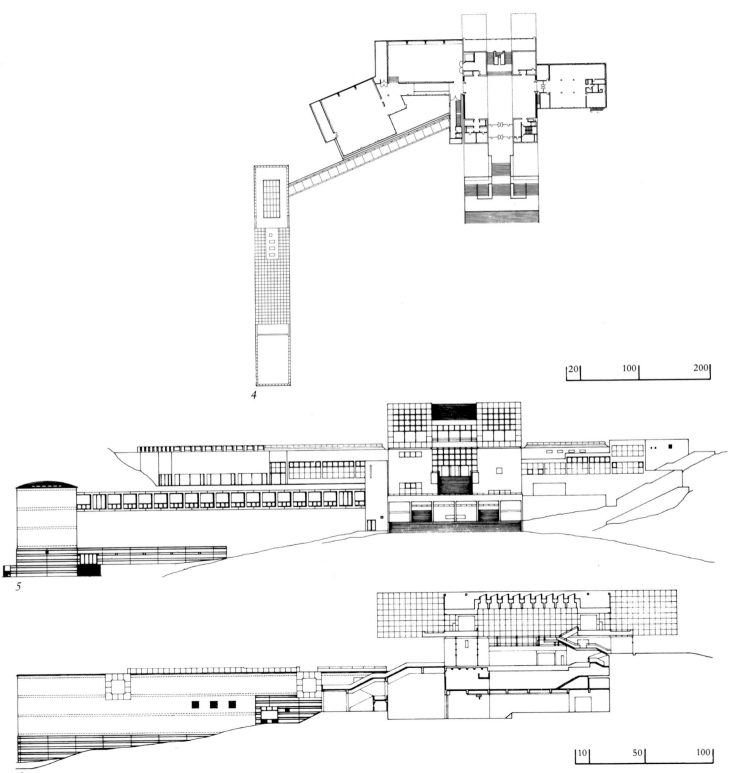

4

|20| 100| 200|

5

6

|10| 50| 100|

4. Entrance-level plan.
5. Front elevation.
6. Section through the entrance, with the annex
   in the background.
7. Axonometric.

   Overleaf:
8. The main approach to the museum.

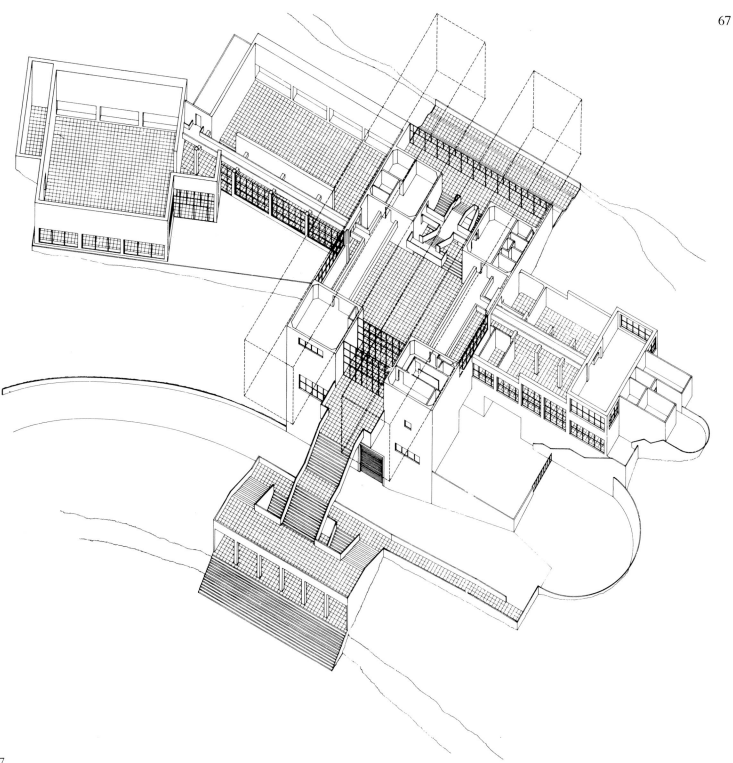

9. *Detail of the entrance hall.*
10, 11. *Interior views.*

10

11

12. *View of the annex.*
13. *The annex sculpture garden.*
14. *The atrium between the annex and the main building.*

72

12

13

15, 16. *Interior circulation areas.*
17. *The grand staircase.*

74

15

16

Kitakyushu Central Library
Kitakyushu, Fukuoka, Japan, 1973–74

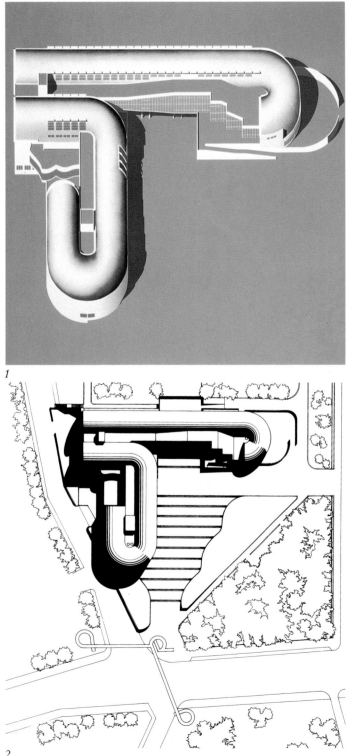

1

2

This project, which came directly after the Fujimi Country Clubhouse, also features a big, double-barrel-vault roof. The program called for an independent cultural facility housing the city's central library, a historical museum, and an audiovisual resource center, all combined on one site. The scheme gathers all of these elements within one architectural form, unified by the barrel vaults.

In one short section the two vaulted roofs run parallel. One soon turns away from its partner, and then turns in on itself again, while the other continues on in the same direction, ending in a short "hook." The first vault covers the historical museum; the second tops the library and, in its hook, the audiovisual center. The barrel vaults are composed of two precast-concrete panels connected to each other at the central top section, forming three-pin arches covered by copper sheets. Three kinds of precast-concrete forms are used for the roof base—one for linear parts and two fan shapes for curved parts—and the top line of the vault is horizontally supported. The height of the rooms underneath is adjusted for various levels using base sections of cast-in-place concrete, resulting in rooms in a wide range of sizes. The precast ribs are left exposed, and the rhythmical articulation of rooms is visible in the ceilings.

Parallel to the gradually rising floor levels in the library building is an interior sloping path. Forming an L shape, the long rear elevation faces onto a park, and the approach by foot to the building is on this side. From the other side of the library building the keep of the town castle can be seen.

The museum is devoted to exhibitions of ancient dwellings and other structures of the region, as well as of historical materials relating to the area's culture. At one end of the museum is a large stained-glass "rose window" designed by Isozaki. It is a colorful representation of a diagram—created by the philosopher Baien Miura, who was born nearby— that expresses the ideas of the cosmos and nature in terms of the Oriental concept of yin and yang. The restaurant facing it has an external form determined by Isozaki's "Marilyn Monroe" curve. These elements serve as a contrast to the historical architectural forms of the vaults and the rose window.

30   150   300

1. *Axonometric (silk screen).*
2. *Site plan.*
3. *View from the street, showing the curved barrel-vault roof.*

3

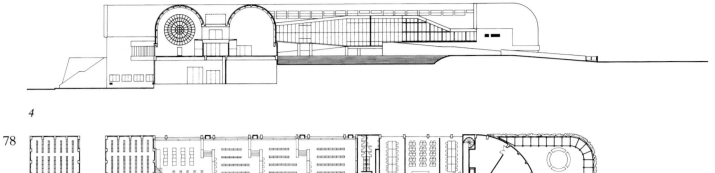

4

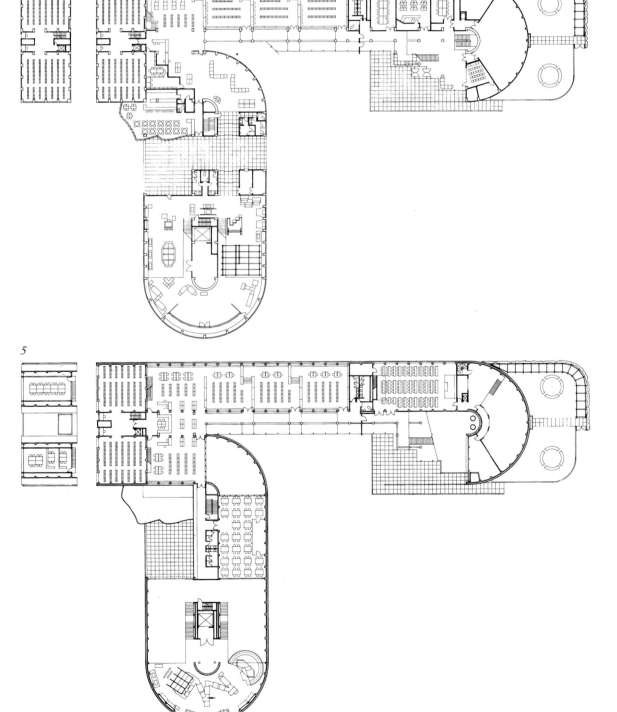

5

6

10   50   100

4. *Section through the museum wing, with the rose window at left.*
5. *First-floor plan.*
6. *Second-floor plan.*
7. *Axonometric showing the assembly of the prefabricated concrete shells.*
8. *Structural axonometric.*

Overleaf:
9. *Exterior view of the vaulted roof.*

7

8

10. *Detail of the exterior.*
11, 12. *Exterior views.*

11

12

13. *The rear facade.*
14, 15. *The rose window, from outside and inside.*

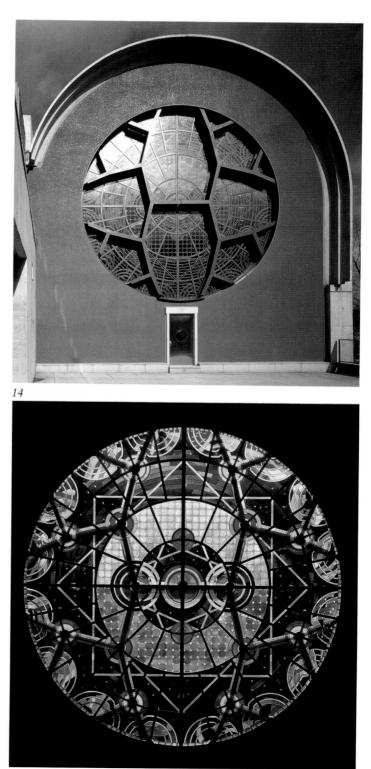

14

15

16. The entrance hall.
17. View from the second-floor mezzanine.
18. The structural ribs of the winding vault.

17

18

Gunma Prefectural Museum of Fine Arts

Takasaki, Gunma, Japan, 1971–74

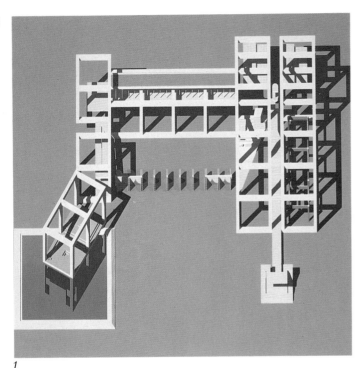

1

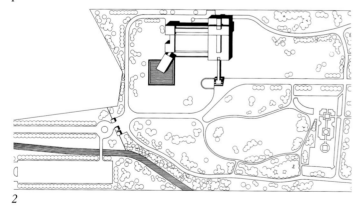

2

The first of Isozaki's many commissions for modern and contemporary art museums was received from Gunma Prefecture in 1971. After the cultural revolutions of 1968 and the exhausting work on the national project Expo '70, Isozaki felt that there was no other way to proceed in design and in the analysis of architectural programs than to trace every form, every concept, back to its origins. Only pristine, essential structures seemed to offer hope of finding new points of departure. The Gunma Prefectural Museum of Fine Arts was the first of Isozaki's designs to be executed in this spirit.

The cube—the equilateral volumetric unit—was clearly the form to begin with for the new approach. The design problem then became developing the spatial distribution from arrangements of and continuities between this basic shape as applied to the requirements of the program. The cubic framework was also taken up as a metaphor for the art museum of today, where the gallery has become a kind of port into and out of which artworks move. No mere structural device, the cube here represents the idea of the art gallery as void.

The design is based on the interaction of two architectural systems: the skeletal parti of forty-foot cubes (the basic structure) and the exhibition spaces, stairways, administrative offices, lighting, and so on (the supplemental structure). The series of cubes, laid out on an expansive lawn in a parklike setting, takes the form of one large rectangular block, which houses the main exhibition space, and two shorter, projecting wings. The first of these is perpendicular to the central block and contains the entrance hall. The second, angled off the building's primary axis, holds a gallery for traditional Japanese art. This wing is elevated above a square reflecting pool, with an open terrace at the first-floor level.

The entire south side of the building is clad in four-foot-square panels of aluminum or glass, creating a gleaming, gridded facade. Although the rear (north) elevation was also meant to be covered in aluminum, it was left in exposed concrete due to financial constraints.

Principles of framing, grids, flush surfaces, and other aspects of this design were later applied to the new master plan for the Brooklyn Museum.

500 | 1000 |

1. *Axonometric (silk screen).*
2. *Site plan.*
3. *Facade detail, showing the terrace and the reflecting pool.*

3

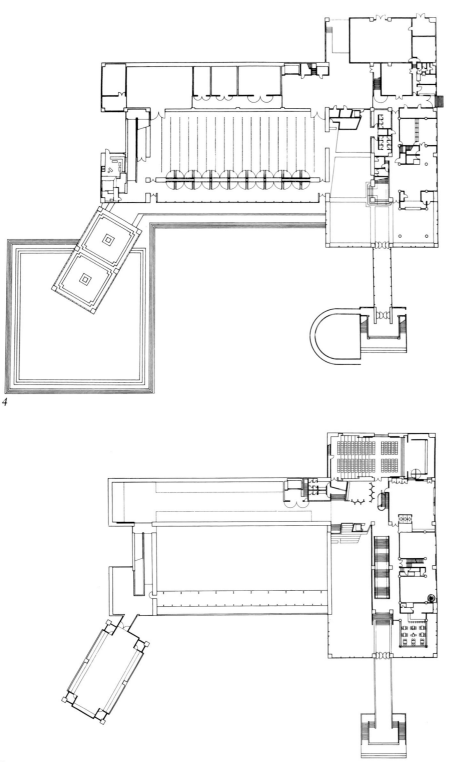

4

20 | 100 | 200 |

4. *First-floor plan.*
5. *Second-floor plan.*
6. *Front elevation.*
7. *Side elevation.*
8. *Section through the entrance.*

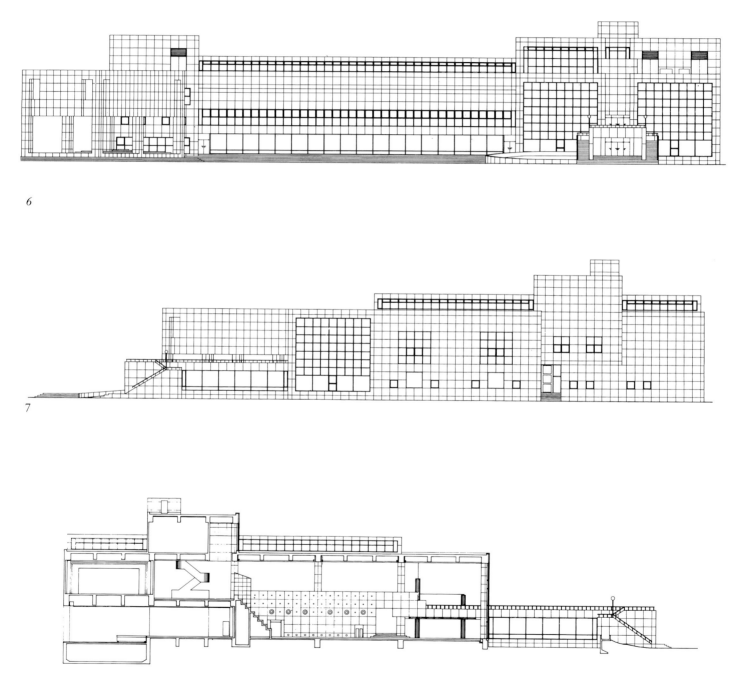

6

7

8

<table>
<tr><td>10</td><td>50</td><td>100</td></tr>
</table>

92

9

10

9. The gallery for Japanese arts hovering over
   the man-made pool.
10. View through the pilotis.
11-13. Details of the entrance block facade.

11

13

12

94

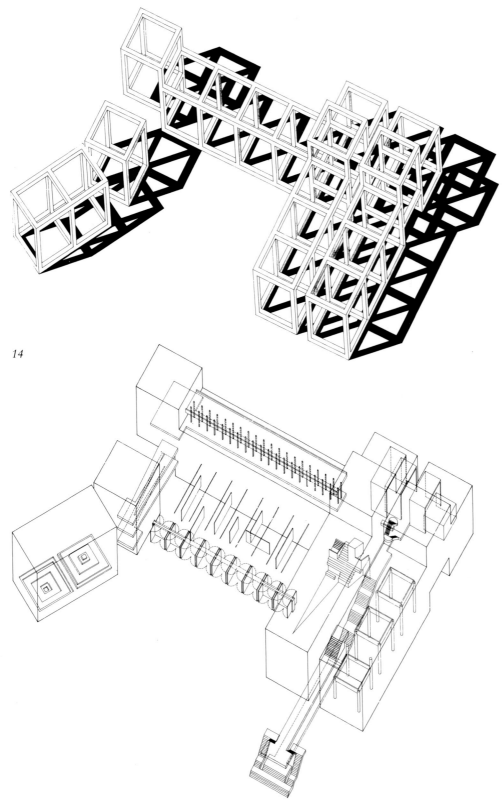

14

15

14. Conceptual axonometric of the basic
    structure.
15. Conceptual axonometric of the supplemental
    structure.
16. First-floor gallery.
17. The main staircase.
18. The entrance lobby.

Overleaf:
19. The museum in its park setting.

16

18

17

West Japan General Exhibition Center

Kitakyushu, Fukuoka, Japan, 1975–77

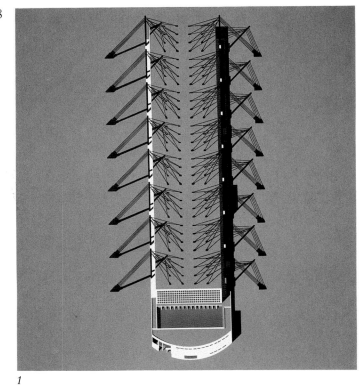

From the very early stages of this design, the intention was to fill the building with metaphors of water. The only way to deal effectively with the setting—a former port, where large-scale elements such as cranes, oil tanks, chimney stacks, and warehouses coexisted in a disorderly and arbitrary manner—was to treat the structure symbolically. The row of steel pillars that support the wires of the suspended roof resemble the masts of boats with their sails down, or the steel frames of a long-span bridge. The 165-by-560-foot exhibition space was meant to have a thin, wavy covering to evoke the image of looking up at the sparkling water's surface from below; but due to the tight budget the structure was left exposed. The courtyard to the office block was also filled with water, creating the illusion that the entire building was adrift.

2

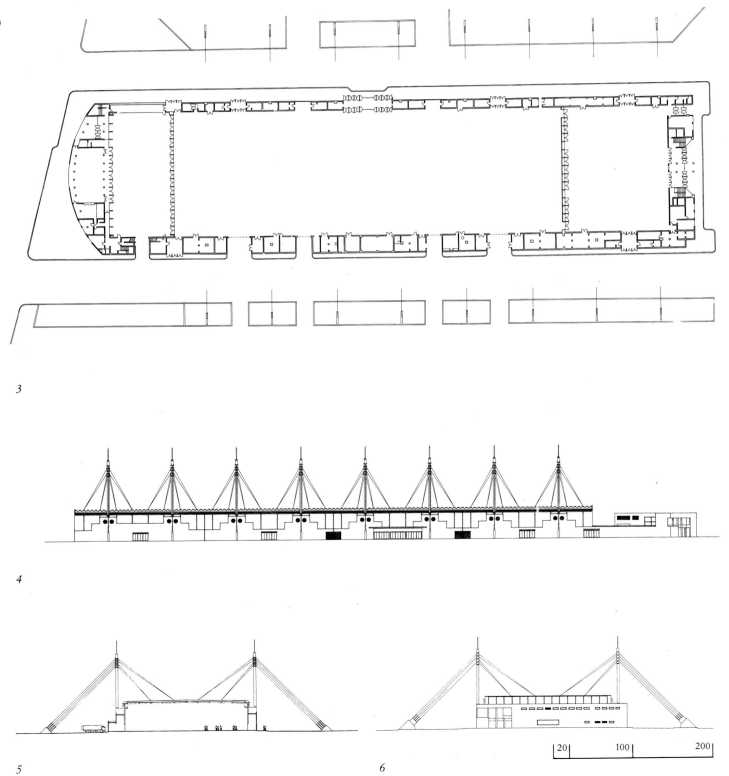

100

3

4

5

6

20 100 200

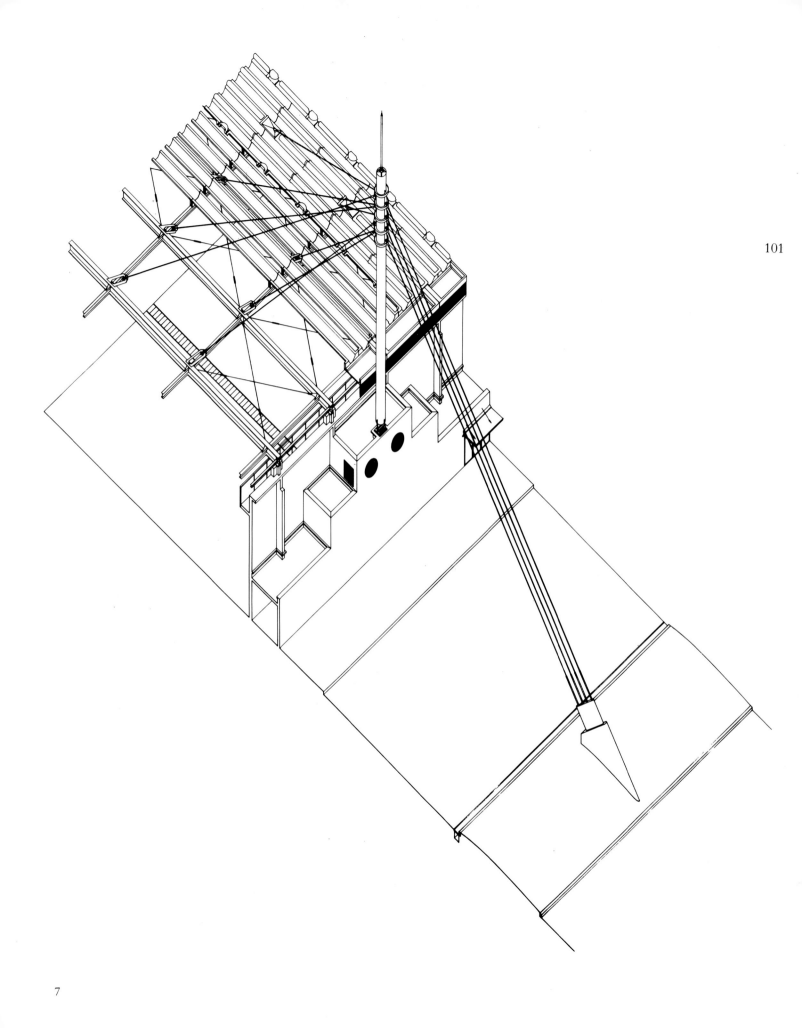

8

9

8. *View from the pool.*
9. *View from the main street.*
10. *The exhibition space.*

Kamioka Town Hall
Gifu, Japan, 1976–78

1

The initial plan for this building, to be located in the middle of the remote mining town of Kamioka, was for a rather low structure that would remain inconspicuous among the surrounding houses, with their tarred tin roofs. This design was rejected, however, and a building that contrasted with the dark atmosphere of the town was requested instead. The final design is a structure with an exterior of gleaming silver aluminum that resembles a spaceship.

Several basic forms are combined in this building, which also has an unusual combination of finishing materials (aluminum and granite). The cubic structure of the main entrance for the executive offices is faced in pink granite. A double-cylinder form houses the reception area on the lower floor and an assembly hall on the upper floor. The area in between, in certain respects an extension of the entrance block, is used for offices; Isozaki's "Marilyn Monroe" curve provides a softening effect here.

1. Axonometric (silk screen).
2. Exterior view of the assembly hall, with
   offices underneath.

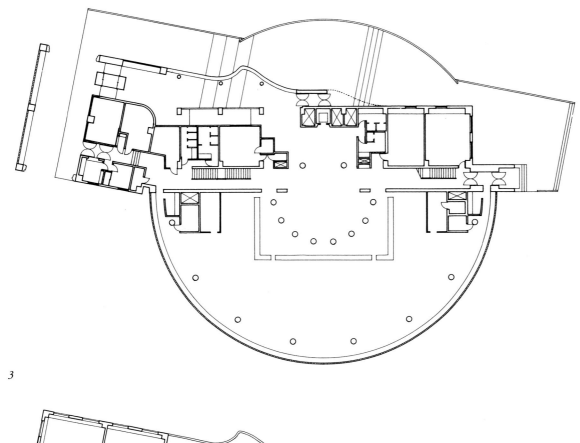

3

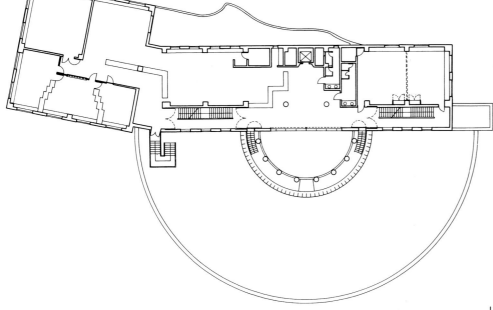

4

3. *First-floor plan.*
4. *Third-floor plan.*
5. *Elevation of the entrance cube (left) and the assembly hall (right).*
6. *End elevation.*
7. *End elevation of the entrance cube.*
8. *Section.*

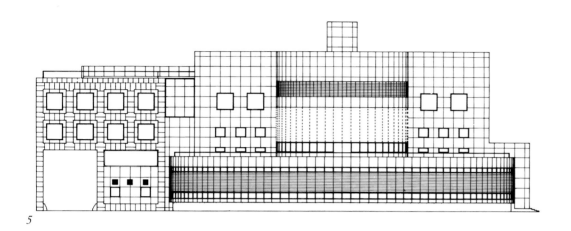

5

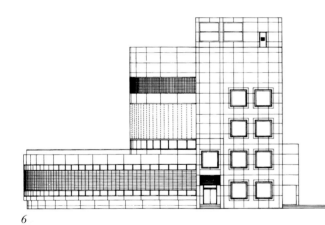

6

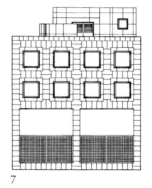

7

8

9. The town hall in context.
10. Detail of the exterior.
11. View from the roof terrace.

10

11

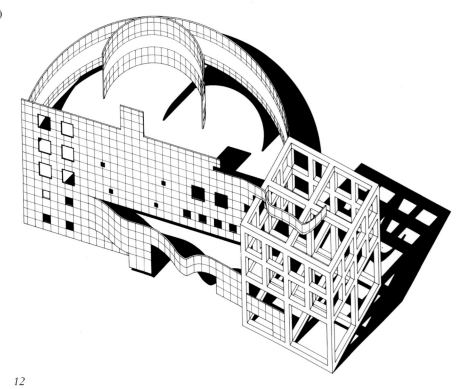

12

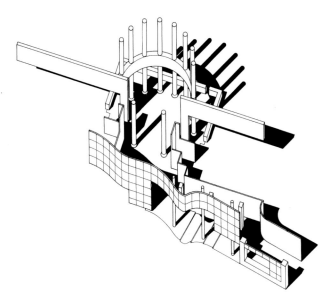

13

12. *Axonometric showing the entrance cube's*
    modular frame.
13. *Axonometric diagram of public circulation.*
14. *Axonometric.*

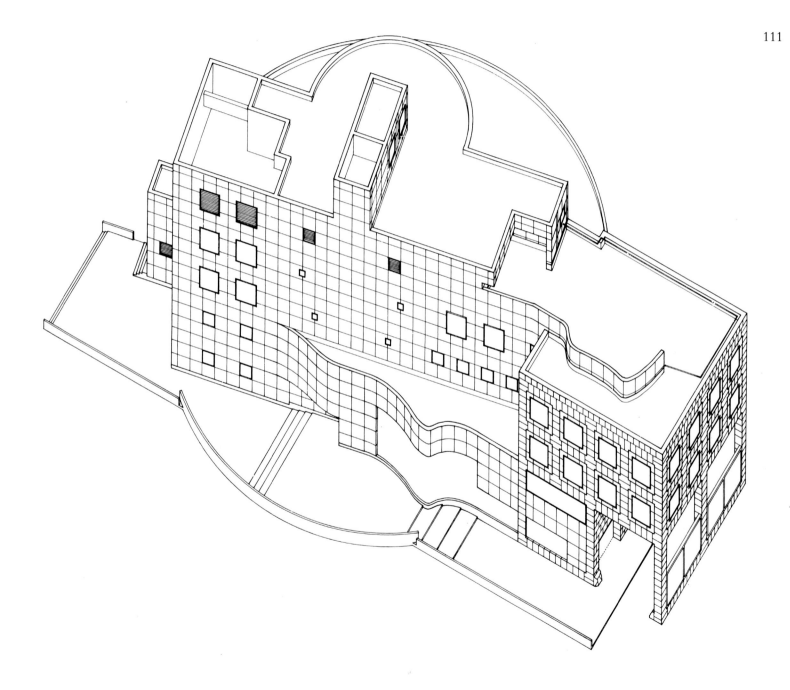

15, 16. Interior views.
17. The semicircular reception area.

112

15

16.

Nakayama House

Oita, Japan, 1964

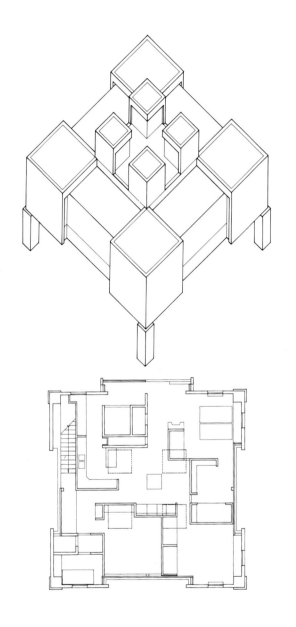

1

2

Located in the downtown area of a city that was on the verge of high-rise development, this project called for a clinic and a residence in separate buildings (an urban residence type called a *machiya* in Japanese) that was protected from outside views. The image underlying the design was inspired by the handling of light and atmosphere in Vermeer's paintings. The quartered streetfront windows of old Dutch town houses are referred to here in the four clerestory windows grouped in the center of the roof, but they are transformed by the need to have daylight entering at an angle from above.

Although the desire was to design a three-dimensional composition of pure Platonic forms, it did not seem feasible because the method of lighting dictated a specific division of rooms and structures. This problem was resolved only by departing from modern architecture's credo that spatial division should conform to function. The solution was two completely unrelated internal systems—the primary structure (determined by the lighting method), and the layout for furniture, storage spaces, and domestic artifacts—which were designed separately and simply put together. Discontinuities and skewed elements appear throughout, perhaps most distinctly in the relationship between the clerestories and the placement of equipment, and pointing out these disjunctions is one of the main design themes.

Before the big buildings went up, the Nakayama House stood on its own in serene isolation; it was not long, however, before it was completely surrounded. But this hermetic microcosm was designed to be insulated from the outside world, to have its autonomy secured as land, space, and sky were closed off all around. The design was severely criticized by many observers at the time because it so completely cut off its surroundings; but it was a particular response to a very special program and was not intended as a general solution.

10   20   40

1. Axonometric.
2. Floor plan.
3. Night view.
4. Corner elevation.

115

3

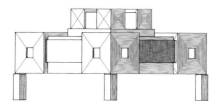

4

117

6

7

Yano House

Kawasaki, Japan, 1973–75

118

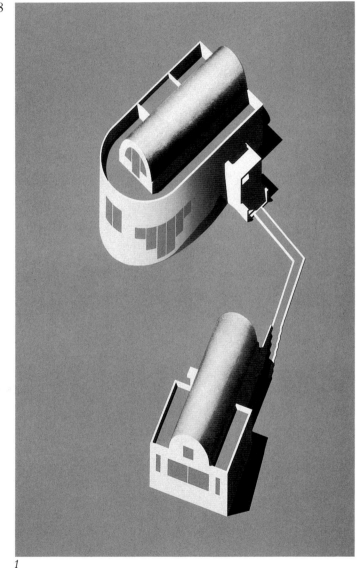

Of the two separate structures here—a clinic and a house—the design for the latter was derived from an earlier project, the Responsive House, whose cross section is now extruded in one direction. The principal daytime domestic space—the living and dining area—is situated on the first floor. The suspended spherical bedroom of the Responsive House is transformed here into a central vaulted structure containing a study and a bedroom.

The primary ceiling height is determined by the varying elevation of the site, which slopes down toward the south. On the exterior the house looks very simple, with only one and a half floors, but a complex spatial composition is developed through five interior levels connected by stairs. Thin concrete plates are used for the walls and the roof vault to enclose the interior space, while large windows in the living room establish continuity with the outside. On the south side, however, the view is obscured from eye level downward to maintain the sense of stability in the living room. The vaulted bedroom and study are structurally united in one continuous whole, which, at the south elevation, ends in a perfect semicircular surface: another element designed to emphasize the sense of interior enclosure.

The interior dimensions in the Yano House had to be carefully controlled in order to balance the large architectural components, like the vault roof, within the concrete composition. Even more important in this respect are two cylindrical columns in the center of the living room. Aside from their obvious purpose of supporting the second floor, they are indispensable in establishing a centripetal center in a space with a curved wall and rather odd window forms. Although the columns were meant to be highly symbolic elements, in the end they were unfortunately thicker than intended, revealing the limitations of reinforced concrete.

1

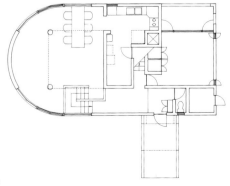

2

| 10 | 20 | 40 |

1. *Axonometric (silk screen).*
2. *Entrance-level plan.*
3. *The house in its setting.*
4. *Entrance elevation.*
5. *Elevation of the semicircular end.*

3

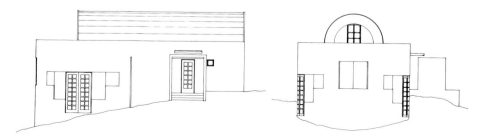

4

5

6. *The entryway.*
7. *The living room.*
8. *The house extending into the landscape.*

120

6

7

Kaijima House
Tokyo, 1976–77

1

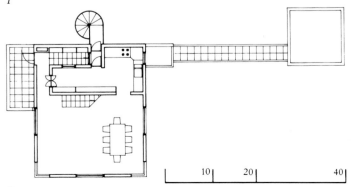

2

3

Two cubes of different sizes are placed on the lawn. The smaller one contains a gateway and a machinery room; the bigger one is a home with a T-shaped cross-vault top sheltering the bedrooms. As in the Yano residence, the bedroom forms present a womblike image. In contrast, the main floor, which is a public area, is made up of right angles. The scheme explores the question of whether a simple cube can effectively contain a residence. Will the cube have to be modified to such an extent that the original form is barely recognizable? The goal was to create a design where the pure three-dimensional structure and the architectural message are in perfect balance.

4

1. Axonometric (silk screen).
2. First-floor plan.
3. View from the rear, showing the double barrel-vault roof.

Hayashi House

Fukuoka, Japan, 1976–77

124

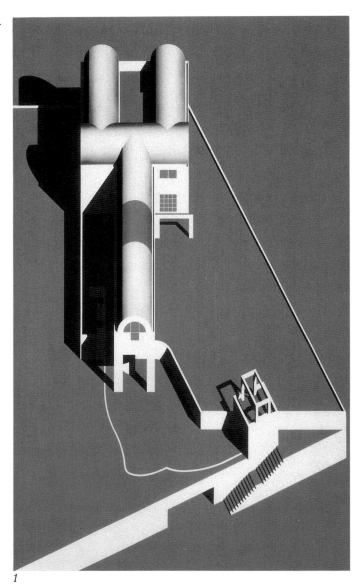

1

The site for this residence in the low hills of the western part of Fukuoka City was flattened out on two levels behind an existing retaining wall. The view to the southeast stretches far and wide, taking the eye over the Tsukushi plain, which is punctuated by groups of houses nearby, hills in the middle distance, and silhouetted mountains at its boundary. To secure this view, the main structure of the two-story, thirty-eight-foot-square house is placed over the retaining wall, with the southeast elevation rising from it.

A long "nose" section extends more than forty feet from the front "face" of the house down toward the entrance, which opens onto a small enclosed area inside a "folly" gatehouse. A path meanders through steps, stepping stones, and other elements to compose the approach to the main entrance. A prism-topped atrium stairwell, providing access from the entrance up to the main part of the house, runs along the northwest interior of the nose. Slope and stairs cover the level difference between the two sections of the site. The stairwell extends through all four interior levels of the nose, connecting the basement rooms, the ground-floor entrance hall, the mezzanine, and the children's rooms here, as well as the two floors of the main structure.

Roofing consists of a two-pronged fork of tunnel-vault sections. The vaulted rooms in the house proper and the nose are all bedrooms, and low-ceilinged side areas of the house have frames and partitions for the bathroom, closets, and other rooms. A double-height living room occupies one third of the house, and side alcoves have windows on the southeast elevation. Between the alcoves is a dining room with double doors opening onto the terrace.

10   25   50

2

3

4. The entrance foyer.
5. The dining room.
6. Detail of the intersecting vaults.

4

5

1. *Axonometric (silk screen).*
2. *First-floor plan.*
3. *View from the street.*

Karashima House

Oita, Japan, 1977–78

128

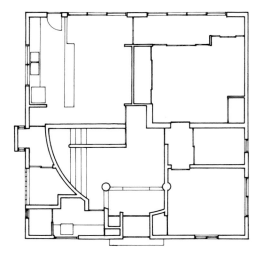

1

The biggest problem in the design of this house, which faces onto a busy street near a bustling shopping center in the city of Oita, was reducing the traffic noise as much as possible. To this end, most of the south (street) elevation is in exposed concrete and glass blocks; openings are kept to an absolute minimum. In dividing the space of the basic square plan, circulation and service areas are assigned to the southern section, while the rooms on the north side are in the quiet zone shielded from the road.

The function of the double-height atrium hall as the central space—a kind of interior courtyard—is emphasized by its prominent semicircular shape and the gentle light falling from the glass-block wall at the top. The half-cylinder form constitutes the only element animating the external view of the otherwise reticent front facade. In this sense its function is similar to that of the pilasters that give distinction to a piano nobile.

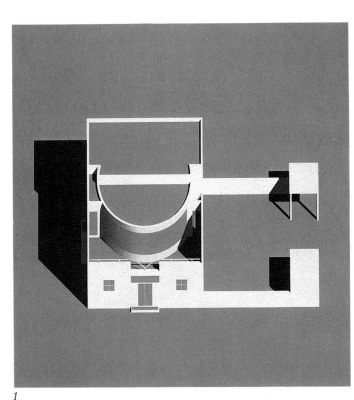

5 10 20

2

3

4. *The entrance.*
5. *The stairs to the second floor.*
6. *Detail of the double-height atrium hall.*

130

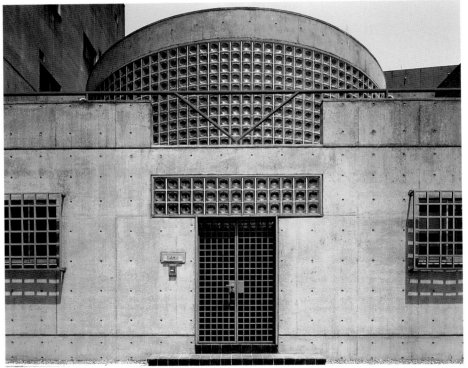

4

5

6

Aoki House

Tokyo, Japan, 1977–78

132

Beyond the requirements of site and program, the shape and character of this small urban residence were determined by severe restrictions on materials and an extreme simplification of the skeleton. Structurally it is made up of four void slab portal units, the ends left open, stacked on top of each other. With this slab system, stairways can be located only on the outside. At the top of the structure is a vaulted roof, but here it is larger than in previous residences (eighteen instead of twelve feet in diameter), and it is pierced on one side by a much smaller one. Exterior and interior walls and ceilings are finished in exposed concrete; only the flooring receives special treatment, with Japanese *genshoseki* stone and carpeting. The basement and first floor serve as gallery space for the owner to show his metalwork; the second floor is his studio; the third has private rooms; and the loft area under the small vaulted roof holds the dining room and kitchen.

The large vault is obscured from view around the house by parapets at the fourth-floor level. Ascending a series of narrow stairways, one encounters it only at the parapet level, coming upon the door quite suddenly. Entering the vault is akin to being pushed unexpectedly from the wings onto a stage, as the door opens onto the "stage scenery": a single granite slab partition obscuring the dining room, an elliptical stained-glass window designed by Aiko Miyawaki floating above, and two of Isozaki's Marilyn chairs.

1

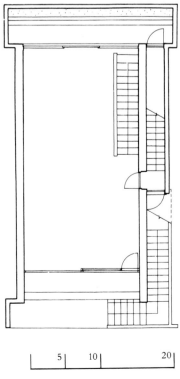

5   10   20

2

1. *Axonometric (silk screen).*
2. *Floor plan.*
3. *View of the first-floor gallery.*
4. *Detail of the top vault.*

3

4

Irahara House

Fukuoka, Japan, 1979–80

134

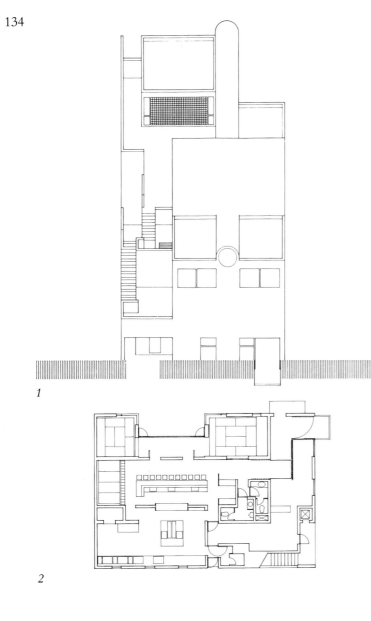

1

2

3

The owner of this building runs a restaurant out in the country, where Isozaki would stop whenever he went to the area on business. As time went on, their conversations led to his designing the restaurant-residence. It is a Japanese-style building, but all of the "soft" materials traditionally found inside have been replaced with "hard" ones. Gray tiles have been laid on the exterior, and the front yard is partitioned by an *inuyarai* aluminum fence.

10 | 25 | 50

1. *Axonometric.*
2. *Floor plan.*
3. *The entrance.*
4. *View from the street.*
5. *Longitudinal section.*

4

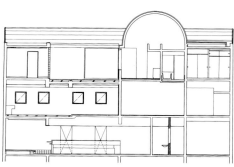

5

Nakagami House
Fukui, Japan, 1982–83

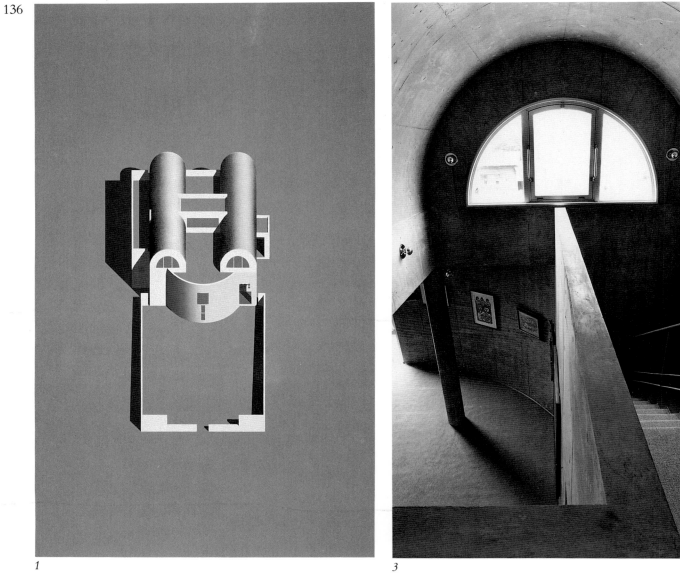

1

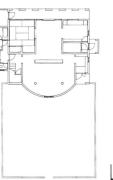

2

3

For buildings in areas that experience heavy snowfall, like the location of this house, a special architectural technology would seem to be required, but once again the appropriate solution seemed to be the favored vaults. The specifications required a salon space for lovers of art; the walls and ceiling of the space remain bare to accommodate a large collection of prints.

10   25   50

1. Axonometric (silk screen).
2. Floor plan.
3. View of the exhibition space from above.
4. Front facade, showing the barrel-vault roof.
5. Transverse section.

137

4

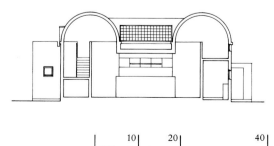

| 10 | 20 | | 40 |

5

Björnson Studio/House

Venice, California, 1981–86

138

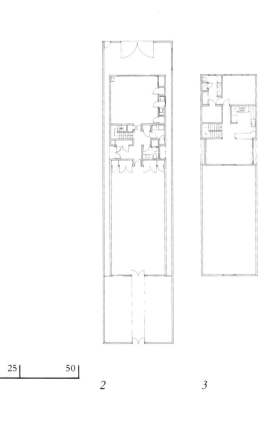

1

This studio and residence faces a narrow street not far from the oceanfront road along Los Angeles' Venice Beach, known for its rollerskaters. It was originally designed as a guest house for artists, and the program called for a studio and basic living quarters that would permit a visitor to stay and work for an extended period of time.

The site was 30 by 118 feet, and, naturally, a number of constraints were imposed by building codes. The maximum building volume possible on the site was determined to be equivalent to three and a half twenty-four-foot cubes. Two cubes were allocated to the studio, one to the living quarters, and the stairs and kitchen were placed in between. Since there were no views to speak of, the walls were left blank and skylights were created by slicing corners off the cubes.

When the design was complete, the client herself decided to move in. Being a collector of modern art, she has made the building into something more than just a residence. The studio has become a gallery, which is also used as a living room and work space. The terrace has been converted into a dining room.

The design goals were to take advantage of the southern California sun and to create an environment that would mesh with the modern art on display. The materials used were therefore typical of those found in an art gallery: wood flooring and gypsum board painted white. The exterior walls are stucco on two-by-fours, a form of construction that is almost indigenous to California.

| 10 | 25 | 50 |

2   3

4

Responsive House
1968–69

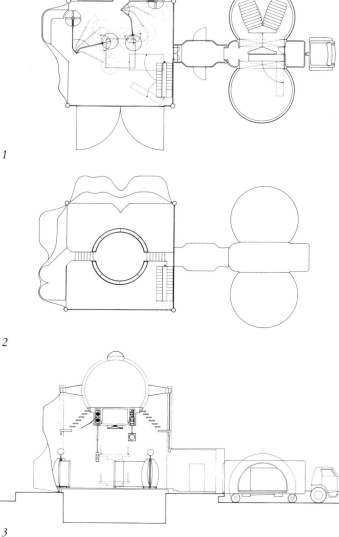

1

2

3

This project is a model of a technological house designed to be maximally responsive, allowing occupants to change layouts at will based on simple domestic devices like Japanese *shoji* screens. The hinge is the key to this solution.

Structural Framework for Spatial Responsiveness
The cube is the three-dimensional figure that holds the maximum volume with the minimum dimensions; the sphere holds the maximum volume with the minimum surface area. They are primary forms for three-dimensional structures like buildings and can be manipulated into any desired shape. Here a sixteen-foot-diameter sphere, suspended within the frame of a twenty-four-foot cube, rises to form a domed roof.

Big Furniture Robots
Three movable walls are used to define interior space, and hence domestic behavior. One of these walls is in fact a stairway giving access to the enclosed spherical room above; the other two have equipment units built in. The stairway can be rotated to create a study area in this living-room space. For example, a dining area can be created on either side of the kitchen wall—and this is done with only casters and two hinges. The front section contains a compound unit with folding table, shelves, lighting fixtures, and other elements in the most primitive kind of domestic robot. The three robots here make the cube section of the structural system responsive to day-to-day activities in the home.

Instant Environment
A versatile interior included in this design is that of the camper, which allows residents to take off to the country and stop overnight wherever they like with their own instant environment. In response to fluctuations in the volume of domestic activity, the spaces within this hybrid form, created with the most up-to-date technology, can be flexibly sectioned.

Membrane Boundary
Highly elastic, thermally insulated, semitransparent, and very weather-resistant, the membrane on the cube makes it possible to push the interior components beyond the floor edges. Two of the walls are made of this material, but the other two are solid: one is fixed to provide connections to the camper, and the other is divided into two sections that completely open out. When they are open, the mirrored surfaces inside reflect exterior light into the interior, mixing spaces at the boundary as internal and external perspectives interpenetrate.

1. First-floor plan.
2. Second-floor plan.
3. Section.
4. View of the model, showing the camper and
   the immobile house.

143

4

Electronic Media Environment

Changing the positions of the robots allows for a physical compression or expansion of interior spaces, the efficient functioning of which, of course, requires advanced electronic equipment. In addition to TVs and telephones, a data-bank terminal is necessary. Information-processing systems like videos, facsimile machines, and speakers have an important place in helping inhabitants to sift through waves of received and transmitted information. Hanging these devices from the ceiling is the most space-efficient way to accommodate them. The interior space can then be divided into upper and lower sections by the hanging deck, which forms the floor of the spherical room.

Overall Mechanism

The cube of the immobile house is static. The mobile house of the camper injects dynamism, playing the temporary living space against the permanent.

House of Nine Squares
1980

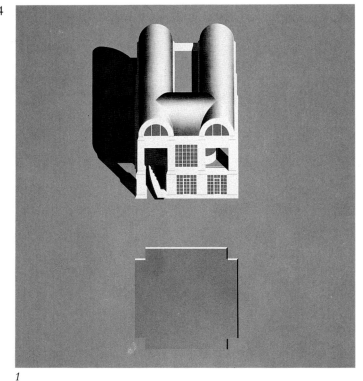

144

1

To establish a residence as architecture, two conditions must be satisfied: a concise spatial formalism not amenable to further reduction must be visible in the plan; and the essence of the house must find expression in its structure.

Nine squares defined by sixteen independent columns form the plan of this house. Centripetal symmetry keeps the framework structurally stable. Ideal for a residence, the system has been used in room layouts for Japanese private houses and in the spatial forms for villas created by Palladio and his contemporaries. It is a primeval type of space division, created by primitive man drawing a mandala of the cosmos on the ground.

The home has a very powerful effect on the formation of the mental life and personal history of the individuals who live in it. Roof, windows, hearth, and other architectural elements, used through history in endless repetition, acquired symbolic associations that penetrated to the minds and personalities of residents. But these concrete forms have in recent times been completely purged of their overt symbolic qualities, often having deteriorated to nightmares of style or kitsch. Be that as it may, the design of domestic architecture cannot escape the need to transform the house into a symbolic system. The essence of the home has to be expressed in as much detail, as many fine points, as possible. Here the vaulted roof, supported by a system of independent columns, is the principal player in the piece. With its very human scale and its gesture of internal enfolding, the vault perfectly embodies the essence of home.

1. Axonometric (silk screen).
2. First-floor plan.
3. Second-floor plan.
4. Third-floor plan.
5. Rear elevation.
6. Side elevation.
7. Section.

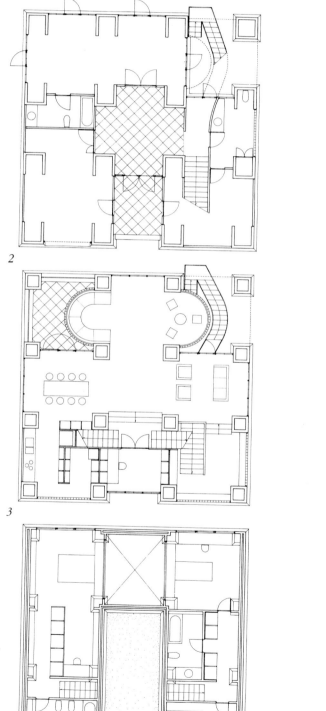

2

3

4

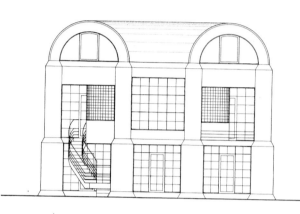

5

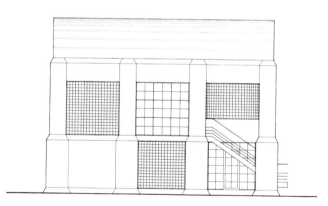

6

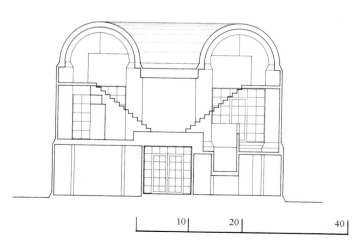

7

| 10 | 20 | | 40 |

Thatched Hut Folly
1983

1

In many ways the small teahouses scattered throughout Japanese gardens are comparable to the follies found in Western landscape architecture. This design for a thatched hut folly brings together rustic elements from Japan and the West into one structure. Its aim, however, is not to create an "integrated" style but to revive the centuries-old tradition of the tea ceremony, in which the teamaster arranges objects—whether works of art or functional articles—to be contemplated and appreciated for their aesthetic appeal. In this folly, traditional rustic objects, as well as more modern industrial materials, are combined in an "arrangement" whose spirit recalls that of the Japanese art.

The folly consists of two parts: a covered garden with a water basin and a waiting bench, and an open space surrounded by a stone wall and divided by a stainless-steel partition. On one side of the partition the tea ceremony is performed; the other side is a preparation area. The hut has a thatched roof, the most common material used for teahouses in Japan since the sixteenth century.

1. *Axonometric (silk screen).*
2. *Exterior axonometric (silk screen).*
3. *Interior axonometric (silk screen).*

147

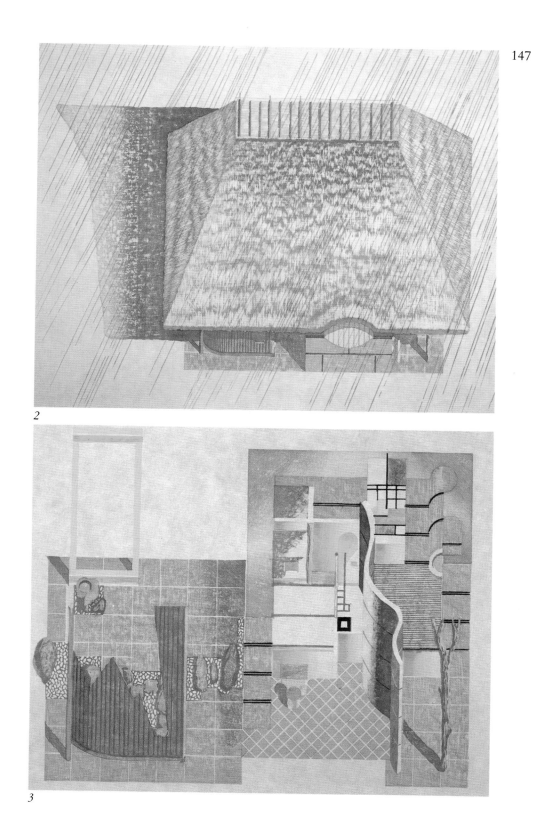

2

3

Tsukuba Center Building

Tsukuba Science City, Ibaragi, Japan, 1979–83

148

1

2

Tsukuba Science City, located forty miles from Tokyo, is a unique phenomenon in Japan. The planners' intention was to centralize in Tsukuba various university and government research facilities that had been scattered throughout Tokyo. But what sets Tsukuba apart from other large-scale "new towns" built in Japanese suburbs after the war is the fact that, along with housing, it provides many of the amenities associated with urban life.

The Tsukuba Center Building was designed as a civic center complex to bring life and activity to the city. It includes a hotel, a concert hall, an information center, a shopping mall, and a community center.

The planning of the town is characterized by its circulation system, in which interconnected pedestrian decks bridge over the vehicular traffic routes at ground level. These bridges provide pedestrian access to the Tsukuba Center Building, located on the primary north-south axis of the town. One level below the pedestrian decks is the focus of the complex, a sunken plaza or "forum," whose design is essentially a reverse quotation of the Campidoglio in Rome.

A concert hall and an information center with audiovisual equipment occupy the south block of the building, with shops arranged around the sunken plaza. The east block consists of two cubes. The larger one houses the hotel and contains the entrance hall on the first floor, a restaurant and coffee shop on the second, and banquet halls of various sizes on the third and fourth. The fifth through tenth floors hold the guest rooms, and the top floor contains a sky lounge and a restaurant. The smaller cube, which has been rotated off the plaza's axis and sliced off on one corner, is a separate banquet hall.

On the sides of the building that face vehicular traffic zones, the exterior is relatively simple and unarticulated, while the sides facing the plaza display a wide variety of forms and finishes. Here the ground floor is rusticated, using locally quarried granite and artificial stone. The upper parts of the building are clad in silver tile—with glazed and unglazed pieces forming a pattern—and aluminum panels, which are used to cover curved surfaces or to highlight specific parts. Geometric shapes—triangles, semicircles, cubes, cylinders—are found on the facade, as are references to traditional architectural forms like columns and arch details. No single, organized system defines or unifies the overall design; each element has its own distinctive character.

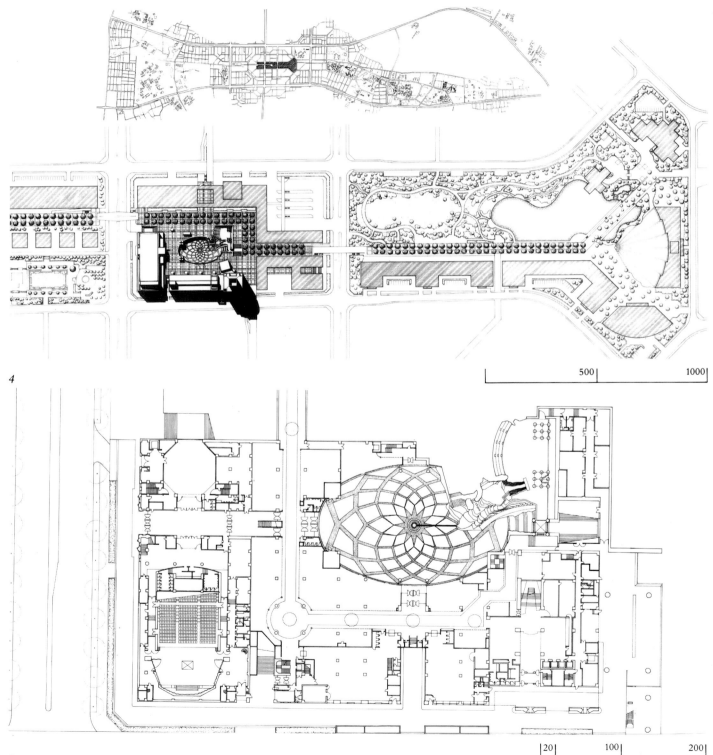

500   1000

20   100   200

4. *Site plan.*
5. *First-floor plan.*
6. *Second-floor plan (pedestrian level)*
7. *Third-floor plan.*

Overleaf:
8. *The street facade of the building from the parking area.*

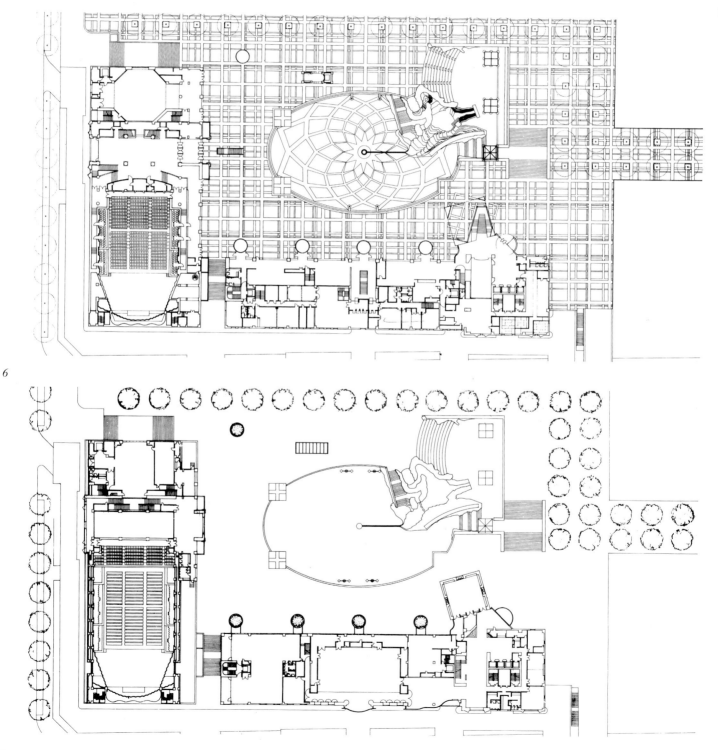

6

7

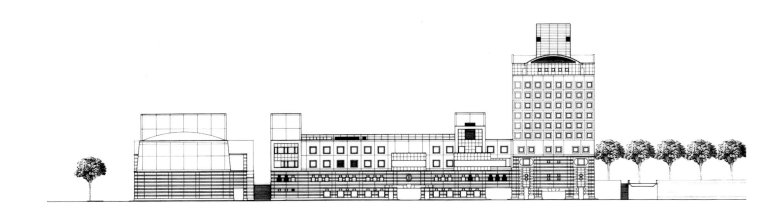

9

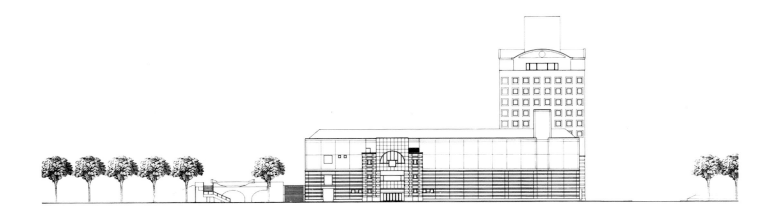

9. *Elevation of the concert hall (left) and the hotel (right).*
10. *Elevation of the concert hall.*
11. *Section through the plaza and the concert hall.*
12. *Transverse section, with the concert hall beyond.*
13. *Section through the concert hall.*

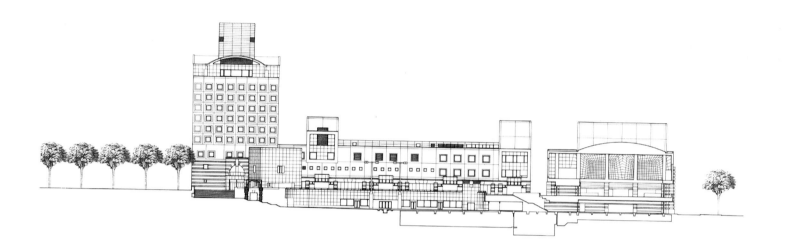

11

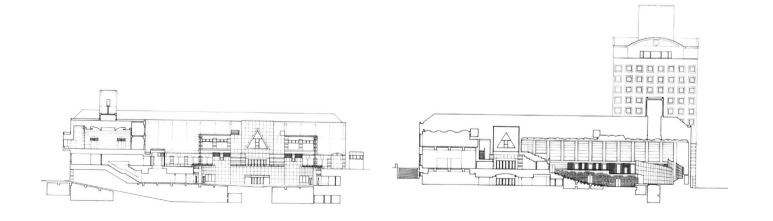

12   *13*

14. *View from the plaza.*
15. *The entrance to the concert hall.*
16. *Detail of the exterior finish.*
17. *View from the concert hall.*

156

14

15

16

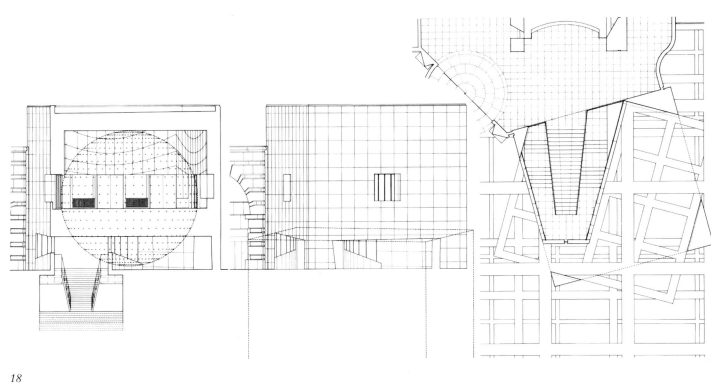

18

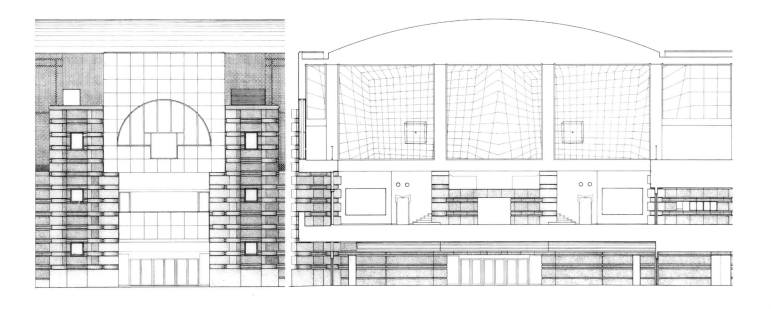

19

20

10 25 50

159

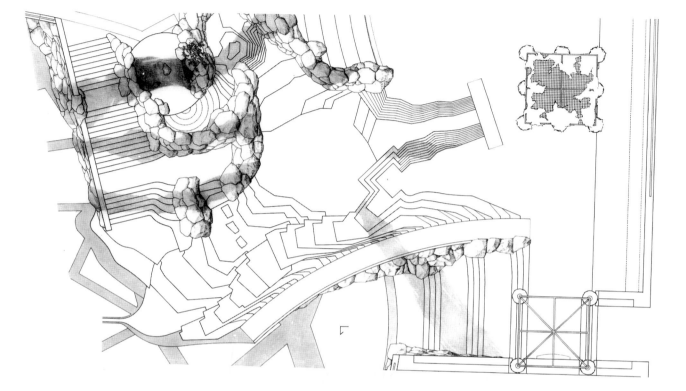

21

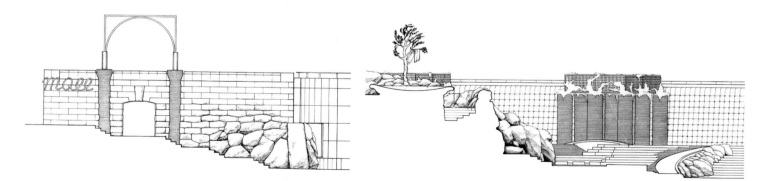

22

10   25   50

23. The interior of the concert hall.
24. Detail of the lighting in the banquet hall.
25. The grand stair of the hotel.

24

25

26. *View from the sunken plaza.*
27. *Outdoor stage elements.*
28. *The plaza amphitheater.*

26

27

Okanoyama Graphic Arts Museum
Nishiwaki, Hyogo, Japan, 1982–84

This museum was built to house the works of Tadanori Yokoo, a graphic artist who was born in Nishiwaki, a city in the area known as the "navel" of Japan. The museum is located at the intersection of the imaginary lines of 35° north latitude and 135° east longitude, which determines Japan's standard time.

The galleries holding Yokoo's works from the 1960s through the 1980s are arranged in a series, like the cars of a train. The architecture of these spaces is intentionally neutral to draw attention to the works themselves. Anterooms between the galleries that chart the development of the artist's style have a more distinct character, with paint and tiles used for their architectural effects.

Offices, a seminar room, and storage areas are also located within the gallery building. At the center of the long western wall of the museum stands a small meditation building topped by a pyramid whose proportions are drawn from those of the Egyptian pyramids. The artist's studio is set off on its own, separated from the main building by a tile-paved central garden.

164

1

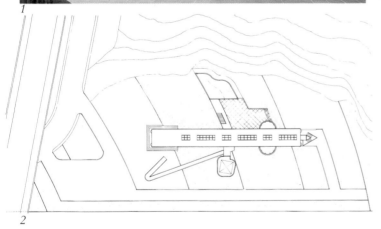

2

20 | 100 | 200

1. *View from the terrace.*
2. *Site plan.*
3. *View from the main approach.*

3

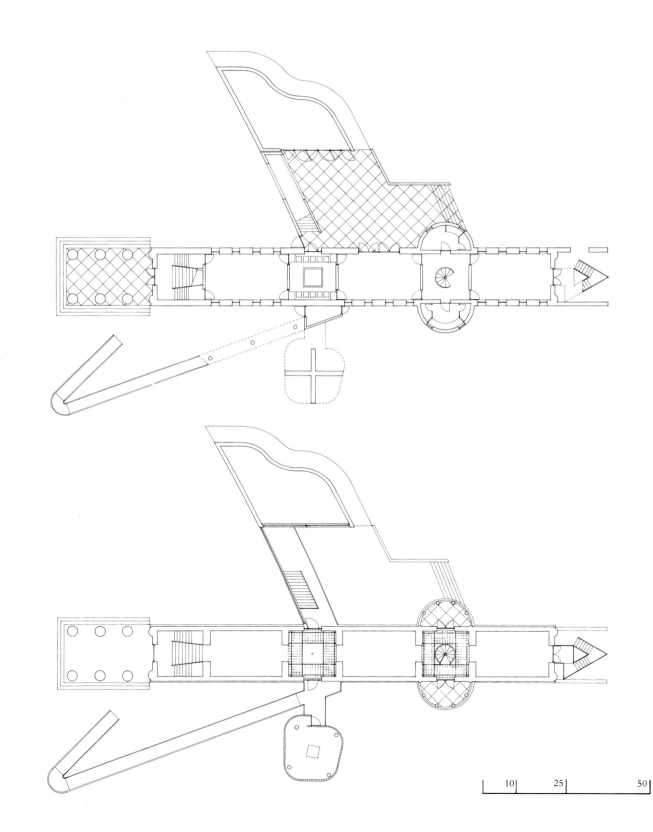

4

5

10   25   50

4. *First-floor plan.*
5. *Second-floor plan.*
6. *Side elevation.*
7. *Front elevation.*
8. *Longitudinal section.*
9. *Transverse section.*

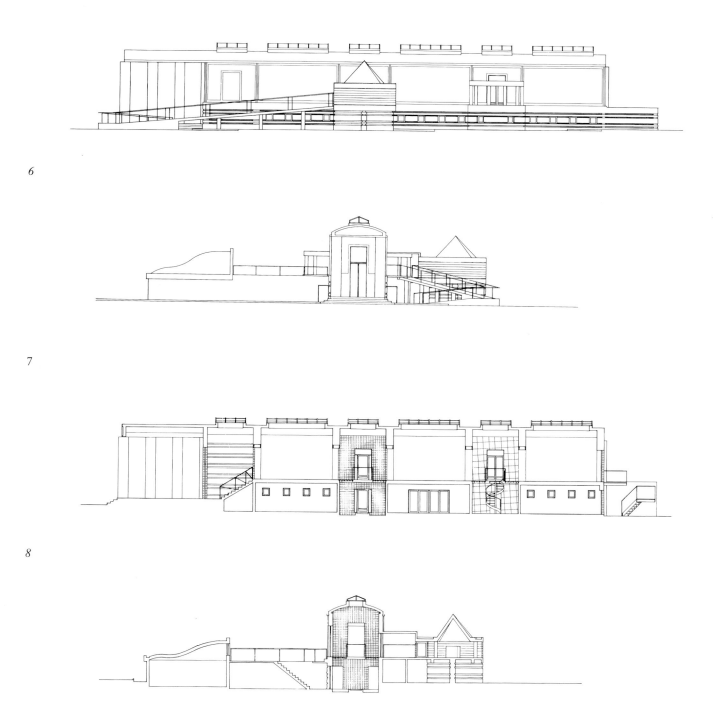

6

7

8

9

10

11

10. *The entrance.*
11. *The meditation room.*
12. *One of the galleries.*

12

14

Phoenix Municipal Government Center

Phoenix, Arizona, 1985

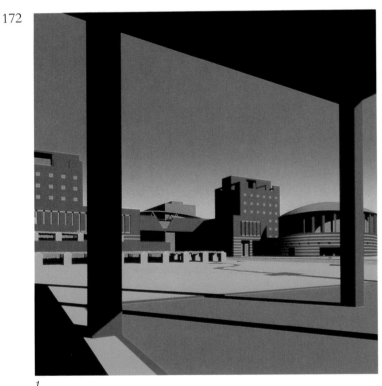

1

The purpose of this project was to give structure to the urban fabric of downtown Phoenix, Arizona's capital. The program called for an integration of the present city hall and the former city hall (built in 1929); an expanded police station; the prosecutor's office and courts; a new fire station; a city council building; and other, nongovernment facilities, such as a theater, offices, and retail space. The buildings would be located on a ten-block site adjacent to the old city hall.

This proposal includes a City Gate—a bridge connecting two of the blocks and crossing over Washington Street, the main axis leading to the state capitol. The columns of a City Colonnade tie new and old facilities together and provide shade from the strong southwestern sun. Within the central six blocks of the downtown area, this colonnade and several clusters of buildings surround a park that incorporates water, rocks, sculpture, and pavilions in a desert setting. At the center of the park is the Phoenix Pavilion, a multipurpose building whose setback form and materials— red and beige sandstone, terra-cotta tile—evoke the traditional Pueblo-Deco style.

2

1. View from the Phoenix Pavilion (silk screen).
2. Interior perspective of the City Council Chamber (silk screen).
3. Perspective of the City Gate.
4. Aerial perspective (silk screen).

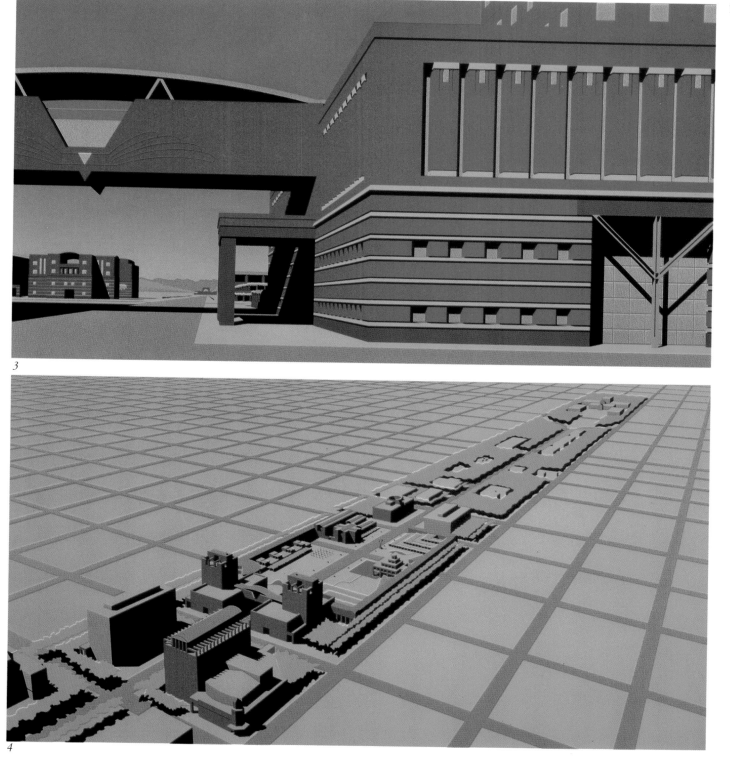

3

4

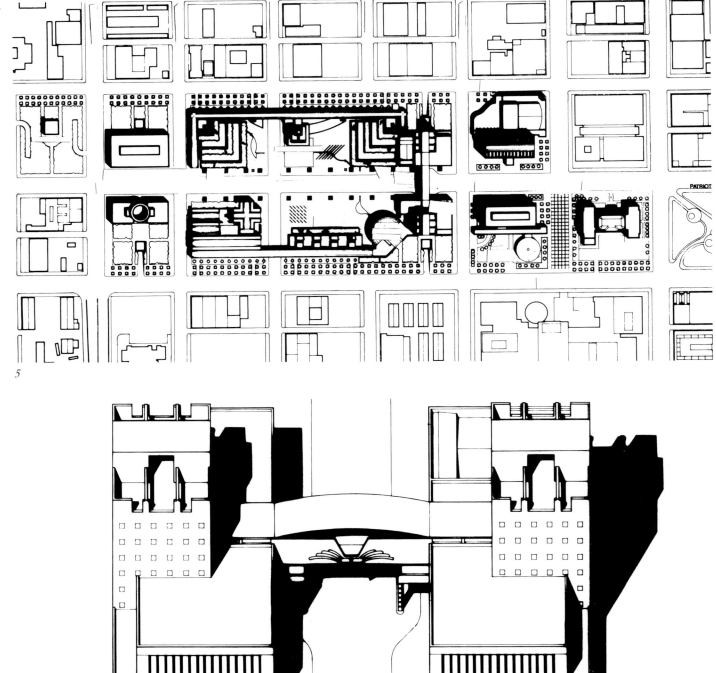

5

6

5. Site plan.
6. Axonometric of the Municipal Government
   Building.
7. Model of the entire site.

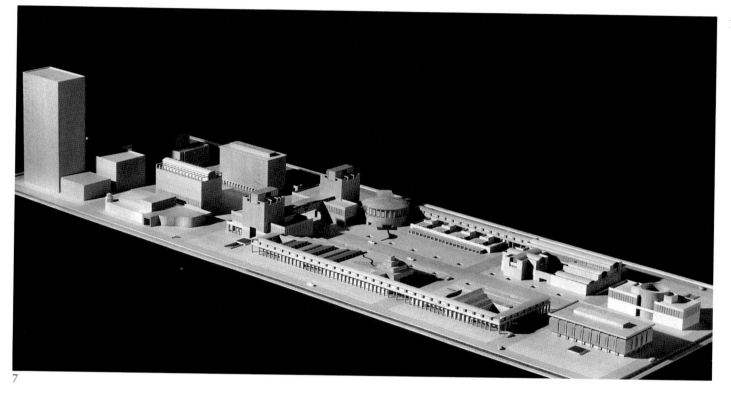

7

New Tokyo City Hall

Shinjuku, Tokyo, 1985–86

1

In need of a new metropolitan government building for a three-block site amidst the skyscraper slabs west of Shinjuku Station, the city held an invitational competition for a facility to replace the seriously overextended building in Marunouchi. Despite the division of the site into two blocks on one side of the street and one on the other side, the competition specifications seemed to call for a design that was, as much as possible, integrated into a single structure. This would both establish the presence of the new city hall within its imposing surroundings and improve the efficiency of administrative operations. In response to the program, this scheme has a somewhat independent international conference center and an open area occupying one block, with administration offices and the Metropolitan Assembly on the two blocks across the street.

The basic building type for a city hall, established historically in the West, is adapted here to its function as the hub of city government activities, and advanced technology is used to redefine this traditional architectural form. The four basic elements of the standard Western typology— tower, front square, great hall, and ceremonial space—are abstracted, and they emerge anew, transformed into a landmark radio tower, a festival plaza, a great atrium, and an international conference center. A spherical council chamber floats symbolically at the top of the city hall building. For more efficient communication between departments, office spaces are arranged with vertical and horizontal networks of circulation and information routes. Both as city hall architecture and as a functional system, this subtly modulated set of spaces of varying densities is far better adapted to the needs of city administration in the high-tech era than any standard spatial configuration in a skyscraper could be.

Office space is provided by the four main blocks, which consist of seventy-eight-foot cubic superframe structures with departments assigned according to the organization of the city government. The front and back office areas are linked by four connecting cubes and bridges hanging in the huge atrium (300 feet high and 1,000 feet long), which is topped by a pyramidal skylight. This great atrium, entered through the main entrance at the base of the radio tower, constitutes the heart of the new city hall in both symbolic and functional terms. Communications with government facilities throughout the city are improved by the 820-foot-high radio tower, which is suspended by steel rods in the frame at the top of the entrance building.

500 | 1000 |

1. *Interior perspective (computer-generated rendering).*
2. *Site plan.*
3. *Exterior perspective (computer-generated rendering).*

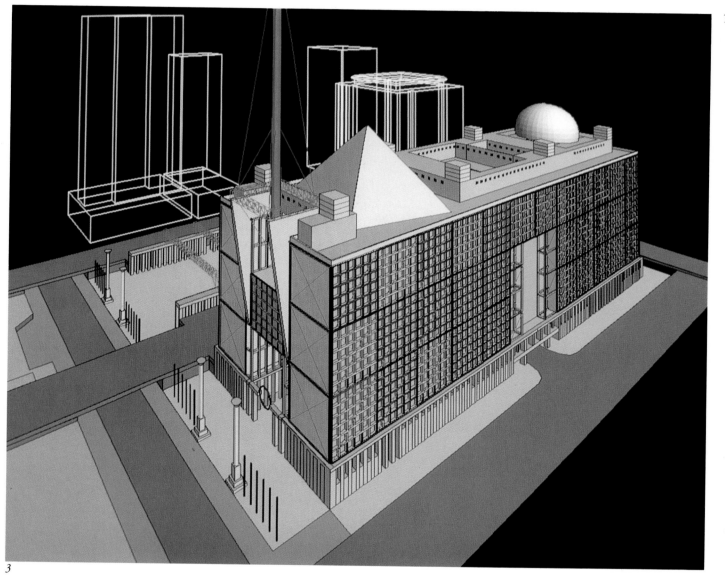

3

4. Model of the proposal among the neighboring high rises.
5. Model, showing the pyramidal skylight and the spherical council chamber.
6. Model, showing the radio tower above the entrance.

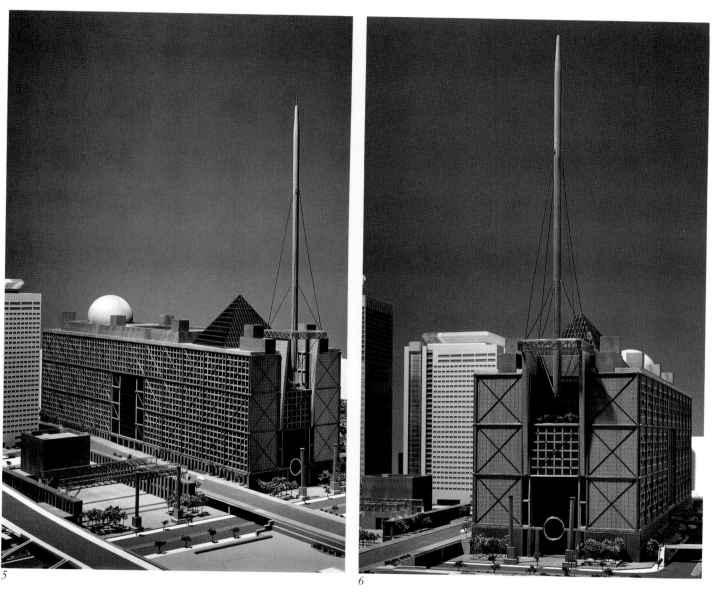

5

6

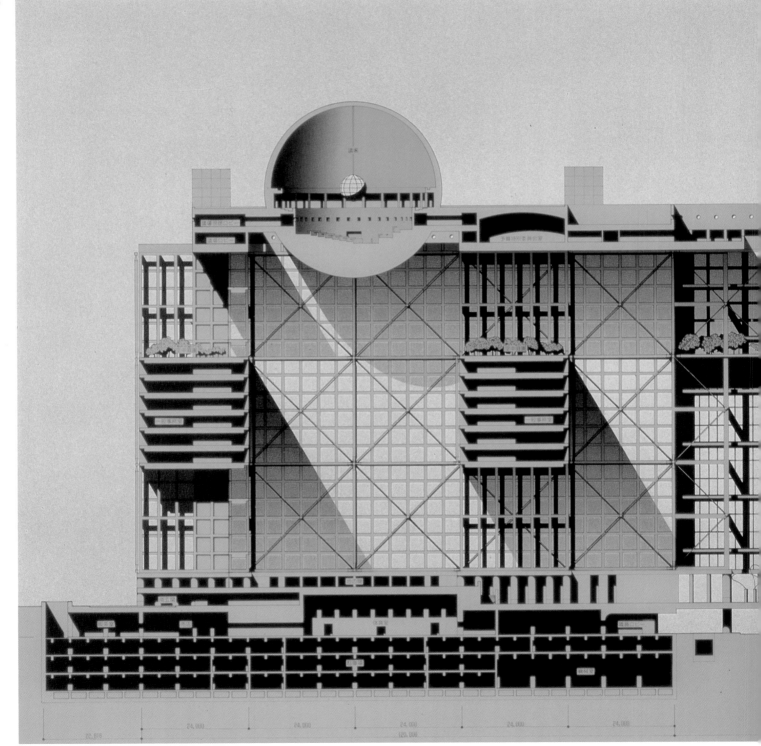

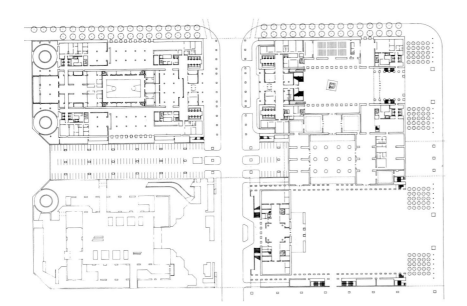

8

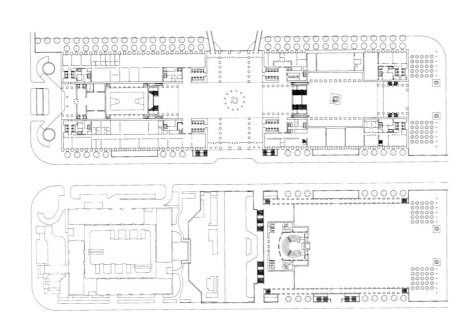

50 200 500

9

183

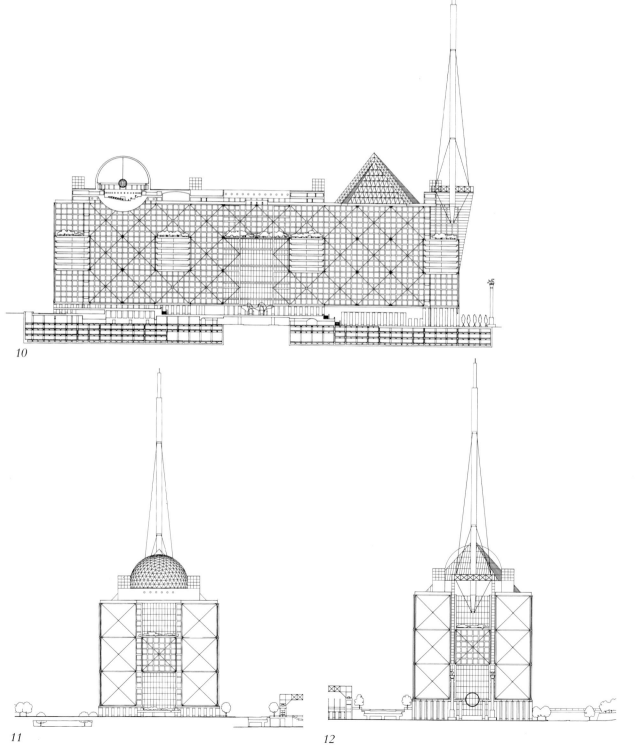

10

11   12

The Museum of Contemporary Art, Los Angeles

Los Angeles, 1981–86

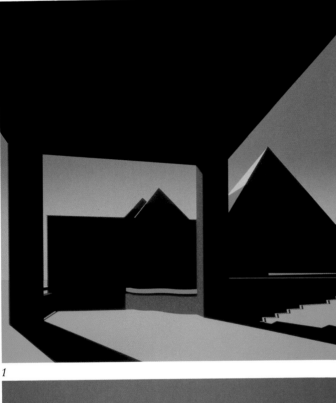

1

2

The Museum of Contemporary Art (MOCA) is located at the center of the California Plaza mixed-use development in the Bunker Hill section of downtown Los Angeles. Although California Plaza will be realized in stages, MOCA is now bounded by an office tower on the south, residential condominiums on the east, and Grand Avenue on the west. The museum sits atop and partially within the parking structure of the plaza.

Along with 24,500 square feet of exhibition space, the museum building includes an auditorium, a library, a café, a bookstore, and office and support areas, which are located on different levels.

The museum presents itself to the street as two structures bracketing a sculpture court and a lower entry court. Pyramids, cubes, and a semicircular vault rest atop walls of red Indian sandstone on a base of red granite. Bands of polished sandstone alternate with bands of larger, rusticated pieces to create a subtle pattern of horizontal striations. On the north, the copper-sheathed vaulted library bridges over the pedestrian path, forming a symbolic gateway to the museum. Beneath this gateway is a green aluminum-clad cube that houses the ticket booth. On the south are three pyramids: the large pyramid, whose lower portion is clad in copper, serves as a skylight for the entrance gallery, while the small pyramids provide illumination for one of the exhibition galleries. Eight more small pyramids, as well as twelve linear skylights, allow natural light into other galleries.

The sculpture court, which overlooks the entry court below, is the focus of the various museum facilities that open onto the plaza level, including the bookstore and the office lobby. From the sculpture court visitors descend the grand stair to the entry court, which gives access to the galleries. This sunken entry allows for maximum ceiling heights in the exhibition areas while conforming to the height limitations of California Plaza. The entry court, the lobby, and the café are finished in the same materials—floors of granite, and walls of white crystallized glass and sandstone—creating the impression of one open, continuous space.

Within the museum the galleries are characterized by variations in proportion, shape, and quality of light, both natural and artificial.

3

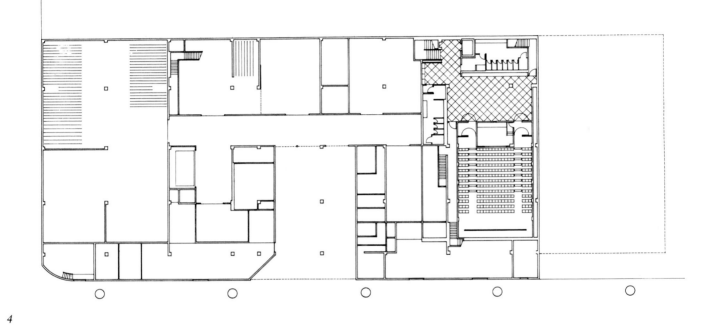

4

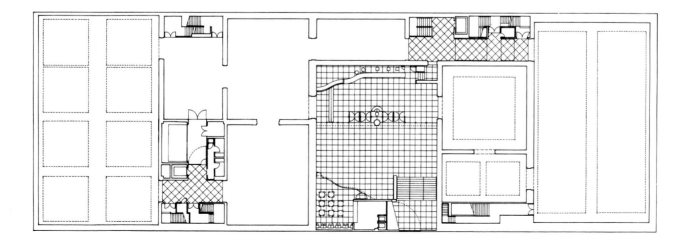

5

10   50   100

187

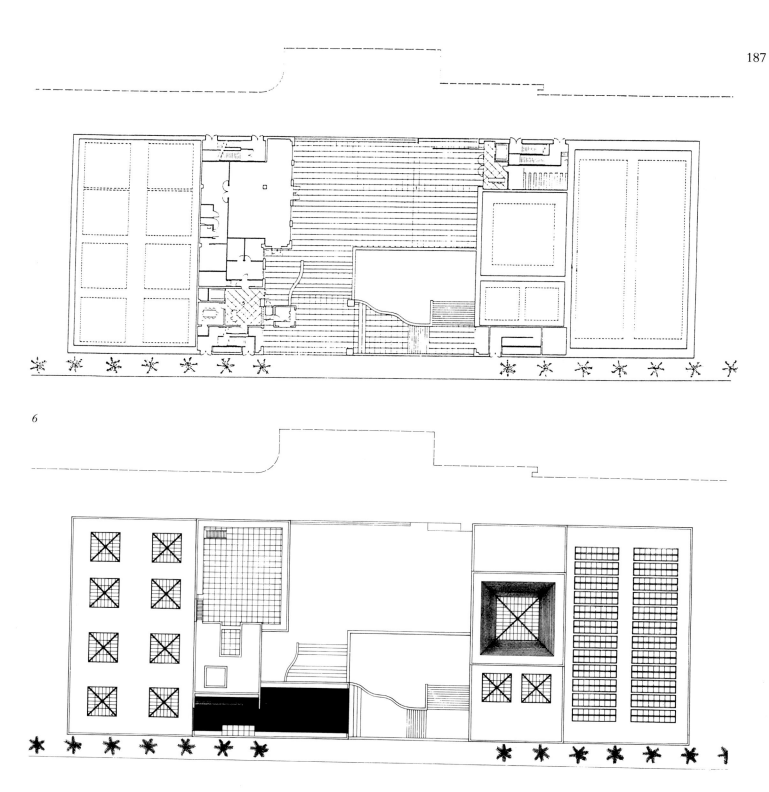

6

7

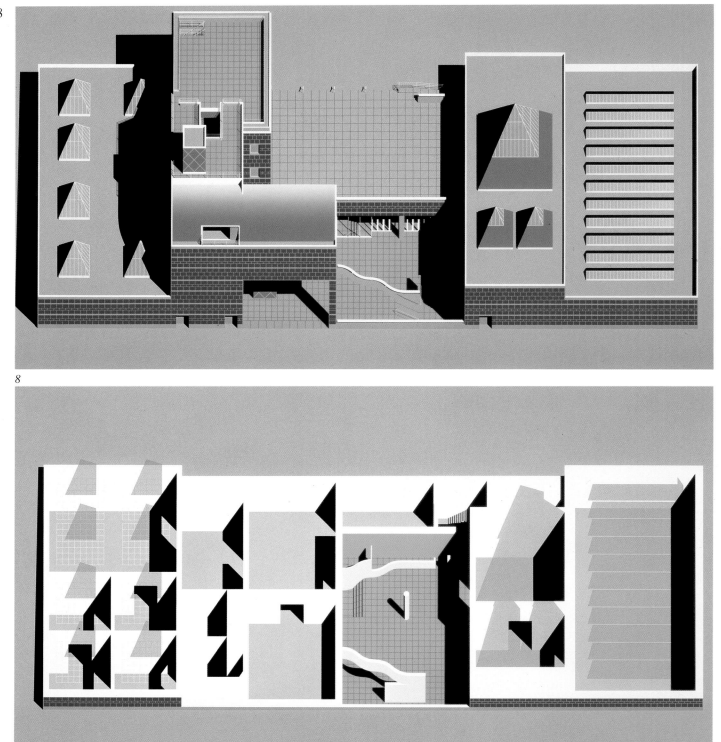

8

9

8. *Overall axonometric (day).*
9. *Axonometric of the galleries (day).*
10. *Overall axonometric (night).*
11. *Axonometric of the galleries (night).*

189

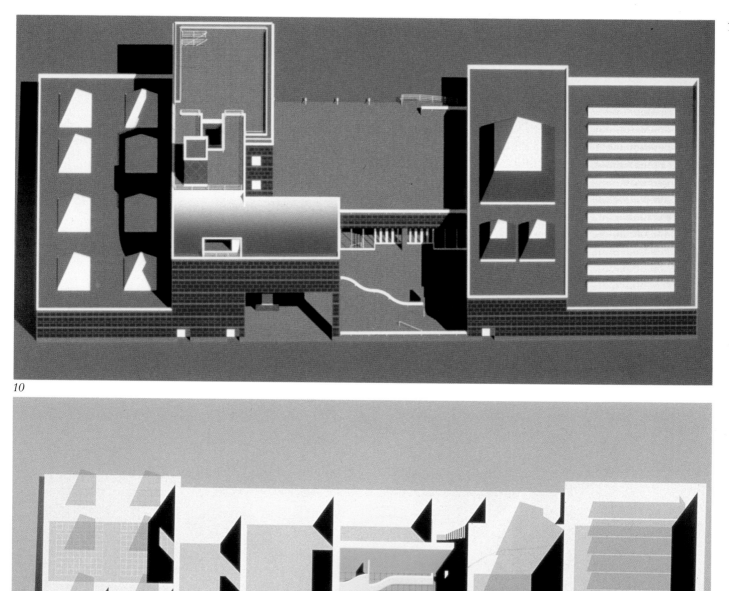

10

11

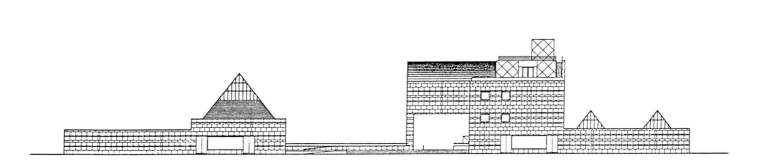

12

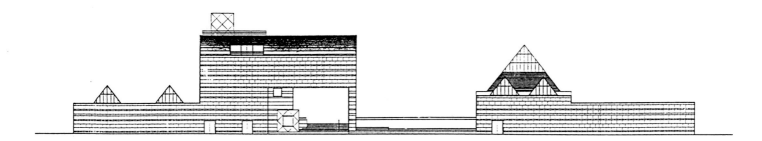

13

12. *Rear elevation.*
13. *Entrance elevation.*
14. *Longitudinal section.*
15. *Transverse section through the entry court,*
    looking toward the principal galleries.
16. *Transverse section through the entry court,*
    looking toward the ticket booth.

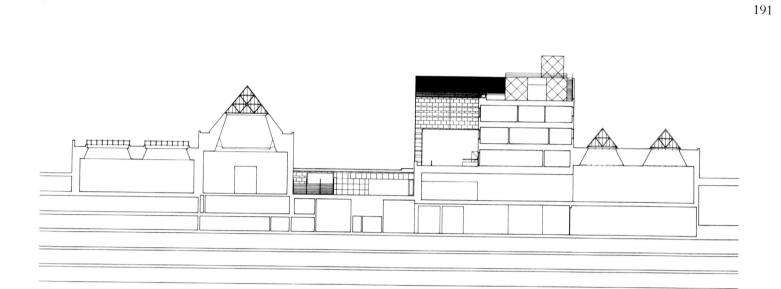

14

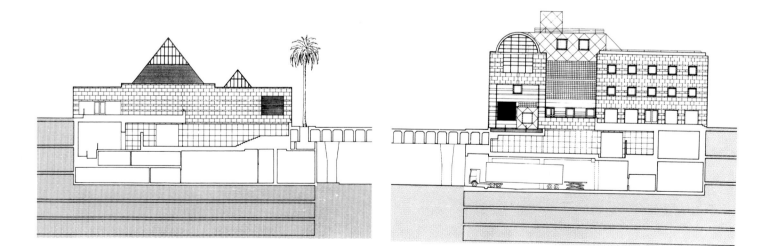

15   *16*

Staff Offices

17. *Detail of the exterior.*
18. *View from the plaza level.*
19. *View from the entrance hall.*

18

19

20. *The entrance lobby.*
21. *Interior stairs.*
22. *One of the galleries.*

194

20

21

Daniel Templon Foundation

Sophia-Antipolis International Park, Valbonne, France, 1986

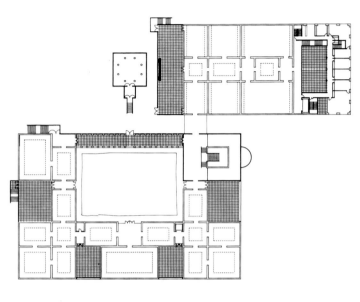

|20| |100| |200|

With funds raised from private donors, the Daniel Templon Foundation financed the construction of this contemporary art museum on a twelve-acre site in the new Sophia-Antipolis International Park, located on the outskirts of Nice. The foundation's goals in building the museum complex were to gather a permanent collection, host temporary exhibitions, sponsor arts events, and provide studios for artists.

The overall plan includes not only the art gallery but also seven separate structures that house studios, a chapel dedicated to art, a reception area, and administrative offices. The gallery, which surrounds a central garden, has two areas: one for displaying the permanent collection, and one for temporary shows. Bridges, terraces, and various levels are used to accommodate changing exhibition needs. The entire gallery can also be opened up into a single space.

Other facilities include a museum store, located near the first-floor entrance, storage and warehouse areas, a 150-seat auditorium, a restaurant, and a vaulted-ceiling library.

1. Floor plan.
2. Section (silk screen).
3. Perspective (silk screen).

197

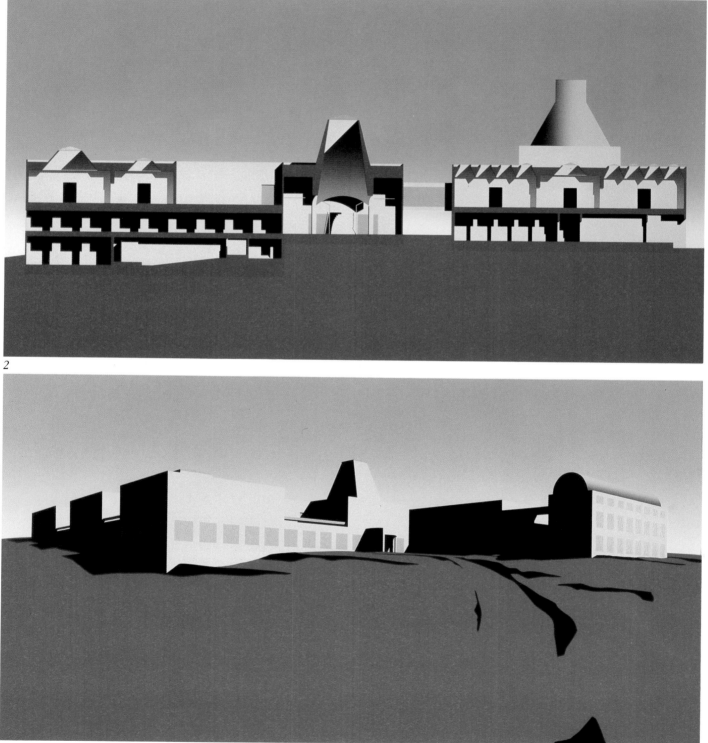

2

3

4. *View of the model, showing the main approach.*
5. *Model, with the library vault in the foreground.*
6. *Section through the gallery entrance, with the library vault beyond.*

198

4

5

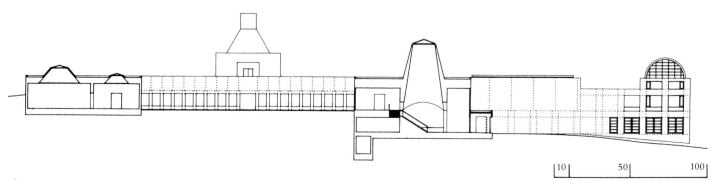

6

10   50   100

The Brooklyn Museum

Brooklyn, New York, 1986–

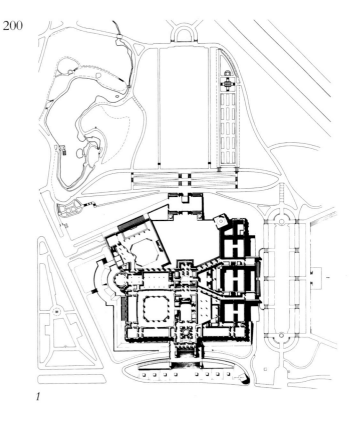

1

2

|50| 200| 500|

In 1893 McKim, Mead & White won the original design competition for the Brooklyn Museum, a building situated adjacent to the Botanic Garden and near Olmsted and Vaux's Prospect Park, Grand Army Plaza, and the Brooklyn Public Library. The centerpiece of their Beaux-Arts–style proposal was a huge dome over a great hall, with arms radiating out in all four directions, each wing enclosing its own courtyard. Construction was begun on the basis of their 1.5 million-square-foot design, but it was never completed: only the front wing with the facade and one block surrounding a courtyard on the east side were built.

The social function of the art gallery has changed in the hundred-year interim since the design, and it has become extremely difficult to extend the existing structures solely by adjusting the original master plan. The directors of the museum proposed a fundamental review of the master plan with which to organize projected stages of expansion and improvement through the year 2020.

After several rounds in the design competition for a new master plan, the jury selected the proposal by the Arata Isozaki/James Stewart Polshek team. The design respects the McKim, Mead & White scheme, draws out the

1. Site plan, piano nobile level.
2. Longitudinal section (silk screen) through the obelisk and the great hall.

201

North-South Section

principles of its internal development, and links the new elements with the existing structures. Connections with the past are embraced through the development of contemporary architectural perspectives on the Beaux-Arts original. This was achieved by a commitment to the following principles:

1) Order: Contemporary forms like frames, grids, panels, and flush surfaces were given equal weight with the five orders of the Beaux-Arts style.

2) Composition: Disposed in biaxial symmetry, the original composition concept is preserved.

3) Manipulation: The section functioning as the keystone is restored to its original condition. The vista to the Botanic Garden is broadened, and its axis is partially rotated in order to create space for an outdoor sculpture garden. Even beyond the limits of physical structures, the design lets the original plan emerge in the floor and ground patterns.

The new master plan calls for approximately 400,000 square feet of renovations and one million square feet of extensions, including parking.

202

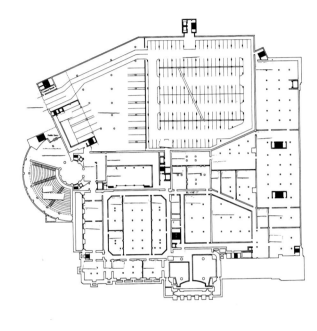

3

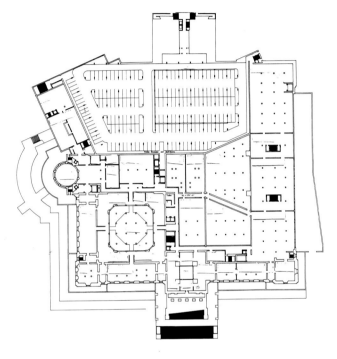

5

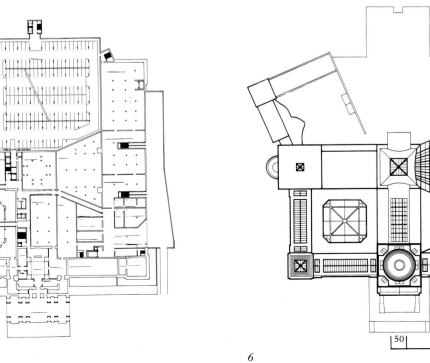

4

6

204

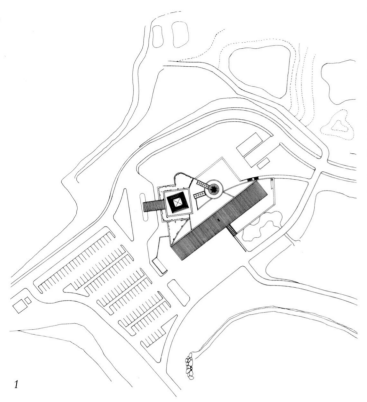

1

The Musashi-kyuryo Country Club, which features an eighteen-hole golf course, is located in western Saitama prefecture, in a corner of the Oku Musashi Natural Park. The golf course cuts through foothills 1,000 feet in altitude, from which the skyscrapers of Tokyo can be seen. A winding mountain road leads to the sloping golf course; an access road following the ridge leads to the clubhouse. This building is the main feature of the plan, and the program required that its interior provide a view of the natural surroundings.

The split-level design makes use of the gently rolling hills. The entrance hall is centrally located. A half flight up are the dining facilities; a half flight down are the locker room, shower room, and starting terrace. Japanese cedar trees in the area and large rocks that were unearthed during construction were used in the building as much as possible; four cedar logs, each four feet in diameter and sixty-five feet tall, seem to support the obelisk-style tower that rises from the entrance hall. The interior is naturally lit through louvered skylights in the tower. In contrast to the enclosed entrance hall, the restaurant has expansive windows, which reach to the slanted roof and then continue horizontally, granting a broad view. The exterior of the clubhouse is mainly of green stacked stone and pink stucco; the roof is of copper plate.

|30| 150| 300|

2

206

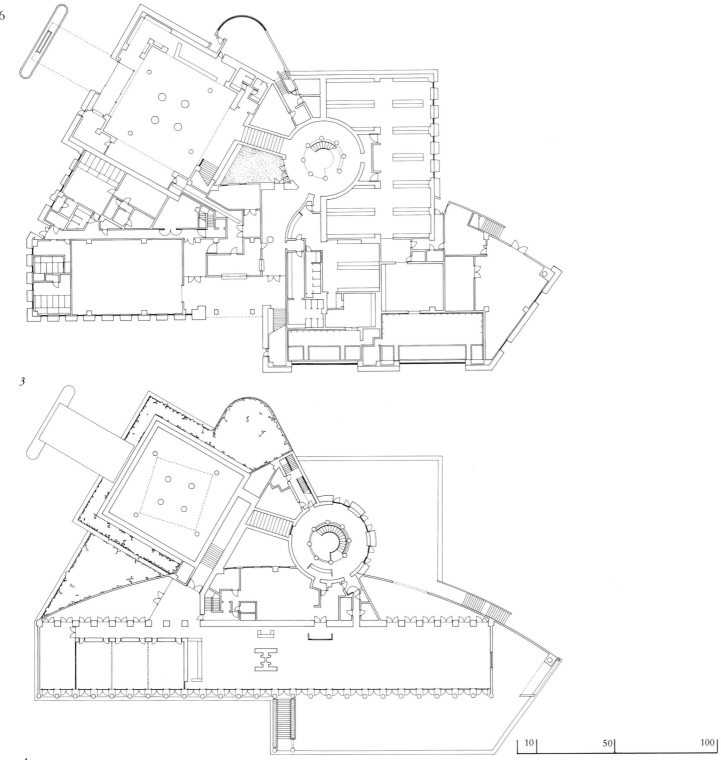

3

4

10   50   100

3. First-floor plan.
4. Second-floor plan.
5. Elevation of the restaurant overlooking the
   golf course.
6. Entrance elevation.
7. Section through the restaurant.
8. Section through the lobby.

Overleaf:
9. View from the hill above.

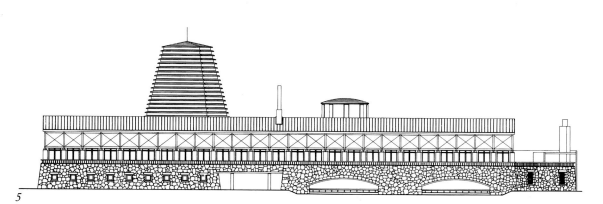

5

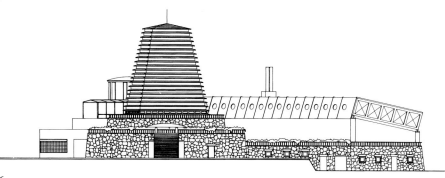

6

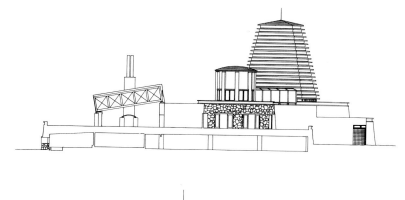

7

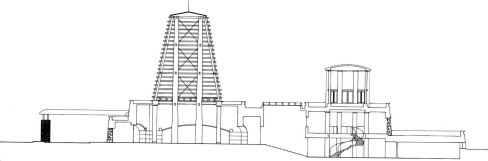

8

10. *The symbolic columns in the lobby.*
11. *The restaurant.*
12. *View of the obelisk skylight.*

10

11

13. The entrance portico.
14. View from the second-floor terrace.
15. The obelisk at night.

212

13

14

15

Palafolls Sports Pavilion

Palafolls, Spain, 1987–

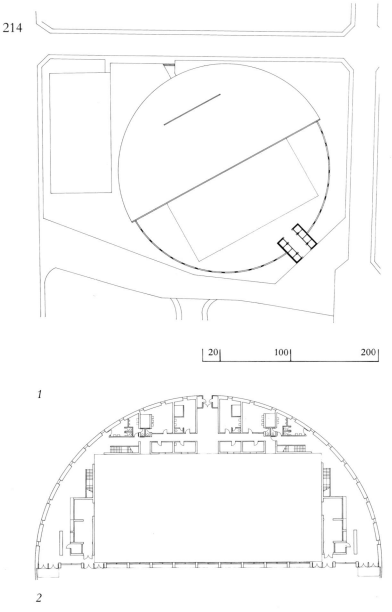

1

2

20 | 100 | 200

10 | 50 | 100

Palafolls is located approximately thirty-five miles northeast of Barcelona and two miles inland from the resort area of the Costa Brava. The site for this sports pavilion lies outside the old city section in an area designated for redevelopment. Almost completely flat, the pavilion area is enclosed in a circular 220-foot-diameter brick wall, with the southern half covered by a space-frame roof and the northern half forming the front court. The shape of the roof is determined by the dimensions required of the arena for the different types of sports competitions it will hold and the number of spectators.

A total of 1,717 ball joints and 7,298 pipes were used in the space-frame roof, which is supported by steel columns in triangular truss formations, built into the north facade of the sports hall, and independent reinforced-concrete columns included in the encircling brick wall. Zinc plates forming the exterior roof surface are laid on a base of wood boards patterned internally by the space frame to create the ceiling. This roof generates a dome space with a maximum height of forty-six feet.

Inside, the rectangular arena is cut from the semicircular plan using dividing walls built of concrete blocks. Seating, lobby, changing rooms, storerooms, and other facilities fill the volume between the exterior brick wall and the internal concrete-block walls.

The arena was planned basically as an indoor gymnasium, and its foreground views to the north are cut off by the outer wall across the front courtyard. From the courtyard itself, on the other hand, the view includes the beautiful lines of the facade set against the nearby hill crowned with the ruins of the old Palafolls Castle. Interior and exterior spaces enable the new sports pavilion to be used for city events like festivals, concerts, plays, and conventions. It will thus function as one of the most important public spaces in the city.

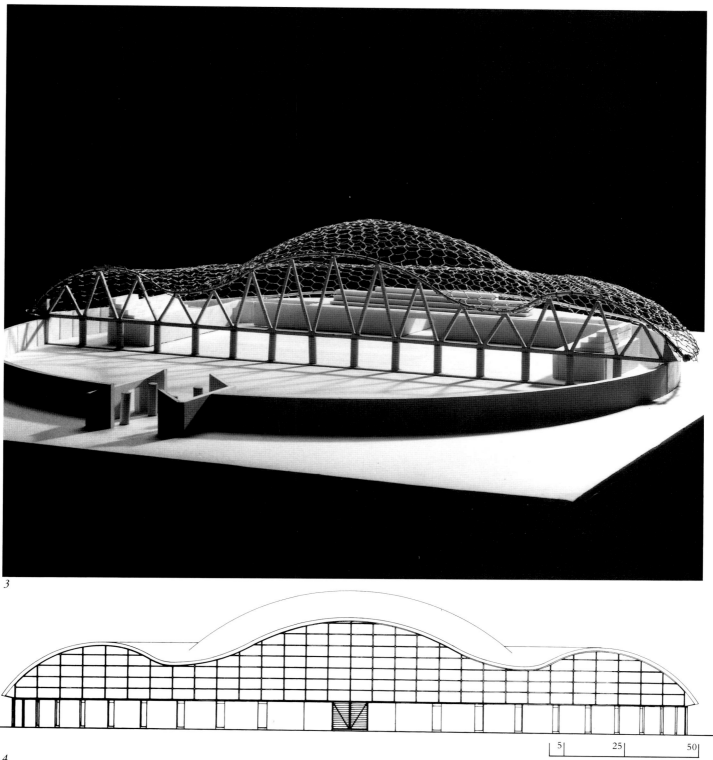

3

4

5   25   50

Hara Museum ARC

Gunma, Japan, 1987–88

216

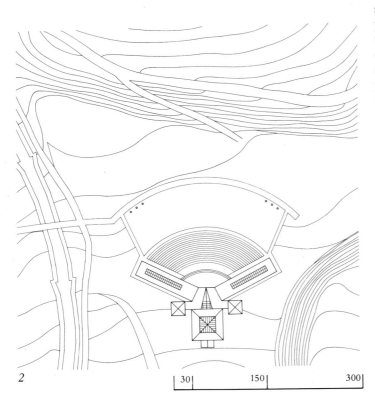

1

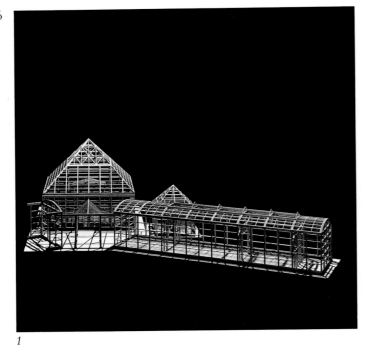

2

|30| |150| |300|

The Hara Museum ARC is about two hours by car on an expressway from Tokyo. The site is on a ranch, and nearby are the Ikaho Hot Springs and summer resort facilities, including a golf course.

The design had to meet two special conditions. ARC was to be an annex of the Hara Museum—the only gallery in Tokyo dedicated exclusively to contemporary art—but it was to be open only in the warmer months (from April to November). Since the ranch itself is a tourist site, performances such as outdoor concerts had to be accommodated by a partially open area of the building. The director of the museum, Toshio Hara, is also involved in the lumber business, and he stipulated a timber construction from the start.

A pastoral area, a wood structure, a small, private museum, a location far from the center of Tokyo—what these have in common is a marginal character. They reveal a critical attitude toward the many museums now being constructed in Japanese cities—all of them huge, public, and authoritarian.

Focused around a pyramid-topped room almost the same size as that under the largest pyramid at MOCA, two perpendicular wings reach out to either side. Access to all three galleries is from the central entrance loggia, where the composition is opened out. To the left and right of the lobby are, respectively, the office and the rest rooms, with small pyramidal roofs. To provide maximum hanging space on the walls there are no windows; illumination comes from the skylights, the only interior sections where the structural frame is exposed. As befits a gallery for contemporary art, the interior exhibition walls are all painted white. But the wood of the exterior and the lobby section is stained black, the pyramid roofs are black slate, and the vaulted roofs are covered with zinc plates. This completely black exterior emphasizes the unchanging geometric presence of the structure within the seasonal variations of the natural surroundings.

Although the structure is wood, it by no means uses the traditional Japanese system of framing. The walls and roof have been assembled as integrated planes, and the arches spanning them are of glue-laminated timber. An effort was made to prevent the structure from evoking, as wood construction is apt to do, any association with things Japanese.

1. Model of the wood frame.
2. Site plan.
3. View from the outdoor amphitheater.

3

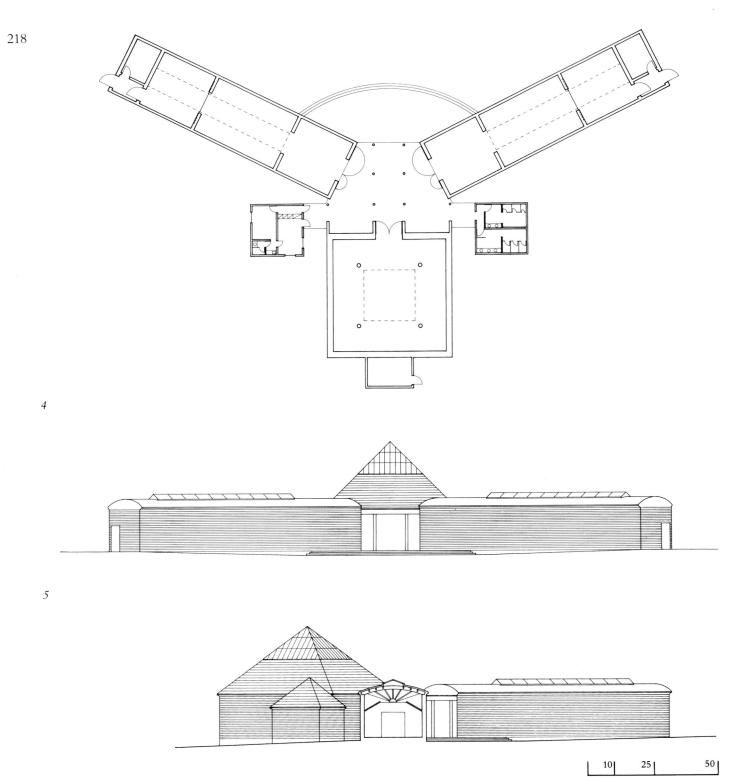

4. *Floor plan.*
5. *Front elevation.*
6. *Section through one of the galleries.*
7. *One of the galleries.*

218

4

5

6

| 10 | 25 | 50 |

1. Site plan.
2. Principal elevation.
3. View of the model.

Kashii Twin Towers

Fukuoka, Japan, 1989–

The population of Kashiihama, a suburb of Fukuoka City, has increased rapidly in recent years. Twenty acres of reclaimed land was designated for a housing complex containing 400 units to accommodate new residents.

Two high-rise towers in the center of the site hold half the units; the rest are distributed among several medium-height blocks around the perimeter of the site to give shape to the residential area. The landscaping was designed especially around the open spaces generated by this layout. Twin towers, an urban formation, and landscaping were the key elements behind the overall configuration of the complex.

Isozaki designed the central twin towers, and commissions for the design of the seven peripheral housing blocks were given to Oscar Tusquets, Christian de Portzamparc, Osamu Ishiyama, Mark Mack, Rem Koolhaas, Steven Holl, and Andrew MacNair. Martha Schwartz undertook planning for the landscaping, which will include follies by Zaha Hadid and Daniel Libeskind that were originally created for the International Garden and Greenery Exposition in Osaka.

Both towers are approximately 400 feet high; one is circular and the other square in plan. While the use of the standard twin-tower form—typified by the World Trade Center in Manhattan—gives the structures the symbolic force to establish the identity of the design, it is undermined here by treating the buildings as imperfect reflections of each other.

The lower and top floors of the towers contain sports and other public facilities, and residences are located on the remaining floors. The buildings are linked by a bridge between the towers suspended 330 feet above the ground; the bridge connects with a public elevator on the outside of the cylindrical tower to form the major public circulation network. This design's combination of residential and other functions with a vertical circulation network has important implications for the future of high-rise multifunctional architecture.

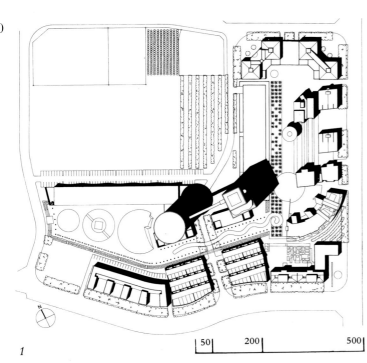

1

| 50 | 200 | 500 |

2

3

222

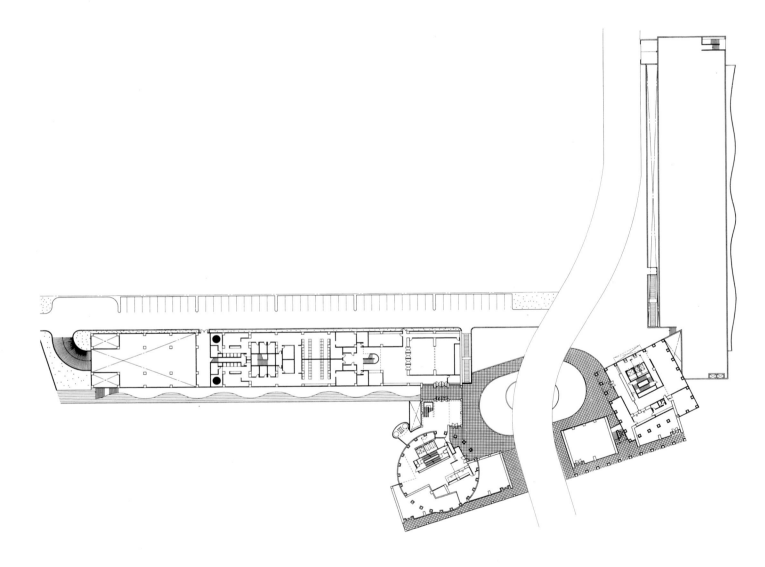

20 | 100 | 200 |

4. Ground-floor plan.
5. Section of the round tower (left) and the
   square tower.

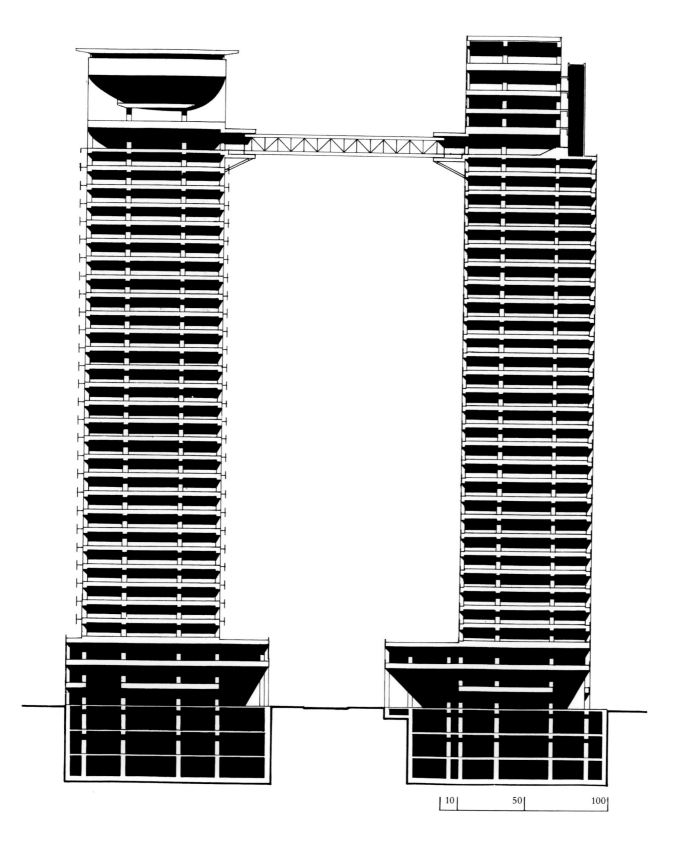

10 | 50 | 100 |

5

International Friendship Pavilion, Expo '90

Osaka, Japan, 1988–90

1

50 | 200 | 500 |

In late 1988 Konosuke Matsushita, the founder of Matsushita Electric Industrial Company, donated funds to establish a commemorative foundation on the occasion of the International Garden and Greenery Exposition in Osaka (the Flower Expo). Charged with constructing and managing Expo facilities that would symbolize friendship with other countries, the foundation was to maintain one of the structures after the fair ended as a permanent reminder of its ideals. Carrying the main burden of the international character of the Expo, the International Friendship Pavilion required sufficient space to accommodate exhibitions and events. Design and construction had to be completed in a limited time of only fifteen months.

The site reserved for the museum, on the north side of the main gate, slopes upward to a height of twenty-five feet. This situation was exploited to establish a broad perspective over the central circulation point linking the Expo's three regions: mountain, street, and field. Raised over the exposition site, the building stands in the position of a villa in relation to the overall plan of the park, which approximates the Belvedere form of Western garden design.

The pavilion has three principal functions: it holds an event hall for 300 people, a VIP room and related hospitality facilities for overseas guests, and an extensive exhibition space for foreign exhibits. A double-height event hall, for which natural light was not necessary, is cut into the ground; the twenty-five-foot difference in level determined its height. The floor, walls, and ceiling of the hall are all movable, and the most advanced technology is used both out front and backstage. VIP and other rooms are arranged on the second floor in front of the event hall. Partially external to the main structure, the third-floor exhibition space is a kind of lobby.

Adopting a truss system in the sixteen-foot-high fourth-floor exhibition room made it possible to cantilever the floor about sixty-five feet on each side of the lower floors. The truss system is enclosed in double glass walls—frosted glass for the exterior walls, and glass coated with patterned ceramic for the interior. Skylights and perforated metal form the ceiling, and the entire interior is filled with natural light uniformly distributed throughout the day.

The placement of the large-volume exhibition spaces on the third and fourth floors, above the plateau level, established a strong spatial quality while minimizing earth-moving work.

225

2

226

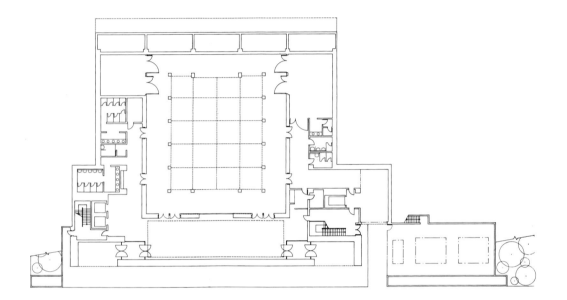

3

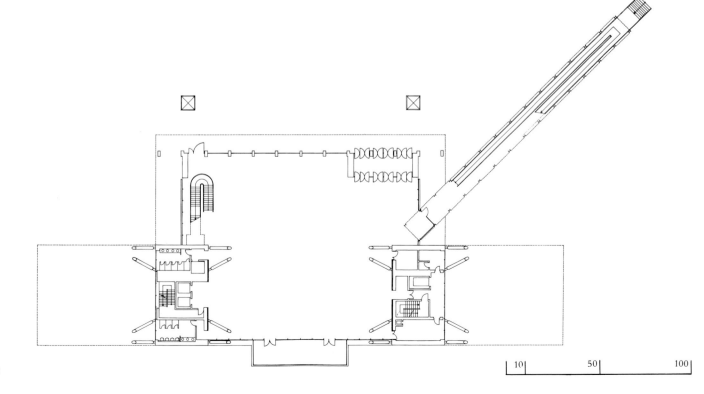

4

| 10 | 50 | 100 |

227

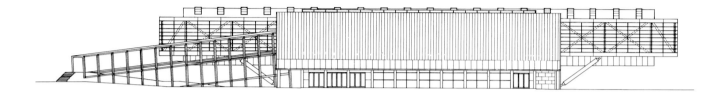

5

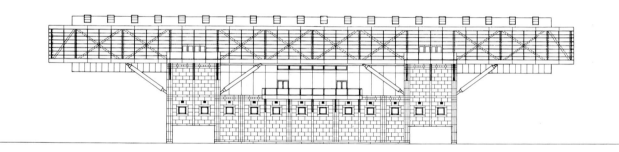

6

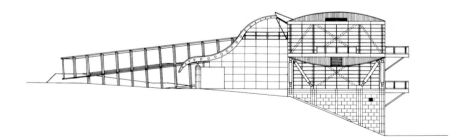

7

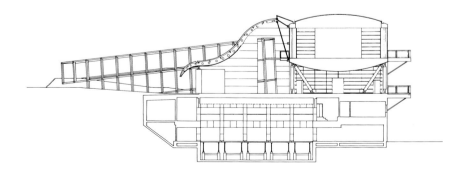

8

9

10

9. The entrance stairs under the cantilever.
10. View from the entrance ramp.
11. View from the top of the entrance stairs.

Overleaf:
12. The entrance lobby.

11

1. Axonometric (silk screen).
2. Site plan.
3. View of the tower from between the theater
   and the conference hall.

Art Tower Mito

Mito, Ibaragi, Japan, 1986–90

232

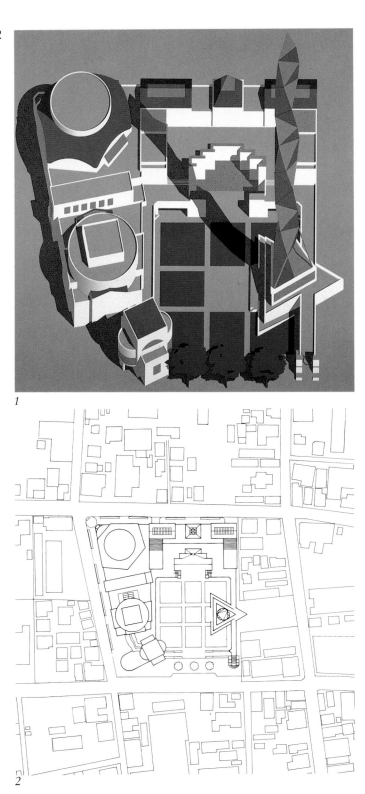

1

2

The Art Tower Mito occupies a block in the old part of Mito, one street away from the old highway that passes east to west through the city. More than half of the site is to be given over to an urban square, and the facility itself is designed as a townscape around the square. It is a small redevelopment project from the point of view of Mito as a whole, but this urban environment is intended to be a new cultural core that will stimulate the reorganization of the surrounding area, away from the linear development along the highway.

The new complex is arranged around the square, which has a green that is open to the public day and night. It includes a 330-foot-high symbolic tower (100 meters, commemorating Mito's centennial), a theater, a concert hall, and a gallery of contemporary art. Although drama, music, and art activities are accommodated in separate facilities, the spaces are close to one another and have a common area so that interrelationships can develop across different fields. The theater and the concert hall are located along the western street, and between them is the entrance hall for the entire complex, which will be equipped with a pipe organ. On the northern street, behind a cascade on the square, are offices, curatorial rooms, a restaurant (on the first floor), and the gallery (on the second). A two-story conference hall is located on the southwestern corner of the square. Underground facilities include rehearsal and dressing rooms, art-storage space, and a 250-car parking garage.

The square is accessible from all directions. One passes under three large oaks (on the south side), alongside the symbol tower (the east), behind the cascade (the north), or through the entrance hall (the west).

50   200   500

3

234

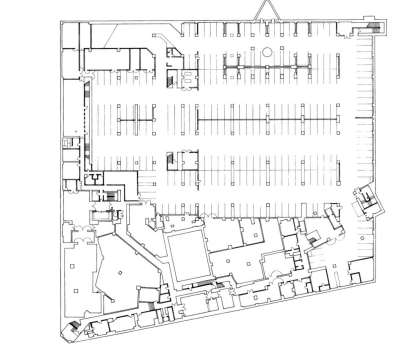

4

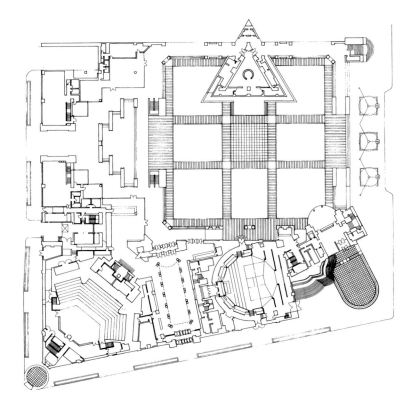

5

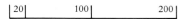

4. Basement plan.
5. First-floor plan.
6. Second-floor plan.
7. Roof plan.
8. Plans of the upper levels of the theater.

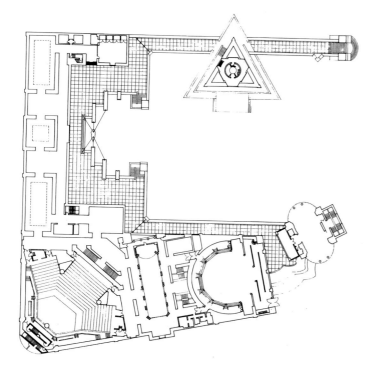

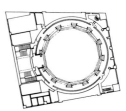

6

8

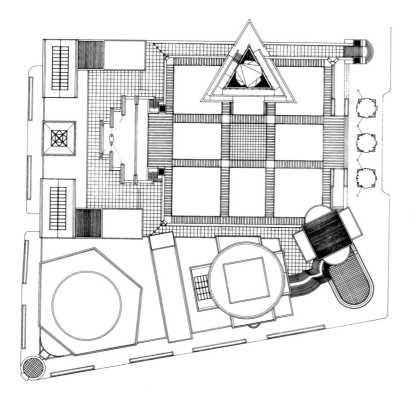

7

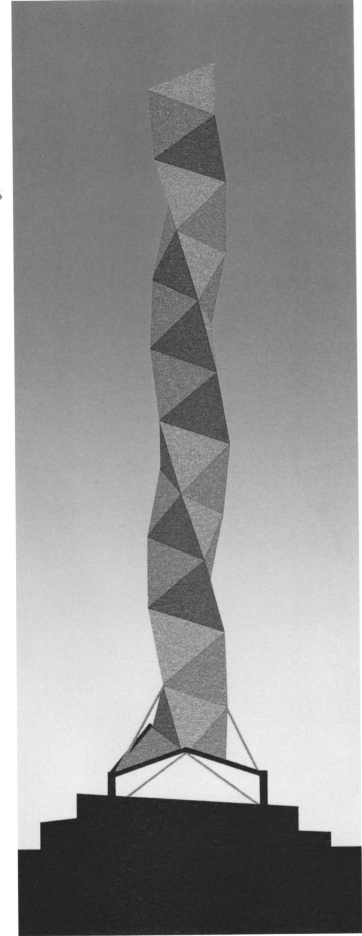

9. Tower elevation (silk screen).
10, 11. Perspectives (silk screen).

10

11

238

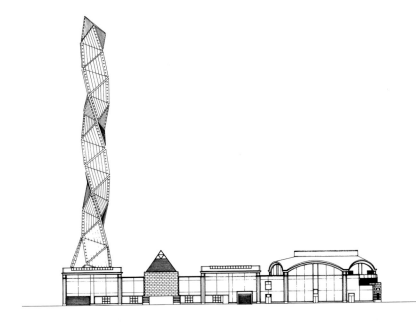

12

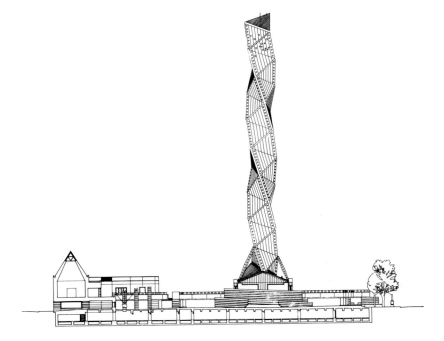

13

12. *Elevation of the gallery (left) and the concert hall (right).*
13. *Section through the gallery.*
14. *The plaza.*

15

16

15. *Exterior of the gallery.*
16. *Exterior of the concert hall.*
17, 18. *Exterior views of the theater.*

17

18

19. *Facade of the entrance hall.*
20. *The tower base.*
21. *The tower at night.*

242

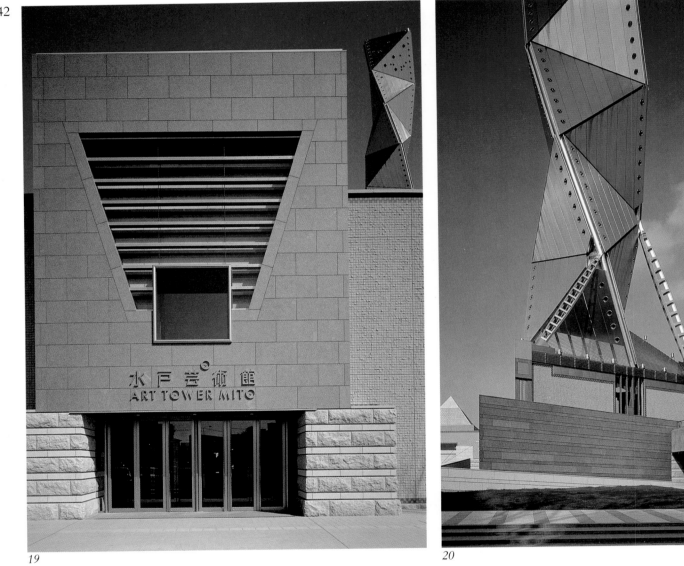

19

20

244

22

24

23

25

22. *The entrance hall.*
23. *The tower lobby.*
24. *One of the galleries.*
25. *Interior of the concert hall.*
26. *View of the onyx window from inside the entrance hall.*
27. *Interior of the theater.*
28, 29. *Interior circulation areas.*

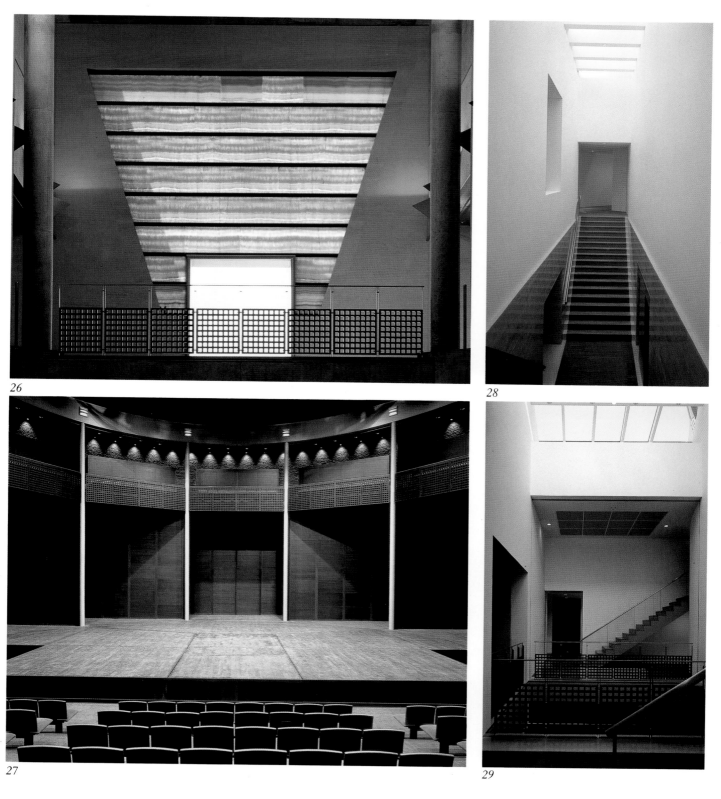

26

28

27

29

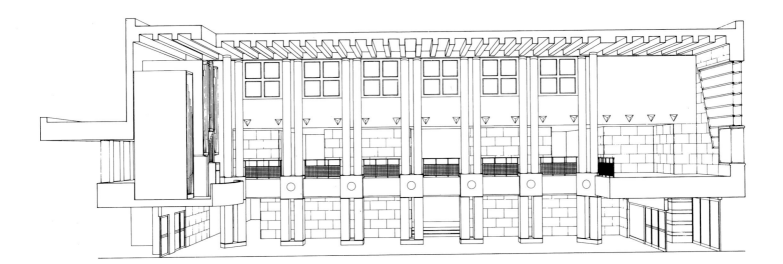

30

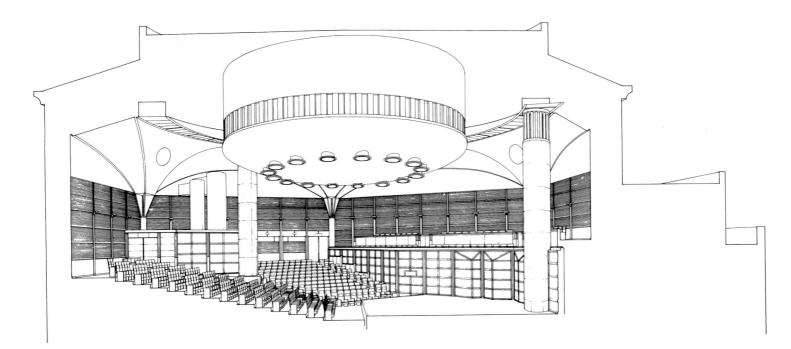

31

30. Section perspective of the entrance hall.
31. Section perspective of the concert hall.
32. Section perspective of the theater.

Overleaf:
33. Detail of the conference hall interior.

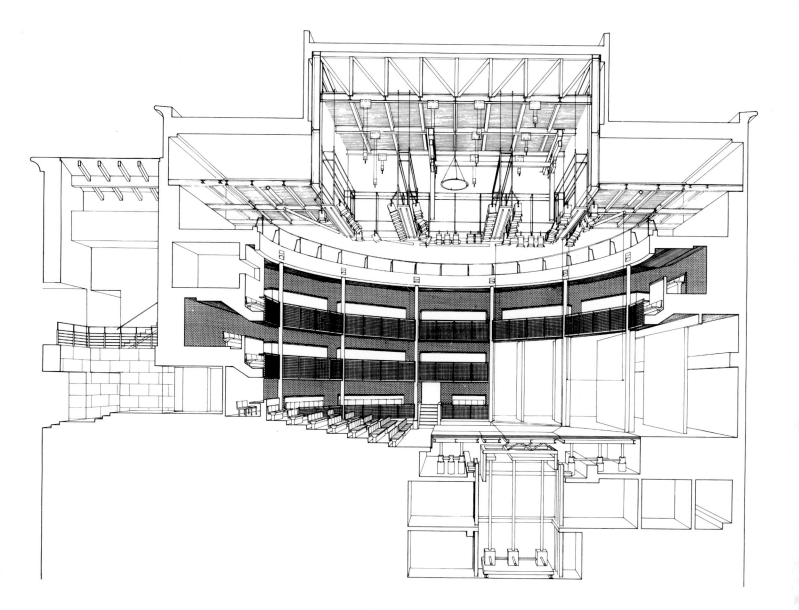

Kitakyushu International Conference Center
Kitakyushu, Fukuoka, Japan, 1987–90

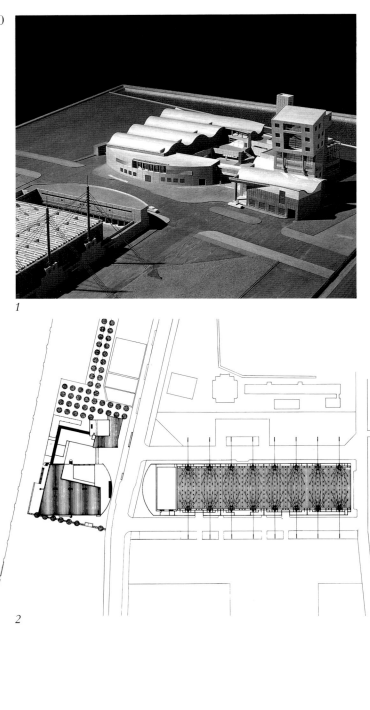

250

1

2

The new conference center stands between Isozaki's West Japan General Exhibition Center, built in 1977, and the wharf on the seafront. The idea of an extended convention center along the lines of the German-style *Messe* has been under study for several years, and more exhibition spaces and related facilities are still in the planning stages. But together with the existing building, the addition of the International Conference Center completes the core of the planned complex, situated on the north side of Kokura Station.

The axis of the General Exhibition Center intersects the line of the wharf at a 13° angle. The new building is divided into two architectural systems: one on the extension of the existing axis, and the other on an axis parallel to the wharf. The integral wing houses the conference and banquet halls, while the ensemble wing, whose composition is developed around an unusual "leaning" tower, holds a large conference-room block, large and small meeting rooms, the convention bureau, and other offices.

Waveform roofing is used on both the integral wing and the conference-room block of the ensemble wing. The roof over the conference hall, enclosing a large void, is a five-inch-thick reinforced-concrete shell covered with highly salt-resistant lead sheets. It reaches a maximum span of eighty-eight feet across the main axis. Under its surface is a secondary curve pre-stress line, worked out with the aid of computer simulations. Perhaps the two most important design elements are the waveform roofs and the leaning tower: the former represents the sea; the latter, the ships that sail on it.

The ceiling and interior walls of the 600-seat conference hall have gentle curves that echo the undulations of the roof, and metal plate and natural stone are used in some parts against the white oak walls. The hall has two 200-inch high-definition monitor screens, and the same equipment can be found in the large and small meeting rooms. This advanced technology allows for international conferencing. In the 1,000-person banquet hall, a large colonnade of columns finished in serpentine stone supports the exposed ceiling, from which a vast number of halogen lamps are suspended by stainless-steel wire, sparkling like stars.

The leaning tower is eight stories high, providing a view all the way to the main island of Honshu. All other sections of the building are three stories.

1. *Overall view of the model, with the West Japan General Exhibition Center on the left.*
2. *Site plan.*
3. *Model, showing the new facilities in relation to the exhibition center.*

3

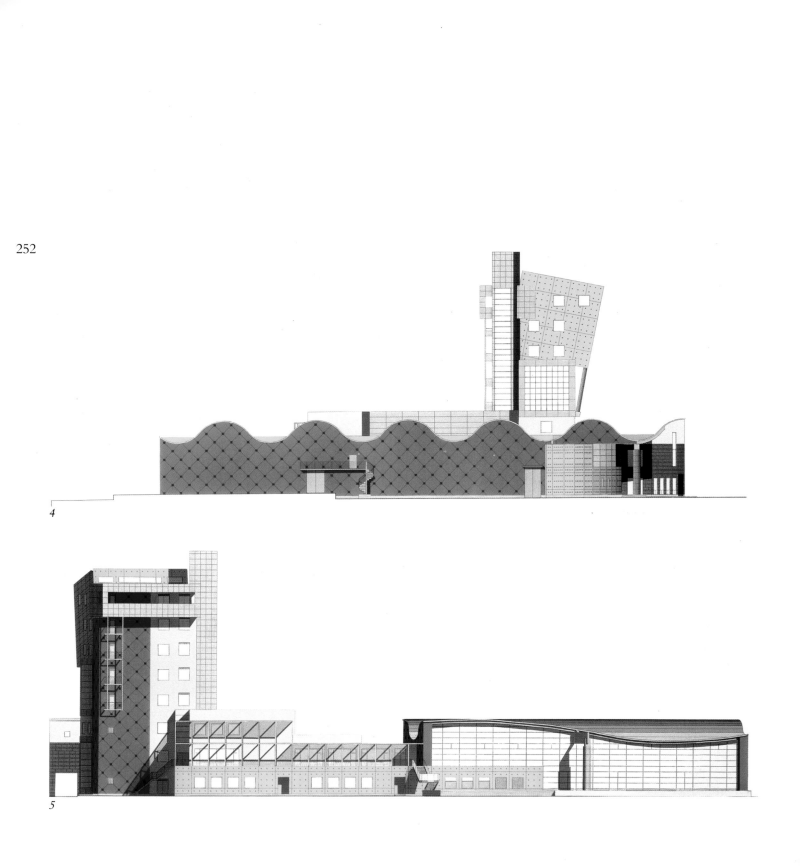

4

5

4. *Side elevation.*
5. *Waterfront elevation.*
6. *View of the main entrance.*

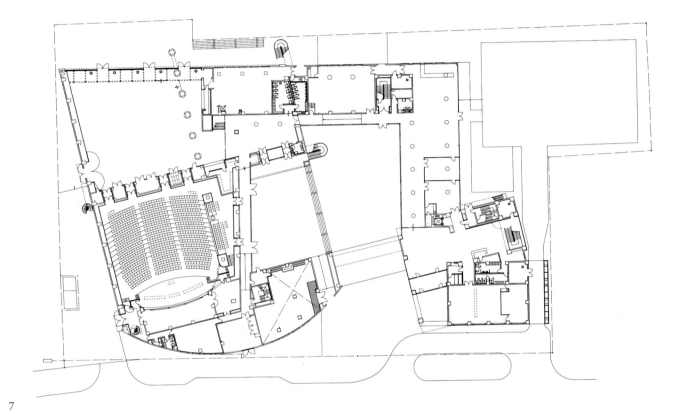

7

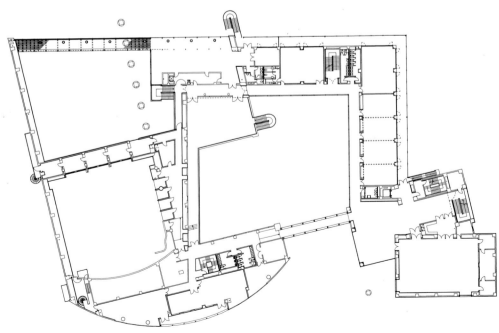

10 50 100

7. *First-floor plan.*
8. *Second-floor plan.*
9. *Entrance elevation.*
10. *Side elevation.*
11. *Section through the conference hall.*

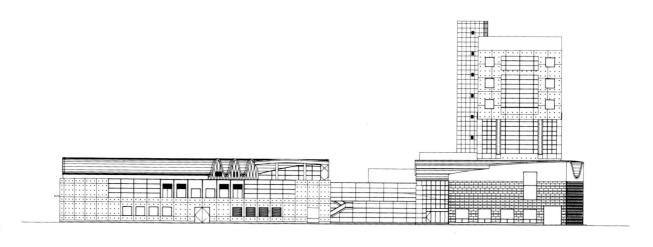

9

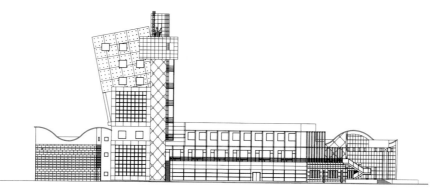

10

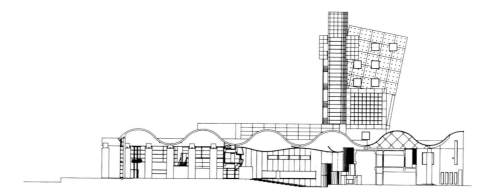

11

Sant Jordi Sports Hall

Montjuic, Barcelona, 1983–90

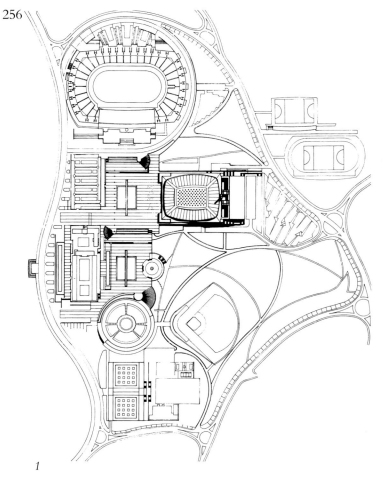

1

This sports hall has been designed as one of the central facilities at Montjuic, the main event area for the 1992 Olympics in Barcelona.

The sports hall has been planned to include an ice hockey rink, a 200-meter track, and other sports facilities; it can also accommodate concerts, conventions, exhibitions, and other non-sports uses. Spectators enter the hall from the square on the north side; athletes, service staff, and press approach from the street on the south side, where the level is fifty feet lower than the north entrance. Between the main arena and the secondary arenas are circulation areas, locker rooms, dressing rooms, restaurants, and offices.

The hall is covered with a double-layer, dome-shaped space frame whose construction was specially designed: three hinged sections are jointed horizontally and assembled in a folded state on the ground before being raised in the air and fixed in their final shape. The roof makes reference to the mountain on which the building is situated; soaring 148 feet above the arena floor at its highest point, it provides the structure with an airiness that is often lacking in the design of similar sports halls. Perforated-metal screens allow for light control within the space frame. Brick, stone, tile, zinc, and other local materials have been used in a variety of ways for the interior and exterior finishes.

200   1000   2000

2

258

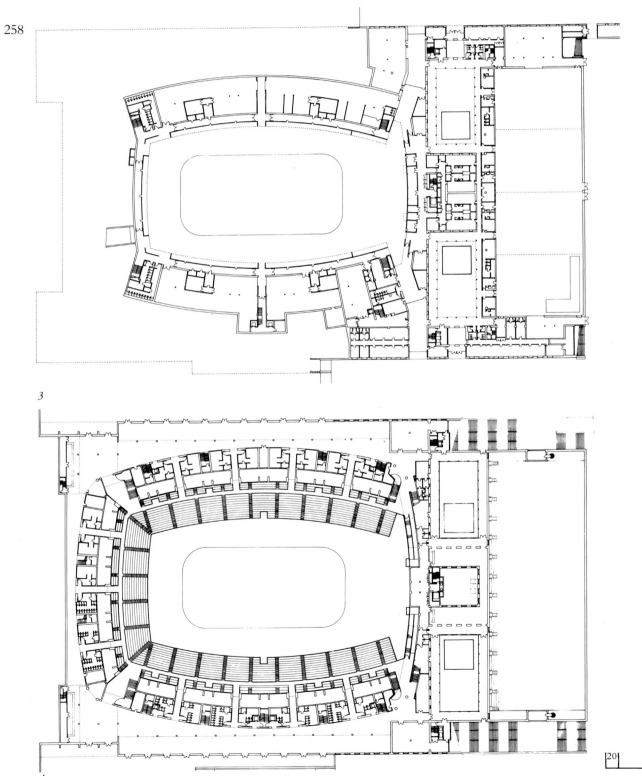

3

4

20 100 200

259

3. First-floor plan.
4. Fourth-floor plan.
5-7. Model of the structural system showing the
   roof assembly and lift-up construction
   process.

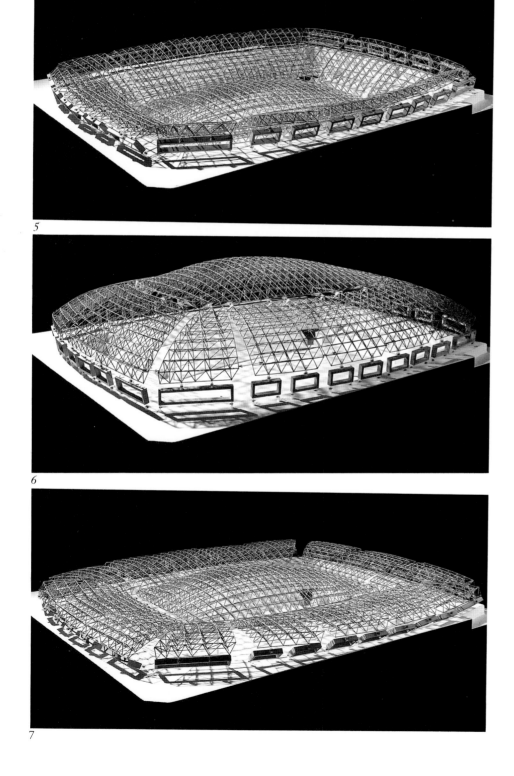

5

6

7

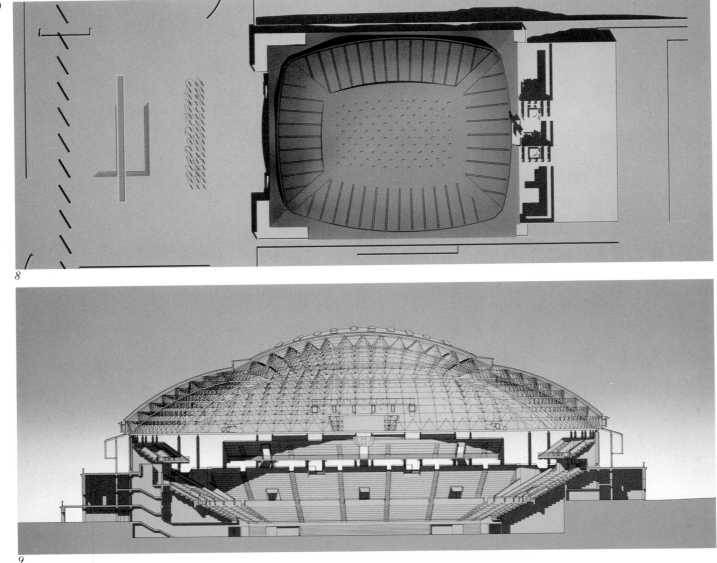

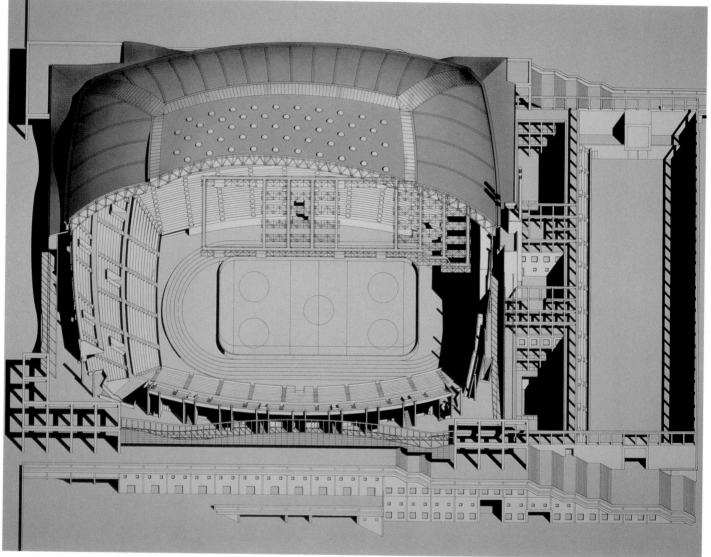

10

262

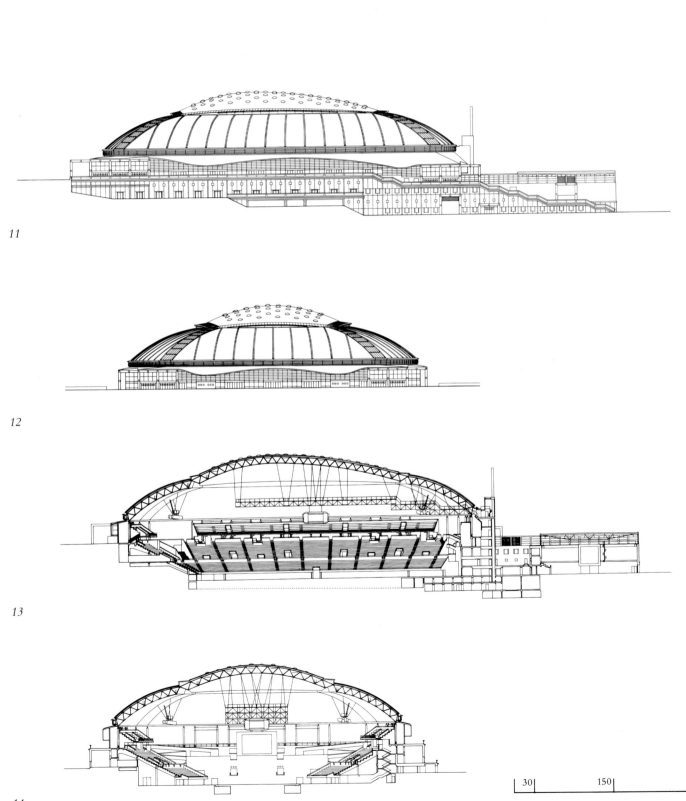

11

12

13

| 30 | 150 | 300 |

14

11. Side elevation.
12. Front elevation.
13. Longitudinal section.
14. Transverse section.
15-18. Section diagrams showing the roof
    structure and lift-up construction process.

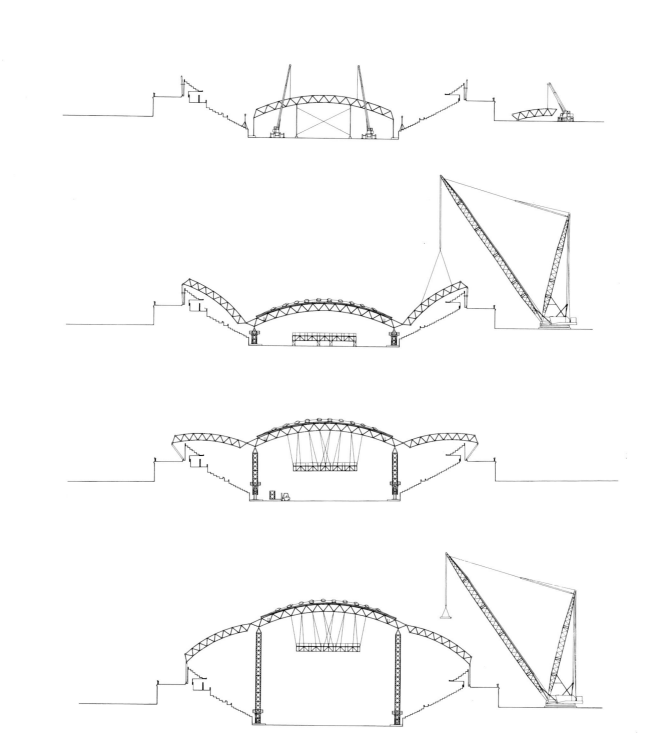

15

16

17

18

264

19

19. Perspective of the original competition entry (silk screen).
20-22. Drawings of the competition entry (silk screen).

20

22

21

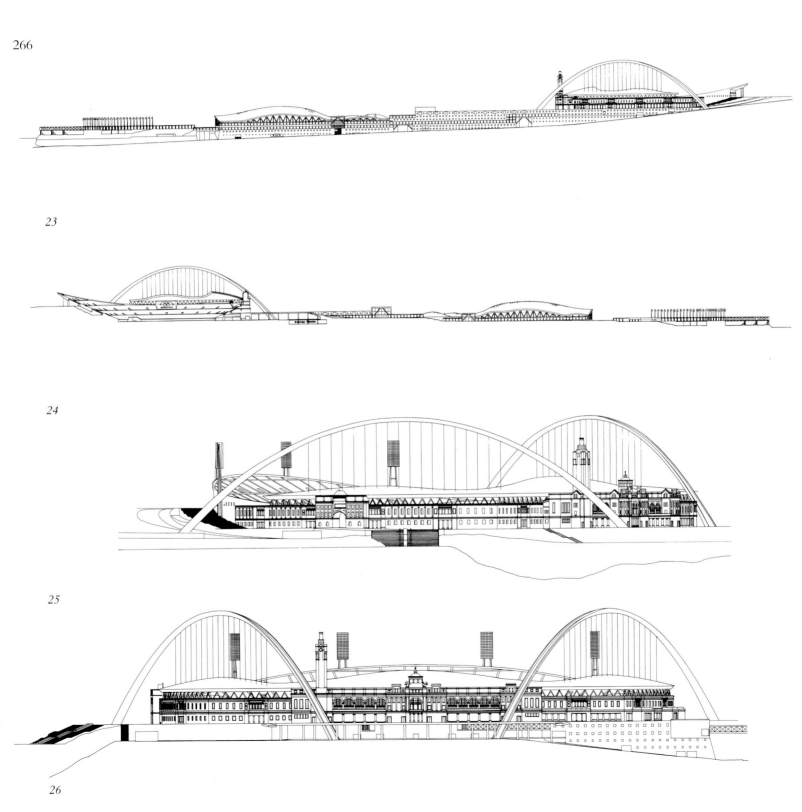

266

23

24

25

26

23-26. *Drawings of the competition entry.*
27. *Aerial perspective of the competition entry.*

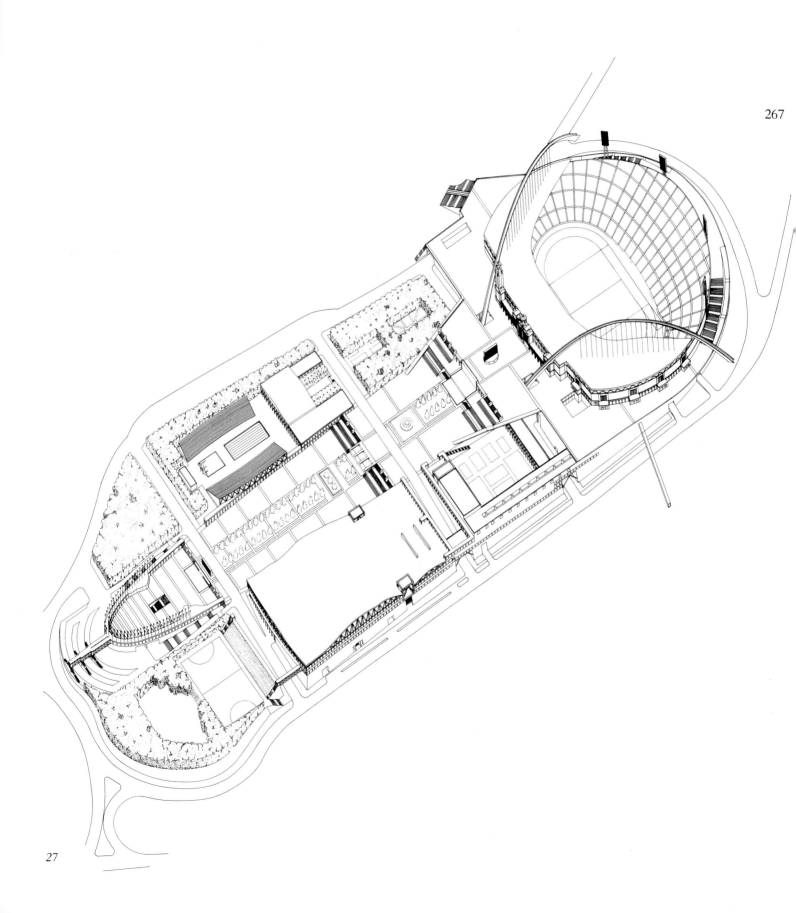

The Disney Building

Lake Buena Vista, Florida, 1987–90

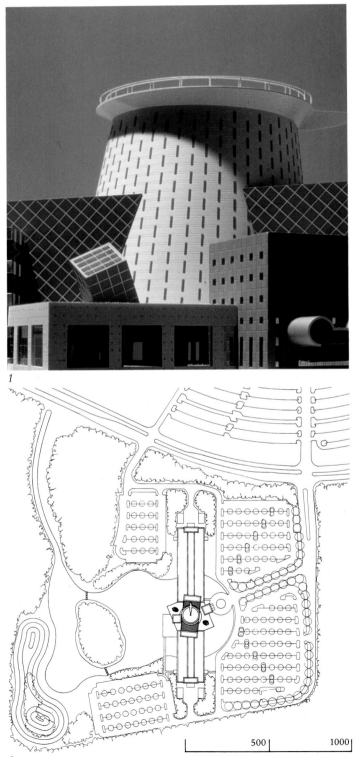

1

2

500   1000

Walt Disney World, just outside Orlando, Florida, is on a vast site of 29,000 acres, an area twice the size of Manhattan. Walt Disney's dream was to construct a model of the city of the future here; theme parks such as the Magic Kingdom, EPCOT Center, and Disney/MGM Studios have already been built on the site.

Disney Village, the area near the main entrance to Walt Disney World from the freeway, is the site for the headquarters of Disney Florida Operating Divisions, collected in a single building.

With a total length of 820 feet on a north-south axis, the building is divided into three blocks. Almost all office functions are contained in two long north and south four-story blocks in identical designs. Each block is laterally divided by an atrium on the central axis. Skylights on the office-block roofs allow daylight to pour into this interior/exterior space; bridges and stairways provide connections across the divide. Aluminum and reflective glass are flush on the curtain wall, creating a smooth, continuous exterior.

Between the two wings is the entrance lobby, an ensemble of forms grouped around a huge truncated cone. The cone, 120 feet in diameter at its base and 120 feet high, stands as the functional and visual focus of attention, inviting people into the building. The long axis of the entrance is turned slightly off the central axis, breaking up the longitudinal mass of the office blocks. A variety of materials, colors, patterns, shapes, and structures in this area provide distinctive accents to the architecture. The walls colliding with the cone are blue, and red cube skylights are inserted into the roof of the entrance block. A huge stylus atop the cone throws shadows into the interior space, forming a sundial indicating the time and seasons. Check patterns in two types of red granite are used to cover two other elements of the entrance block, one containing an entrance hall, the other a conference room at the third-floor level. Access to this conference room is provided by a bridge passing through the cone. The main entrance to the building is covered by the "Mickey" canopy, which pierces the cube leading directly into the open courtyard in the cone.

The building straddles the east end of an artificial lake, a prominent feature of the landscaping. The lake surface, the architectural composition, and the color scheme combine to establish the presence of this flagship building at the forefront of Walt Disney World.

1. Detail view of the model.
2. Site plan.
3. View of the model.

3

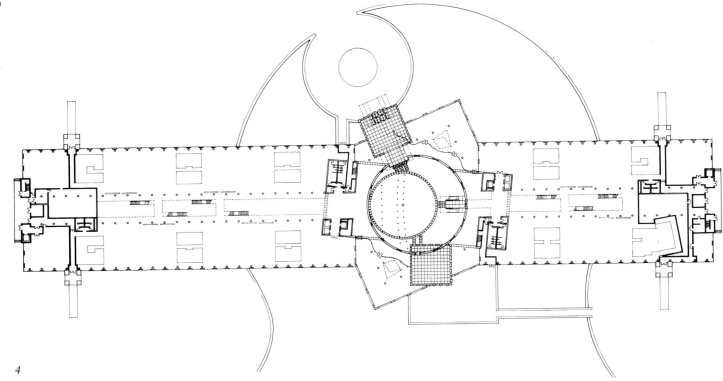

4

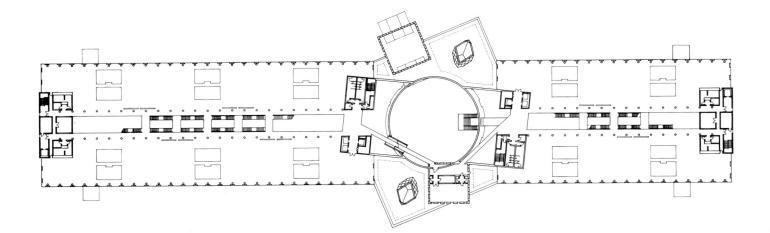

20 100 200

5

271

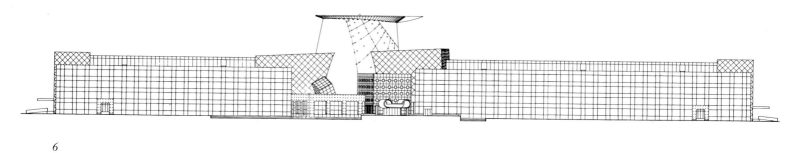

6

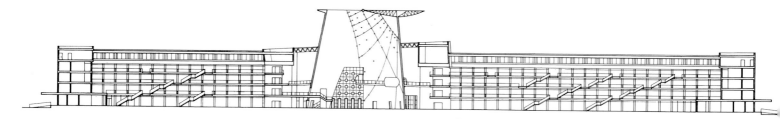

7

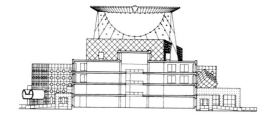

8

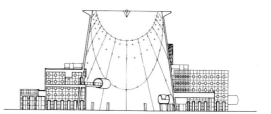

9

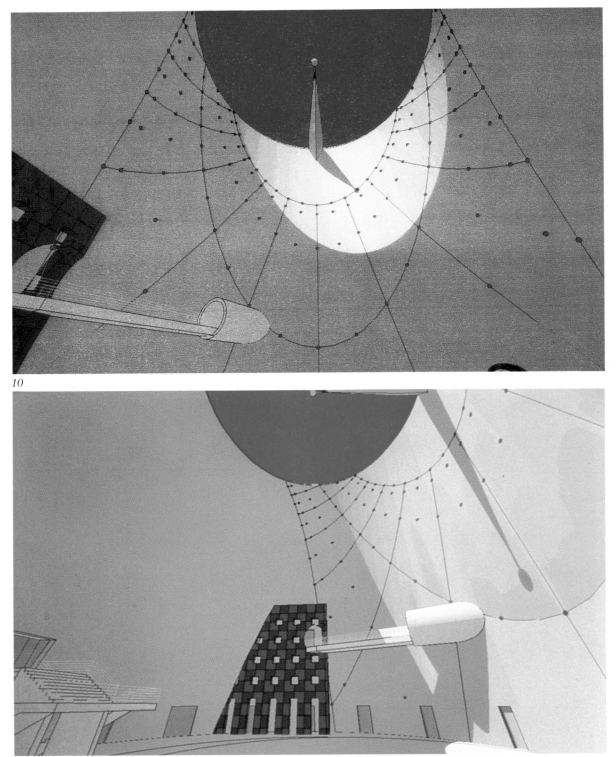

10

11

10, 11. *Interior perspectives (computer-*
       generated renderings).
12. *Section model showing the sundial.*

JR Ueno Railway Station Redevelopment

Tokyo, 1988–

274

1

2

This project is part of redevelopment plans for the Ueno Railway Station, one of the main terminals in Tokyo for suburban and intercity trains. The proposed redevelopment focuses on improving the station itself and strengthening its functions. The program calls for a 1.1 million-square-foot hotel, a 900,000-square-foot department store, a theater, an art gallery, and additions and extensions to reconfigure the interior of the station. The total floor area will comprise 2.8 million square feet.

The colossal slab over the station, devoted mainly to hotel guest rooms, is formed of five 165-foot-square units stacked on top of a quadrant block. It will soar 1,000 feet into the air. The joint sections of the hotel tower units contain machine rooms and function as buffer zones in case of earthquakes or fire. Four huge buttresses support the tower in front and back.

In the upper section of the quadrant block is the department store, which envelops the central concourse of the station itself. Interior circulation routes at Ueno Station are extremely complex because there are two levels of platforms. An 80-foot-high, 330-foot-long void contains the new organization of the concourse interior, which improves circulation patterns for passengers and other users. This void is pierced in its upper reaches by escalators and bridges that are part of the hotel and department-store circulation lines.

An elevated artificial foundation above the railway tracks extends north from under the hotel slab. Placed along this base are gardens, an elliptical hotel banquet hall, the theater, and the art gallery. The placement of elements on the foundation is designed to link the space above the tracks with Ueno Park, which lies across the street on the west side of the station. Just inside the park is a group of cultural facilities, including the Tokyo Metropolitan Festival Hall and the Museum of Western Art. As urban planning, the project thus incorporates a direct relationship to the existing fabric of the city, as well as reformulating the functional type of the railway station. The scheme required a fundamental review of the relation between architecture and the city as part of the design process, and it demonstrated the urgent need for formalization of the techniques and procedures involved in creating massive architecture. Design is scheduled for completion at the end of 1992; construction should be completed in 1999.

500 | 1000 |

1. *View of the model.*
2. *Site plan.*
3. *Superimposed aerial photograph.*

NTV Plaza Project
Shinjuku, Tokyo, 1989–

276

NTV, one of the major TV companies in Japan, has a ten-acre site east of the station in Shinjuku, a district now being developed as the new metropolitan center of Tokyo. Dominated by skyscrapers, the area on the west side of Shinjuku Station has become an important business center, while the east side has long flourished as a commercial and residential neighborhood. Programming for NTV's plan began with the company's desire to erect an art gallery and an opera hall on the site. The art gallery will be approximately the same size as MOCA in Los Angeles, and the concert hall will seat at least 2,000. Also proposed are a 1,000-seat international conference hall; more than one million square feet of offices; a hotel with 200 guest rooms and large and small banquet rooms; commercial space (mainly restaurants); and up to 430,000 square feet of residential space. Including the underground parking garage, the total floor area in NTV Plaza will amount to about 3.2 million square feet.

The program (including the floor area) has not yet been finalized; the illustrations here represent no more than basic concepts, a proposal for the development prototype. The opera hall will occupy the eastern wing of the site. In dramatic contrast, the center of the site will be held by a bundle of three cylindrical towers, approximately 620 feet high, housing offices and the hotel, with banquet halls and other facilities on the lower floors. Between the two wings, an open plaza about 150 feet wide and 650 feet long will run through the complex. Long and narrow, the plaza will draw people into the cultural facilities from the busiest intersection of the district, thus providing a new axis for this part of the city. A public concert hall stands across the road, establishing the south end of the plaza; an elevated block, housing the international conference hall, will act as a gate to the complex over the north entrance.

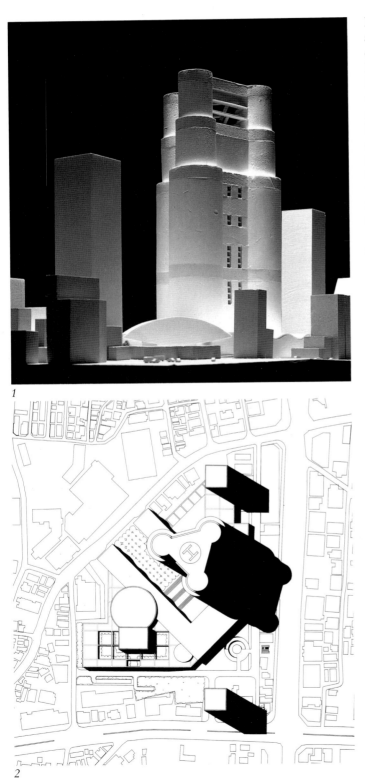

1

2

| 50 | 200 | 500 |

Electric Labyrinth

1968

278

The installation, created for the fourteenth Milan Triennale, was divided into two sections: a maze of sixteen revolving, curved Plexiglas panels, and a huge screen onto which images were cast by three projectors.

The screen was printed with photographs of the devastated, charred remains of Hiroshima after the bomb was dropped; projected onto it, creating a contextual montage, were images of building ruins from cities of the future—brilliant, optimistic visions from the proposals created by Japanese architects in the early 1960s. The projections seemed to say that the fate awaiting all planning proposals, even those that are realized, is one of obliteration, just like Hiroshima.

The revolving panels carried a variety of images: people trapped in urban environments, glimpses of the abused and misused in Japan, visions of hell, late Edo ukiyo-e prints, bombed human bodies, urchins, wastrels, and ghosts. The panels were rotated manually or by signals from an infrared beam; either way, viewers were implicated in their activation.

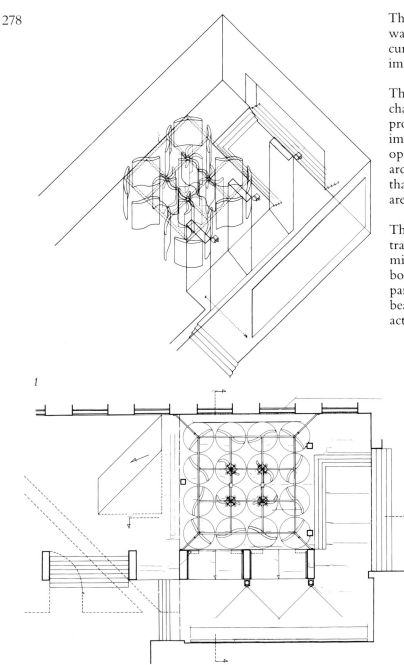

1

2

3

4

"MAN transFORMS"
1976–77

280

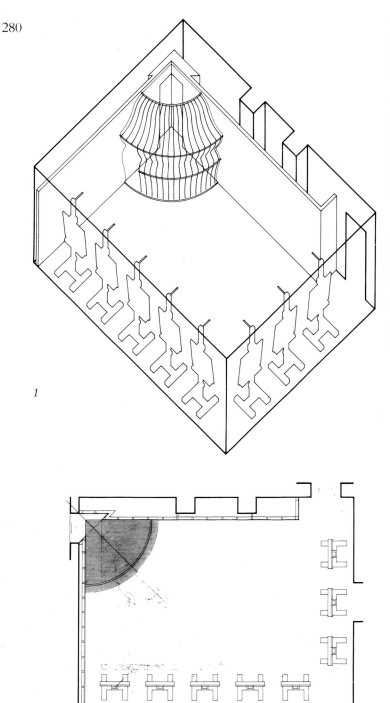

1

2

The overall concept for this exhibition, held at the Cooper-Hewitt Museum in New York, was created by Hans Hollein. Isozaki was responsible for two parts of the exhibition: the Gravity Room and the Angel Cage.

The Gravity Room was arranged to give viewers a sense of this force by pointing out how perception is affected by vertical and horizontal lines. Several photographs of the Leaning Tower of Pisa were hung on the wall (the vertical plane) in front of a slightly inclined surface, which represented the horizontal plane in elements like water and oil.

The Angel Cage was placed among the bird cages in the museum's collection. When viewers reached the exhibition area, they entered the cage, which included a life-size image of an angel based on a Fra Angelico painting. Also interspersed throughout the display were photographs that simulated the view from the inside of a cage looking out. Through photographs and through their own visceral perceptions, viewers were forced to confront the experience of the caged bird.

1. *Axonometric of the Angel Cage installation.*
2. *Plan of the installation.*
3. *View from within the Angel Cage.*

281

"MA: Space/Time in Japan"

1978–81

1

In Japanese both time and space are encompassed by the word *ma,* which means an interval in space or time: the natural distance between one thing and another in a continuity; the spatial interval between one object and another; the natural pause or interval between two or more phenomena occurring continuously. The Western view of space and time as linear, serial continua admits no heterogeneity, but the Japanese sensibility reflects on the nature of the interval. Still lying at the foundations of consciousness in Japan today, the concept of *ma* affects all creations: lifestyles, environments, architecture, art, music, theater, garden landscaping.

This exhibition, organized for the Festival d'Automne in Paris, toured Europe and America. Designed to bring out the concept of *ma* in its diverse manifestations, the exhibition ranged widely, from the traditional *sukiya* style to the latest products of the avant-garde.

Exhibits were grouped around nine subthemes, each explored in its own independent enclosure, which was designed to reveal the theoretical and practical identity of time and space that is *ma.* Conceptual development moved from the sacred to the profane, from pristine aestheticism to everyday life, from sturdy spatiality to the fluidity of time passage.

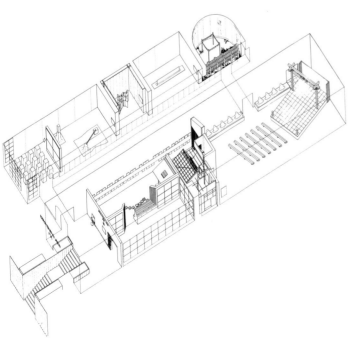

1. The exhibition entrance.
2. Axonometric of the exhibition installation.
3. One of the exhibition sections.

3

"Tokyo: Form and Spirit"

1986–87

284

1

Organized by the Walker Art Center in Minneapolis, this exhibition juxtaposed Japanese cultural artifacts from the Edo period with works by artists currently active in Tokyo to introduce the culture of that city to the American public. Isozaki was asked to organize the installation of the Performing Space and the Walking Space. He worked in collaboration with art director Eiko Ishioka on the Performing Space and painter Tadanori Yokoo on the Walking Space.

The design of the Performing Space was based on the idea that television is the real god of today's society. Numerous TVs were arranged in a configuration common to classical times in both East and West: that of a stage combined with a temple. A TV totem pole was placed in the center of the "temple," and TVs of all sizes were mounted in the floor of the "stage." To reduce them to their primary essence as machines transmitting images, the outer casings of the sets were removed and the inner workings were left exposed.

For the Walking Space Yokoo created a serial work using large ceramic tiles in five groupings that corresponded to the five phases in the history of Tokyo: Edo, Meiji, Taisho, Showa, and the near future. Each phase was represented in an eight-foot-square collage of images of events, person-alities, and scenes prominent in that era. Isozaki designed the "frames" for the pictures to assist understanding of Yokoo's work. A route through the exhibition space was mapped out to lead visitors through the series, which was arranged in a kind of three-dimensional picture scroll.

2

Selected Buildings and Projects

Oita Medical Hall
Oita, Japan, 1959–60
Client: Medical Association, Oita
Consultants: Masami Hanai, Mamoru Kawaguchi, Toshio
Iwamura (structural)
Contractor: Goto-gumi Construction Co., Ltd.

Shinjuku Project
Shinjuku, Tokyo, 1960–61

Peugeot Building
(competition)
Argentina, 1961

Clusters in the Air
Tokyo, 1960–62

Marunouchi Project
Marunouchi, Tokyo, 1963

Iwata Girls' High School
Oita, Japan, 1963–64
Client: Iwata Girls' High School
Design team: Yasuhiko Yamamoto
Consultants: Osawa Laboratory/Tokyo University (mechanical)
Contractor: Goto-gumi Construction Co., Ltd.

Nakayama House
Oita, Japan, 1964
Design team: Noriko Hayashi
Consultants: Yasuo Suzuki Associates (structural); Toshio Ojima
(mechanical)
Contractor: Umebayashi Construction Co., Ltd.

Oita Prefectural Library
Oita, Japan, 1962–66
Client: Oita Prefectural Government
Design team: Yasuhiko Yamamoto, Takahiko Sugiura, Noriko
Hayashi, Masahiro Rokkaku, Noriyuki Miura
Consultants: Osawa Laboratory/Tokyo University (structural);
Toshio Ojima (mechanical); Kiichiro Kurihara (planning)

Fukuoka City Bank, Oita Branch
Oita, Japan, 1966–67
Client: Fukuoka City Bank
Design team: Yasuhiko Yamamoto, Masahiro Rokkaku, Shuichi
Fujie
Consultants: Osawa Laboratory/Tokyo University (structural);
Toshio Ojima (mechanical and electrical)
Contractor: Obayashi Corporation

Kuju-Kao Hi, Cenotaph
Oita, Japan, 1966–67

Fukuoka City Bank, Daimyo Branch
Fukuoka, Japan, 1967–69
Client: Fukuoka City Bank
Design team: Masahiro Rokkaku, Takahiro Nakamori, Koukichi
Shioya
Consultants: Osawa Laboratory/Tokyo University (structural);
Toshio Ojima (mechanical and electrical)
Contractor: Obayashi Corporation

The Festival Plaza, Expo '70
Osaka, Japan, 1967–70
Client: Japan Association for the 1970 World Exposition
Design team: Shuichi Fujie, Koukichi Shioya, Yasuhiko
Yamamoto, Yoshio Tsukio, Yushi Morioka, Takahiro Nakamori,
Noriyuki Miura
Consultants: Yamaki Sekkei Co., Ltd. (structural); Otaki Electrical
Design Office (mechanical); So Kenchiku Kenkyujyo, Yujiro
Isozaki (electrical)
Contractors: Obayashi Corporation, Takenaka Corporation, and
Fujita Gumi Ltd.

Responsive House
1968–69

Fukuoka City Bank, Head Office
Fukuoka, Japan, 1968–71
Client: Fukuoka City Bank
Design team: Noriyuki Miura, Katsuhiko Hamaura, Yasuhiko
Yamamoto, Giheiji Nakayama, Kazuichi Miyazaki
Consultants: Osawa Laboratory/Tokyo University, Yamaki
Sekkei, Co., Ltd. (structural); J.E.S. Urban Equipment, Showa
Equipment Design Office (mechanical)
Contractor: Obayashi Corporation

Fukuoka City Bank, Tokyo Branch
(facade and interior design)
Tokyo, 1970–71
Client: Fukuoka City Bank
Design team: Masahiro Rokkaku
Consultants: J.E.S. Urban Equipment (mechanical); Setsubi
Keikaku Co., Ltd. (electrical)
Contractor: Matsui Construction Co., Ltd.

Fukuoka City Bank, Nagasumi Branch
Fukuoka, Japan, 1971
Client: Fukuoka City Bank
Design team: Eichiro Miyake
Contractor: Shimizu Corporation

Fukuoka City Bank, Ropponmatsu Branch
Fukuoka, Japan, 1971
Client: Fukuoka City Bank
Design team: Yasuhiko Yamamoto, Takashi Ito
Consultants: Yamaki Sekkei Co., Ltd. (structural); J.E.S. Urban
Equipment, Showa Equipment Design Office (mechanical and
electrical)
Contractor: Matsuo Construction Co., Ltd.

Oita Medical Hall Annex
Oita, Japan, 1970–72
Client: Medical Association, Oita
Design team: Takahiro Nakamori, San Joan Jack
Consultants: Masami Hanai, Nanotsu Architectural Laboratory (structural)
Contractor: Goto-gumi Construction Co., Ltd.

Computer-Aided City
Makuhari, Chiba, Japan, 1972
Design team: Takashi Ito, Yoshio Tsukioka

Fukuoka City Bank, Saga Branch
Saga, Japan, 1972–73
Client: Fukuoka City Bank
Design team: Takahiro Nakamori
Consultants: Kimura Structural Engineers (structural); J.E.S. Urban Equipment (mechanical); Setsubi Keikaku Co., Ltd. (electrical)
Contractor: Matsuo Construction Co., Ltd.

Gunma Prefectural Museum of Fine Arts
Takasaki, Gunma, Japan, 1971–74
Client: Gunma Prefectural Government
Design team: Shuichi Fujie, Hiroshi Nishioka
Consultants: Mamoru Kawaguchi & Engineers (structural); Nippon Kankyo Giken Co., Ltd. (mechanical); Setsubi Keikaku Co., Ltd. (electrical); Sotoji Nakamura (teahouse)
Contractor: Inoue Kogyo Co., Ltd.

Kitakyushu City Museum of Art
Kitakyushu, Fukuoka, Japan, 1972–74
Client: City of Kitakyushu
Design team: Eichiro Miyake, Ken Nishida
Consultants: Kimura Structural Engineers (structural); Nippon Kankyo Giken Co., Ltd. (mechanical); Setsubi Keikaku Co., Ltd. (electrical)
Contractor: Shimizu Corporation

Fujimi Country Clubhouse
Oita, Japan, 1973–74
Client: Nakagawa Development Co., Ltd.
Design team: Noriyuki Miura
Consultants: Mamoru Kawaguchi & Engineers (structural); J.E.S. Urban Equipment (mechanical); Setsubi Keikaku Co., Ltd. (electrical)
Contractor: Sato-gumi Co., Ltd.

Kitakyushu Central Library
Kitakyushu, Fukuoka, Japan, 1973–74
Client: City of Kitakyushu
Design team: Yasuhiko Yamamoto, Takashi Ito
Consultants: Kimura Structural Engineers (structural); Nippon Kankyo Giken Co., Ltd. (mechanical); Setsubi Keikaku Co., Ltd. (electrical); Minoru Nagata Acoustic Engineer & Associates (acoustical)
Contractor: Okumura-gumi Co., Ltd.

Katsuyama Country Clubhouse
Fukuoka, Japan, 1974
Design team: Hiroshi Nishioka

Yano House
Kawasaki, Japan, 1973–75
Design team: Hiroshi Nishioka, Masanobu Yuzawa
Consultants: Kimura Structural Engineers (structural); Nippon Kankyo Giken Co., Ltd. (mechanical)
Contractor: Kojima-gumi Ltd.

Shuko-sha Building
Fukuoka, Japan, 1974–75
Client: Shuko-sha Print Co., Ltd.
Design team: Takahiro Nakamori, Itaru Iwasaki
Consultants: Mamoru Kawaguchi & Engineers (structural); Kiuchi Equipment Planning Laboratory (mechanical); Setsubi Keikaku Co., Ltd. (electrical)
Contractor: Kumagai-gumi Construction Co., Ltd.

Kawarayu Project
Kawarayu, Gunma, Japan, 1975
Design team: Shuichi Fujie, Hiroshi Aoki

West Japan General Exhibition Center
Kitakyushu, Fukuoka, Japan, 1975–77
Client: West Japan Industrial and Trade Exhibition Association
Design team: Yasuhiko Yamamoto, Shuichi Fujie, Hiroshi Nishioka, Masanobu Yazawa
Consultants: Mamoru Kawaguchi & Engineers (structural); Inoue Laboratory/Waseda University (mechanical); Setsubi Keikaku Co., Ltd. (electrical)
Contractor: Kajima Corporation

Tomb of Ootomo Sorin
Oita, Japan, 1976–77
Design team: Hiroshi Aoki

Kaijima House
Tokyo, Japan, 1976–77
Design team: Hiroshi Nishioka
Consultants: Yoji Hosokawa (structural)
Contractor: BAU Construction

Hayashi House
Fukuoka, Japan, 1976–77
Design team: Hiroshi Nishioka, Takashi Ito, Eisaku Ushida
Consultants: Mamoru Kawaguchi & Engineers (structural); Inoue Laboratory/Waseda University (mechanical); Setsubi Keikaku Co., Ltd. (electrical)
Contractor: Obayashi Corporation

Kamioka Town Hall
Gifu, Japan, 1976–78
Client: Town of Kamioka
Design team: Shuichi Fujie, Hiroshi Aoki
Consultants: Kimura Structural Engineers (structural); Chubu
Sekkei, Inc. (mechanical); Setsubi Keikaku Co., Ltd. (electrical)
Contractor: Kajima Corporation

Kubo House
Tokyo, 1976–78
Design team: Takashi Ito

Sueoka Clinic
Oita, Japan, 1977–78
Design team: Shuichi Fujie, Hiroshi Nishioka, Eisaku Ushida
Consultants: Mamoru Kawaguchi & Engineers (structural);
Yoshida Design Studio (mechanical)
Contractor: Obayashi Corporation

Aoki House
Tokyo, 1977–78
Design team: Takashi Ito, Masanobu Yuzawa
Consultants: Kimura Structural Engineers (structural); Yoshida
Design Studio (mechanical)
Contractor: BAU Construction

Karashima House
Oita, Japan, 1977–78
Design team: Hiroshi Nishioka, Takashi Ito, Koji Sato
Consultants: Mamoru Kawaguchi & Engineers (structural);
Yoshida Design Studio (mechanical)
Contractor: Goto-gumi Construction Co., Ltd.

Gunma Women's College
(competition)
Gunma, Japan, 1978
Design team: Shuichi Fujie, Hajime Yatsuka, Hiroshi Aoki, Eisaku
Ushida, Makoto Kikuchi

Oita Audio-Visual Center
Oita, Japan, 1977–79
Client: City of Oita
Design team: Shuichi Fujie, Takashi Ito, Masanobu Yuzawa,
Eisaku Ushida, Hiroshi Nishioka
Consultants: Mamoru Kawaguchi & Engineers (structural);
Yoshida Design Studio (mechanical and electrical)
Contractor: Showa Sogo Construction Co., Ltd.

Hakubi Kyoto Kimono School
Tokyo, 1978–79
Client: Hakubi Kyoto Kimono School
Design team: Shuichi Fujie, Eisaku Ushida, Koji Sato
Consultants: Masaya Murakami (structural); Yoshida Design
Studio (mechanical)
Contractor: Taisei Corporation

Ministry of Foreign Affairs, Saudi Arabia
(limited competition)
Riyadh, Saudi Arabia, 1979
Client: Ministry of Foreign Affairs, Kingdom of Saudi Arabia
Design team: Hajime Yatsuka, Makoto Kikuchi, Bruce Goodwin

Employees' Service Facilities of Nippon Electric Glass
Shiga, Japan, 1978–80
Client: Nippon Electric Glass Co., Ltd.
Design team: Shuichi Fujie, Makoto Kikuchi
Consultants: Mamoru Kawaguchi & Engineers (structural);
Yoshida Design Studio (mechanical); Go Design Studio (electrical)
Contractor: Kajima Corporation

Irahara House
Fukuoka, Japan, 1979–80
Design team: Hiroshi Nishioka
Consultants: Yamada Structural Engineers (structural)
Contractor: Kajima Corporation

Tegel Harbor Complex Project
(limited competition)
West Berlin, 1980
Client: Internationale Bauausstellung Berlin
Design team: Hajime Yatsuka, Makoto Kikuchi, Eisaku Ushida
Consultants: Mamoru Kawaguchi & Engineers (structural)
Contractor: Walter Leibender

Etoh Clinic
Oita, Japan, 1980–81
Design team: Hiroshi Nishioka, Hajime Yatsuka, Naoki Inagawa,
Kathryn Findlay
Consultants: Fuji Electric Equipment, Oita (mechanical)
Contractor: Obayashi Corporation

Toga Sanbo Theater
Toyama, Japan, 1981–82
Client: The Japan Performing Arts Center
Design team: Tadashi Murai
Consultants: Inoue Laboratory/Waseda University (structural);
Soei Design Office (mechanical)
Contractor: Nohara-gumi, Takakuwa Construction

Hauserman Showroom at Merchandise Mart
(interior design)
Chicago, Illinois, 1981–82
Client: Hauserman Co., Ltd.
Design team: Takashi Ito, Hideyashu Kuwayama
Consultants: Hauserman Facilities Design Group

House with Three Walls
West Hollywood, California, 1981–82
Design team: Allyne Winderman, Ronald Rose
Consultants: H. Robert Hogan & Associates (structural); Robert
Arneson (mechanical)
Contractor: Yamashita Construction

Amphitheater at Togamura
Toyama, Japan, 1982
Client: Togamura
Design team: Shuichi Fujie, Hideo Matsuura
Consultants: Inoue Kogyo Co., Ltd. (structural); Soei Sekkei (mechanical)
Contractors: Nohara-gumi Construction Co., Ltd., and Takanawa Construction Co., Ltd.

Tsukuba Center Building
Tsukuba Science City, Ibaragi, Japan, 1979–83
Client: Housing and Urban Development Corporation
Design team: Shuichi Fujie, Takashi Ito, Hiroshi Aoki, Makoto Watanabe, Hideo Matsuura, Hiroshi Nagata, Itsuro Shimoki
Consultants: Kimura Structural Engineers (structural); Kankyo Engineering, Inc. (mechanical and electrical); N.H.K. Technical Research Laboratory, Acoustical and Audio-Visual (acoustical); Shiro Kuramata, Yasuhiko Yamamoto (interiors)
Contractors: Toda Corporation, Tobishima Construction, Ohki Construction, and Kabuki Construction

Fukuoka City Bank, Head Office Addition
Fukuoka, Japan, 1978–83
Client: Fukuoka City Bank
Design team: Hiroshi Nishioka, Naoki Inagawa
Consultants: Masaya Murakami (structural); Kyushu Denki-koji Co., Ltd. (mechanical)
Contractor: Obayashi Corporation

Nakagami House
Fukui, Japan, 1982–83
Design team: Shuichi Fujie, Naoki Inagawa
Consultants: Mamoru Kawaguchi & Engineers (structural); Yoshida Design Studio (mechanical)
Contractor: Kajima Corporation

Okanoyama Graphic Arts Museum
Nishiwaki, Hyogo, Japan, 1982–84
Client: City of Nishiwaki
Design team: Makoto Kikuchi, Jun Aoki
Consultants: Mamoru Kawaguchi & Engineers (structural); Yoshida Design Studio, Fujigo Engineers (mechanical); TL Yamagiwa Laboratory Inc. (lighting)
Contractor: Obayashi Corporation

Glass Art Akasaka
Tokyo, 1983–84
Client: Kowa Shoji Co., Ltd.
Design team: Makoto Kikuchi, Masato Hori, Hideki Yoshimatsu
Consultants: Kimura Structural Engineers (structural); Noriyuki Haraguchi, Etsutomu Kashiwabara, Aiko Miyawaki, Shu Takagi, Takashi Fukai, Tadashi Kawamata, Toyomi Hoshina, Kenjirou Okazaki, Shimon Saito, Koichi Somaki, Takashi Fukai (interior installations)
Contractor: Kajima Corporation

Shinoyama Studio
Tokyo, Japan, 1983–85
Design team: Jun Aoki
Consultants: Kimura Structural Engineers (structural); Kankyo Engineering Inc. (mechanical)
Contractor: Takenaka Corporation

The Palladium Club
New York, 1983–85
Client: Muidallap Corporation
Design team: Shin Watanabe, Hiroshi Aoki, Takashi Ito, Ann Kaufman, Masato Hori, Norimitsu Sukeshima, Nagisa Kidosaki
Consultants: Broch, Hesse & Shalat AIA Architects (associate architect); Lovett & Rozman Associates P.C. (structural); Kallen & Lemelson (mechanical); Jules Fisher & Paul Marantz Inc. (lighting); Don Kaufman Color (color); Ecart International, Andrée Putman (furniture)
Contractor: Herbert Construction Corporation; Michael Overington (construction manager)

Iwata Gakuen Gymnasium
Oita, Japan, 1984–85
Client: Iwata Gakuen High School
Design team: Hiroshi Aoki, Jun Aoki
Consultants: Kimura Structural Engineers (structural); Yoshida Design Studio (mechanical)
Contractor: Obayashi Corporation

Iwata Gakuen Dormitory
Oita, Japan, 1984–85
Client: Iwata Gakuen High School
Design team: Jun Aoki, Shuji Miura
Consultants: Kimura Structural Engineers (structural); Yoshida Design Studio (mechanical and electrical)

Phoenix Municipal Government Center
(limited competition)
Phoenix, Arizona, 1985
Client: City of Phoenix
Design team: Hiroshi Aoki, Shin Watanabe, Jun Aoki, Shuji Miura, John O'Reilly
Consultants: Gruen Associates (associate architect); Magadini-Alagia Associates (structural); Baltes/Valentino Associates (mechanical); Jules Fisher & Paul Marantz Inc. (lighting); Bolt, Beranek & Newman (acoustical); Joseph Holgate (civil); A. Wayne Smith & Associates (landscape); Arizona Construction Estimates, Hanscomb Partnership, Futaba Sekisan (cost estimators)

Suffolk County Courthouse
(limited competition)
Islip, New York, 1985
Design team: Shin Watanabe, Kenji Sato, Guen Suzuki, Yasuyori Yada
Consultants: Bentel and Bentel Architects, Planners AIA (associate architect)

Tenjin Five Redevelopment Project
(limited competition)
Fukuoka, Japan, 1985
Design team: Makoto Kikuchi, Hideki Yoshimatsu, Norimitsu Sukeshima

The Museum of Contemporary Art, Los Angeles
Los Angeles, 1981–86
Client: The Museum of Contemporary Art, Los Angeles
Design team: Shin Watanabe, Hajime Yatsuka, Makoto Kikuchi, Ronald Rose, Allyne Winderman
Consultants: Gruen Associates, Los Angeles (associate architect); John A. Martin & Associates (structural); Syska & Hennessy (mechanical); Jules Fisher & Paul Marantz Inc. (lighting); Bolt, Beranek & Newman (acoustical); Chermayeff & Geismar (graphics); Patricia Moritz (entrance sign)
Contractor: HCB Contractors

Björnson Studio/House
Venice, California, 1981–86
Design team: Shin Watanabe, Naoki Inagawa
Consultants: Oimitri Verglin; Klaus Rinke (interiors)
Contractor: Ramfer Inc.

Housing Block 4, House 2
West Berlin, 1982–86
Client: Internationale Bauausstellung Berlin
Design team: Eisaku Ushida, Hans Karl

Yokoo Studio
Tokyo, 1983–86
Design team: Hiroshi Aoki, Eisaku Ushida, Masato Hori
Consultants: Mamoru Kawaguchi & Engineers (structural); Yoshida Design Studio (mechanical)
Contractor: Tamasho Co., Ltd.

Kuroyanagi House
Tokyo, 1983–86
Design team: Takashi Ito
Consultants: Kimura Structural Engineers (structural); Takenaka Corporation (mechanical)
Contractor: Takenaka Corporation

Kitakyushu City Museum of Art Annex
Kitakyushu, Fukuoka, Japan, 1985–86
Client: City of Kitakyushu
Design team: Hiroshi Aoki, Yasuyori Yada, Kazutoshi Imanaga
Consultants: Kimura Structural Engineers (structural); Kankyo Engineering Inc. (mechanical and electrical)
Contractors: Simizu Corporation, Kawaguchi Construction Co., Ltd., and Fukushi-gumi Ltd.

Daniel Templon Foundation
Sophia-Antipolis International Park, Valbonne, France, 1986
Client: Daniel Templon Foundation
Design team: Guen Suzuki, Makoto Kikuchi, Jun Aoki
Consultants: G. X. Marguerita (associate architect); Kimura Structural Engineers (structural); Jules Fisher & Paul Marantz Inc., TL Yamagiwa Laboratory (lighting)

New Tokyo City Hall
(limited competition)
Shinjuku, Tokyo, 1985–86
Client: Tokyo Metropolitan Government
Design team: Hiroshi Aoki, Makoto Kikuchi, Shin Watanabe, Jun Aoki, Shuji Miura, Guen Suzuki, Kenji Sato, Yasuyori Yada, Kazutoshi Imanaga, Yusaku Imamura
Consultants: Kimura Structural Engineers (structural); Toshio Ojima, Kankyo Engineering Inc. (mechanical and electrical)

Museum für Völkerkunde
(competition)
Frankfurt, West Germany, 1986
Client: City of Frankfurt
Design team: Shogo Kishida, Makoto Takahashi, Hikaru Hane

Musashi-kyuryo Country Clubhouse
Saitama, Japan, 1986–87
Client: Musashino Kosei Bunka Jigyo-dan Co., Ltd.
Design team: Hiroshi Aoki, Kenji Sato, John O'Reilly
Consultants: Mamoru Kawaguchi & Engineers (structural); Kankyo Engineering Inc. (mechanical)
Contractor: Taisei Corporation

Ochanomizu Square Building
Tokyo, 1984–87
Client: Shufu-no-tomo Publishing Co., Ltd.
Design team: Makoto Kikuchi, Norimitsu Sukeshima, Hideki Yoshimatsu, Guen Suzuki, Shuji Miura
Consultants: Kimura Structural Engineers (structural); Kankyo Engineering Inc. (mechanical); Minoru Nagata Acoustic Engineer & Associates (acoustical)
Contractor: Obayashi Corporation

Library/Studio, Togamura
Toyama, Japan, 1984–87
Client: International Performing Arts Center
Design team: Kenji Sato
Consultants: So Architect Associates (associate architect); Kimura Structural Engineers (structural); Chubu Sekkei Co., Ltd. (mechanical and electrical)
Contractors: Fujii-gumi Construction Co., Ltd., and Takakuwa Construction Co., Ltd.

Paternoster Square Urban Design Project
(limited competition)
London, 1987
Client: The Paternoster Consortium Ltd.
Design team: Makoto Kikuchi, Yusaku Imamura, Sara Wong

Narimasu Church
Tokyo, 1985–88
Client: Narimasu Church
Design team: Shogo Kishida
Consultants: Hanawa Structural Engineers (structural); Kankyo Engineering Inc. (mechanical)
Contractor: Maeda Construction Co., Ltd.

Hara Museum ARC
Gunma, Japan, 1987–88
Client: Nihon Tochisanrin Co., Ltd.
Design team: Yasuyori Yada, Hiroshi Aoki, Fumio Matsumoto
Consultants: Mamoru Kawaguchi & Engineers (structural); Kankyo Engineering Inc. (mechanical)
Contractor: Inoue Kogyo Co., Ltd.

Anciens Abattoirs Redevelopment Project
(limited competition)
Strasbourg, France, 1988
Client: City of Strasbourg
Design team: Yusaku Imamura, Nazila Shabestari, Marcella Riva

Houtzagerij Sports Hall
The Hague, Netherlands, 1989
Client: Dienst der Gemeentewerken
Design team: John O'Reilly, Nazila Shabestari

Lake Sagami Country Clubhouse
Yamanashi, Japan, 1987–89
Client: Yamada Chiken Co., Ltd.
Design team: Hiroshi Aoki, Fumio Matsumoto, Yasuyori Yada
Consultants: Mamoru Kawaguchi & Engineers (structural); P. T. Morimura & Associates (mechanical and electrical); Brian Clark (stained-glass design)
Contractor: Taisei Corporation

The National Museum of Egyptian Civilization
(interior design and installation)
Cairo, 1985–89
Client: The Egyptian Antiquities Organization
Design team: Shuichi Fujie, Naoki Inagawa, Yusaku Imamura, Kazuyuki Iwanaga, Ko Ono
Consultants: Dr. El Ghazali M. Kesseiba D.P.L.G. & Associates (architect); Toyoguchi Design Associates; Norma Display Co., Ltd.; Tamayo Iemura, Yuzo Itagaki, Mutsuo Kawadoko, Jiro Kondo, Kazuaki Seki, Sahoko Tsuji, Kaoru Yoshinari (historians)

Bond University: Administration/Library/Humanities Building
Gold Coast, Queensland, Australia, 1987–89
Client: Bond University
Design team: Hiroshi Aoki, Kenji Sato, Sara Wong, Kazutoshi Imanaga
Consultants: The Heather Thiedeke Group, Pty. Ltd. (associate architect); McWilliam and Partners Pty. Ltd. (structural); Lincoln Scott Australia, Pty. Ltd. (mechanical, electrical, and elevators); Weathered Howe and Associates, Pty. Ltd. (hydraulic); Norman Desney and Young, Pty. Ltd. (communications); Rider Hunt Gold Coast, Pty. Ltd. (quality surveyor)
Contractor: Thiess Watkins White, Pty. Ltd.

Tokyo Christian College, Chapel
Chiba, Japan, 1988–89
Client: Tokyo Christian College
Design team: Hiroshi Aoki, Fumio Matsumoto, Hiroyuki Fukuyama
Consultants: Mamoru Kawaguchi & Engineers (structural); Kume Architects, Engineers (mechanical)
Contractor: Kajima Corporation

International Exhibits Aqua Hall, Expo '90
Osaka, Japan, 1988–89
Client: Japan Association for the International Garden and Greenery Exposition
Design team: Shuichi Fujie, Hiroshi Aoki, Norimitsu Sukeshima, Kazutoshi Imanaga, Akira Hikone
Consultants: JAS Associates (associate architect); Mamoru Kawaguchi & Engineers (structural); Kankyo Engineering Inc. (mechanical and electrical)
Contractors: Toda Corporation, Tokai Kogyo Co., Ltd., and Matsumura Gumi Corporation

International Friendship Pavilion, Expo '90
Osaka, Japan, 1988–90
Client: K. Matsushita Foundation of Expo '90
Organizer: Eiichi Asai, AAP Co., Ltd.
Design team: Hiroshi Aoki, Kazutoshi Imanaga, Hiroyuki Fukuyama, Akira Hikone
Consultants: Takenaka Corporation Building Design Department (associate architect); Mamoru Kawaguchi & Engineers (structural); Kankyo Engineering Inc. (mechanical); Minoru Nagata Acoustic Engineer & Associates (acoustical); Theater Design Workshop (theater design)
Contractors: Takenaka Corporation, Kajima Corporation, Asanuma-gumi Corporation, and Marumoto Construction Co., Ltd.

JR Yufuin Railway Station
Oita, Japan, 1989–90
Client: Kyushu Railway Company
Design team: Yasuyori Yada, Akira Hikone
Consultants: Mamoru Kawaguchi & Engineers (structural); Nippon Kankyo Giken Co., Ltd. (mechanical)
Contractor: Obayashi Corporation

Sant Jordi Sports Hall
Olympic Ring, Montjuic, Barcelona, Spain, 1983–90
Client: City of Barcelona, 1992 Olympics Office
Design team: Shuichi Fujie, Hiroshi Aoki, Naoki Inagawa, Shogo Kishida, Masato Hori, Kunio Uesugi, Fernando Alvarez, David Correa, Emil Paloma, Eva Serra, Rafael Villasente; Toshiaki Tange (coordinator)
Consultants: Juan Carlos Cardenal Gonzalez (associate architect); Julio Martinez Calzon, Mamoru Kawaguchi & Engineers (structural); Josep Maria Milian, Toshio Ojima (mechanical); Francisco Labastida (hydraulic); INYPESA (electrical); Alfredo Delgado (stage design); Shozo Murakami (acoustical); Takashi Kato (sports facility)
Contractors: Anell Olimpic de Montjuïc, S.A. (construction management); Drogados y Construcciones, S.A., and Orona Cooperativa, Ltd. (steel frame); Drogados y Construcciones, S.A., and COTEX, S.A. Cooperativa, Ltd. (roof finish); COMSA (concrete and finish); CAMUNSA (mechanical and electrical)

Kitakyushu International Conference Center
Kitakyushu, Fukuoka, Japan, 1987–90
Client: City of Kitakyushu
Design team: Shogo Kishida, Norimitsu Sukeshima, Atsushi Aiba, Marcella Riva, Michio Ohashi
Consultants: Mamoru Kawaguchi & Engineers (structural); Kankyo Engineering Inc. (mechanical); Minoru Nagata Acoustic Engineer & Associates (acoustical)
Contractors: Kajima Corporation, Okumura-gumi Corporation, and Daisho Co., Ltd.

Art Tower Mito
Mito, Ibaragi, Japan, 1986–90
Client: City of Mito
Design team: Jun Aoki, Toru Uno, Guen Suzuki, Akira Hikone, Shogo Kishida, Nazila Shabestari
Consultants: Seiichi Mikami & Associates (associate architect); Kimura Structural Engineers (structural); Kankyo Engineering Inc. (mechanical and electrical); Minoru Nagata Acoustic Engineer & Associates (acoustical)

The Disney Building
Lake Buena Vista, Florida, 1987–90
Client: Disney Development Company
Design team: Shin Watanabe, Makoto Kikuchi, Yasuyori Yada, Hisayoshi Ota, Lorissa Kim
Consultants: Hunton Brady Pryor Maso Architects, P.A. (associate architect); O. E. Olsen & Associates, Inc. (structural); Tilden Lobnitz Cooper Inc. (mechanical); Foster, Conant & Associates, Inc. (landscape architect); CRS Sirrine, Inc., Associated Space Design (interior)
Contractor: Holder Construction Company

Project for Site "K"
(limited competition)
San Sebastián, Spain, 1989–90
Design team: Naoki Inagawa, Masato Hori, Kenji Sato, Naoki Ogawa, Yasuyuki Watanabe; Toshiaki Tange (coordinator)
Consultants: Minoru Nagata Acoustic Engineer & Associates (acoustical)

Tokyo University of Art and Design
Hachioji, Tokyo, 1986–
Client: Kuwazawa Design School
Design team: Shuichi Fujie, Norimitsu Sukeshima, Kazutoshi Imanaga, Naoki Ogawa
Consultants: Mamoru Kawaguchi & Engineers (structural); Kankyo Engineering Inc. (mechanical)
Contractor: Obayashi Corporation

The Brooklyn Museum
Brooklyn, New York, 1986–
Client: The Brooklyn Museum
Design team: Shin Watanabe, David Gauld, John O'Reilly, Jun Aoki, Yusaku Imamura, Fumio Matsumoto
Consultants: James Stewart Polshek & Partners (co-architect); Robert Silman Associates (structural); Goldman, Copeland, Batlan & Oxman, P.C. (mechanical); Peter George Associates (acoustical); Jules Fisher & Paul Marantz Inc. (lighting)
Contractor: HRH Construction Corporation (construction management)

Palafolls Sports Pavilion
Palafolls, Spain, 1987–
Client: City of Palafolls
Design team: Shuichi Fujie, Masato Hori; Toshiaki Tange (coordinator)
Consultants: Julio Martinez Calzon (structural)

Marutan Building
Yokohama, Japan, 1988–
Client: Marutan Corporation
Design team: Hiroshi Aoki, Norimitsu Sukeshima, Shigeru Hirabayashi
Consultants: Hanawa Structural Engineers (structural); Kankyo Engineering Inc. (mechanical and electrical)
Contractor: Obayashi Corporation

JR Ueno Railway Station Redevelopment
Tokyo, 1988–
Client: East Japan Railway Company
Design team: Shuichi Fujie, Kenji Sato, Naoki Ogawa, Yasuyuki Watanabe, Joachim Frey, Andrea Held
Consultants: Kimura Structural Engineers (structural); Kankyo Engineering Inc. (mechanical); Akeno Sanitary Engineering Consultants, Inc. (fire regulations)

Tateyama Museum of Regional History, Tenji-kan Hall and Youho-kan Hall
Toyama, Japan, 1989–
Client: Toyama Prefectural Government

Design team: Yasuyori Yada, Akira Hikone
Consultants: So Architect Associates (associate architect); Mamoru Kawaguchi & Engineers (structural); Tyubu Sekkei Co., Ltd. (mechanical and electrical)
Contractors: Shinei-Kensetsu Co., Ltd., Yakuramaki-Kensetsu Co., Ltd., and Yonei-Kensetsu Co., Ltd.

Kashii Twin Towers
Fukuoka, Japan, 1989–
Client: Fukuoka Jisho Co., Ltd.
Design team: Shuichi Fujie, Norimitsu Sukeshima, Hiroyuki Fukuyama, Steve McConell, Brent Tokitsu, Kenji Sato
Consultants: Obayashi Corporation (associate architect, structural, and mechanical); Kimura Structural Engineers (structural); Kankyo Engineering Inc. (mechanical)
Contractor: Obayashi Corporation

NTV Plaza Project
Shinjuku, Tokyo, 1989–
Client: Nippon Television Network Corporation
Design team: Shuichi Fujie, Makoto Kikuchi, Hiroki Kitagawa, William S. Gordon, Jr.

The Washington International University in Virginia
Loudoun County, Virginia, 1989–
Client: The Washington International University in Virginia, Planning and Development Committee
Design team: Shin Watanabe, David Gauld, John O'Reilly
Consultants: Cooper, Robertson & Partners (co-architect); Office of Dan Kiley (landscape architect); Christopher Consultants, Ltd. (site engineer)

Musée d'Art Contemporain de la Ville de Fréjus
Parc Aurelien, Fréjus, France, 1989–
Client: City of Fréjus
Design team: Masakazu Bokura, Sergio Duran
Consultants: François Gauthier Architect (associate architect); F. Størksen (structural); Betibat (mechanical); Peter Rice (curtain wall); Jules Fisher & Paul Marantz Inc. (lighting)

The Izu Museum of Contemporary Art
Ito, Japan, 1990–
Client: E.I.E. International Corporation
Design team: Hiroshi Aoki, Yasuyori Yada
Consultants: Toshihiko Kimura (structural); Kajima Corporation (structural and mechanical); TL Yamagiwa Laboratory Inc. (lighting)
Contractor: Kajima Corporation

NHT Research and Development Center
Nishiharima Technopolis, Hyogo, Japan, 1990–
Client: Hyogo Prefectural Government
Design team: Shin Watanabe, Toru Uno, Yasuyuki Watanabe, Kim Boo-Woong
Consultants: JAS Associates (associate architect); Hanawa Structural Engineers (structural); Kankyo Engineering Inc. (mechanical); LPA (Kaoru Mende) (lighting)

Movie stage design for *The Other Man's Face,* 1965.

Installation of the Japanese section, Venice Biennale, 1976. With Kishin Shinoyama (The House).

"MA: Space/Time in Japan," 1978–81. Organized by the Festival d'Automne, Paris, and the Cooper-Hewitt Museum, New York. Traveled to locations in Europe and the U.S.

"Sofu Teshigawara: Calligraphies and Sculptures," 1981. Seibu Museum of Art, Tokyo.

"Highlights of the Egyptian Museum, Cairo," 1983. Seibu Museum of Art, Tokyo.

"Isamu Noguchi: Space of Akari and Stone," 1985. With Hiroshi Teshigawara (flower arrangement). Yuraku-cho Art Forum, Tokyo.

Stage design for *Bugaku-Hoe,* 1985. National Theater of Japan, Tokyo. With Aiko Miyawaki, Toshimitsu Imai, Kishin Shinoyama, and Kenny Scharf.

"Isamu Noguchi," American Pavilion, Venice Biennale, 1986.

"Gio Ponti, 1891–1979," 1986. Yuraku-cho Art Forum, Tokyo.

"Tokyo: Form and Spirit," 1986–87. With Eiko Ishioka (Performing Space) and Tadanori Yokoo (Walking Space). Organized by the Walker Art Center, Minneapolis, Minn. Traveled to locations in the U.S.

Stage design for *Madama Butterfly,* 1989. Auditorium Maurice Ravel, Lyons, France.

Stage design for *Tsuki-no-kokai, Hi-no-kokai,* 1989. National Theater of Japan, Tokyo.

"La Tour Eiffel: Un Message de 100 Ans (Architecture, Mode, Peinture)," 1989. Gunma Prefectural Museum of Fine Arts, Gunma, Japan.

Selected Exhibitions

1966   "Space and Color." Minami Gallery, Tokyo.

"From Space Toward Environment." Matsuya Gallery, Tokyo.

1968   "Electric Labyrinth," in 14th Milan Triennale.

1972   "Operations Vesuvius." Naples.

1975   "International Exhibition of Architecture Terra–1." The Polytechnic, Wroclaw, Poland.

1976   "Dortmunder Architekturausstellung." Museum am Ostwall, Dortmund, Germany.

"Arata Isozaki." Museum Sztuki, Lodz, Poland.

"Arata Isozaki Retrospective." Art Net Gallery, London.

1976–77   "Angel Cage" and "Gravity Room," in "MAN transFORMS." Cooper-Hewitt Museum, New York.

"Architecture of Quotation and Metaphor: Arata Isozaki Architectural Works 1960–76." Fukuoka Art Gallery, Fukuoka; Gatodo Gallery, Tokyo.

1977   "The Cubic Frame as a Metaphor for the Museum I & II," in 14th São Paulo Biennale.

1977–78   "Gendai to Koe." Traveled to galleries throughout Japan.

1977–80   "Numerals: Mathematical Concepts in Contemporary Art." Leo Castelli Gallery, New York; Yale University Art Gallery, New Haven, Conn.; Dartmouth College Gallery, Hanover, N.H.

1978   "Arata Isozaki." Graham Foundation for Advanced Studies in the Fine Arts, Chicago.

"MA: Space/Time in Japan." Organized by the Festival d'Automne, Paris, and the Cooper-Hewitt Museum, New York.

"A New Wave of Japanese Architecture." Organized by the Institute for Architecture and Urban Studies, New York. Traveled to locations in the U.S.

1979   "Visionary Drawings of Architecture and Planning." The Drawing Center, New York.

11th International Biennial Exhibition of Prints. National Museum of Modern Art, Tokyo.

"Arata Isozaki." Bijutsu-hakubutukan, University of Tokyo.

1980   "City Segments." Organized by the Walker Art Center, Minneapolis, Minn. Traveled to locations in the U.S.

"Façade," in "The Presence of the Past," Venice Biennale.

1980–81   "House of Nine Squares," in "Houses for Sale." Leo Castelli Gallery, New York; James Corcoran Gallery, Los Angeles.

"Architects Make Art." Rosa Esman Gallery, New York.

1981   "Arata Isozaki: Professional Work." Graduate School of Design, Harvard University, Cambridge, Mass.

"Concepts of the Individual House: Arata Isozaki and Others." Spaced Gallery of Architecture, New York.

"Furniture by Architects." Hayden Gallery, M.I.T., Cambridge, Mass.

"Hedendaagse Japanese Kunst." Galerie Nouvelles Images, The Hague, Netherlands.

1981–82   "Window Room Furniture." Cooper Union, New York.

1982   "La Modernité: Un Projet Inachevé." Festival d'Automne, Paris.

1983   "Ten New Buildings." Institute of Contemporary Arts, London.

"Arata Isozaki." Philippe Bonnafont Gallery, San Francisco.

"Drawings by Japanese Architects." Space Museum, Seoul.

"Arata Isozaki: Lead Reliefs, Drawings, and Silkscreen Prints." Rosa Esman Gallery, New York.

"Arata Isozaki: Print Works." GA Gallery, Tokyo.

"Thatched Hut Folly," in "Follies: Architecture for the Late-Twentieth-Century Landscape." Leo Castelli Gallery, New York; James Corcoran Gallery, Los Angeles.

"Drawings for the Museum of Contemporary Art, Los Angeles." Gatodo Gallery, Tokyo.

1985   "Le Affinità Elletive," Milan Triennale.

"Arata Isozaki." Williams Center for the Arts, Lafayette College, Easton, Penn.

"New Public Architecture: Recent Projects by Fumihiko Maki and Arata Isozaki." Organized by the Japan Society, New York. Traveled to locations in the U.S.

"Kagu: Mobilier Japonais." Musée d'Angers, Angers, France.

"The Contemporary Landscape: From the Horizon of Postmodern Design." National Museum of Modern Art, Tokyo.

1986   "Arata Isozaki: Tokyo City Hall Project." 9H Gallery, London.

1986–87   "Arata Isozaki: Drawings and Prints." Max Protetch Gallery, New York.

"Tokyo: Form and Spirit." Organized by the Walker Art Center, Minneapolis, Minn. Traveled to the Museum of Contemporary Art, Los Angeles; the IBM Gallery of Art and Science, New York; the San Francisco Museum of Modern Art.

"Japon des Avant-Gardes 1910–1970." Centre Georges Pompidou, Paris.

"Postmodern Visions: Contemporary Architecture 1960–1985." IBM Gallery of Science and Art, New York; National Museum of Modern Art, Tokyo.

1987   "Eccentric Places: The Architecture of Imagination." San Diego State University, San Diego, Calif.

Documenta 8. Kassel, Germany.

"Arata Isozaki: Ten Recent Projects." GA Gallery, Tokyo.

"Arata Isozaki: Lead Reliefs 1979–1987." Gallery Ueda, Tokyo.

1988   "5 + 5 Museos de Hoy." Palacio de Cristal, Madrid.

"Internationale Bauausstellung Berlin." Sogetsu Kaikan, Tokyo.

"Il Polo Espositivo: Un Tema, Due Architetti." Piazza SS. Annunziata, Florence.

"Arata Isozaki: Lead Reliefs, 1986–87." Kirsten Kiser Gallery, Los Angeles.

"Cleto Munari Collection" (installation). Yuraku-cho Art Forum, Tokyo.

1990   "Arata Isozaki's Sant Jordi Sports Hall." Colegio d'Arquitectos de Catalonya; Colegio Oficial d'Arquitectos de Baleares, Majorca.

Works by Arata Isozaki

Books

Kukan-e (Towards Space). Tokyo: Bijutsu Shuppansha, 1971.

Kenchiku no Kaitai (The Destruction of Modern Architecture). Tokyo: Bijutsu Shuppansha, 1975.

Kenchiku Oyobi Kenchikugai-teki Shiko (Dialogues with Architects and Others). Tokyo: Kajima Institute, 1976.

Kenchiku no 1930 Nendai (The Architecture of the 1930s). Tokyo: Kajima Institute, 1978.

Shuho-ga (Collected Writings, 1969–78). Tokyo: Bijutsu Shuppansha, 1979.

Kenchiku no Shuji (Notes on a Counter-Architecture). Tokyo: Bijutsu Shuppansha, 1979.

Kenchiku no Chiso (Critical Essays on Architects, Designers, and Others). Tokyo: Shokokusha, 1979.

Drawings for the Museum of Contemporary Art, 1981–83. Tokyo: Gatodo Gallery, 1983.

Postmodern Genron (The Principles of Postmodernism). Tokyo: Asahi Shuppansha, 1985.

Ima, Mienai Toshi (Now, the City Invisible). Tokyo: Daiwa Shobo, 1985.

Postmodern no Jidai to Kenchiku (The Postmodern Era and Architecture). Tokyo: Kajima Institute, 1985.

Kenchiku no Performance (Performance Architecture). Tokyo: Parco Shuppan, 1985.

Barcelona Drawings. Barcelona: Gustavo Gili, 1988.

Kenchiku no Seijigaku (The Politics of Architecture). Tokyo: Iwanami Shoten, 1989.

Mitate no Shuho (The Way of Mitate). Tokyo: Kajima Institute, 1990.

Image Game. Tokyo: Kajima Institute, 1990.

Architectural Pilgrimage Series, with Kishin Shinoyama. Tokyo: Rikuyosha. *The Temple of Amun at Karnak* (no. 1, 1980); *The Acropolis* (no. 2, 1985); *Villa Adriani* (no. 3, 1981); *Chiesa di S. Vitale* (no. 4, 1989); *Abbaye du Thoronet* (no. 5, 1980); *Chartres Cathedral* (no. 6, 1983); *Palazzo del Tè* (no. 8, 1980); *Les Salines Royales de Chaux* (no. 10, 1980); *Sir John Soane's Museum* (no. 11, 1990); *The Chrysler Building* (no. 12, 1984).

Essays and Articles

"Light, Color, and Shadow." *The Japan Architect* (May 1968).

"Frank Lloyd Wright's View of Space." In *GA 1: Frank Lloyd Wright: Johnson and Son Administration Building and Research Tower, Racine, Wisconsin. 1936–39,* Yukio Futagawa, editor and photographer. Tokyo: ADA Edita, 1970.

"Archigram as Counter-Culture." In *Archigram.* London: Studio Vista, 1972.

"About My Method." *The Japan Architect* (August 1972).

"Hashi." In *MAN TransFORMS* (catalogue). New York: Cooper-Hewitt Museum, 1976.

"General Remarks: Thoughts on the Wretched State of Japanese Architectural Education." *The Japan Architect* (February 1976).

"The Metaphor of the Cube." *The Japan Architect* (March 1976).

"Rhetoric of the Cylinder." *The Japan Architect* (April 1976).

"From Manner to Rhetoric to...." *The Japan Architect* (April 1976).

"Yano House." *GA Houses 1* (November 1976).

"Tokyo's Chikatetsu." In *Subways* (catalogue). New York: Cooper-Hewitt Museum, 1977.

"Nine Quotation Sources, Nine Metaphors." *The Japan Architect* (October/November 1977).

"City Demolition Industry, Inc." In *A New Wave of Japanese Architecture* (catalogue). New York: Institute for Architecture and Urban Studies, 1978.

"The Notion of Space/Time in Japan." In *MA: Space/Time in Japan* (catalogue). New York: Cooper-Hewitt Museum, 1978.

"A Metaphor Relating with Water." *The Japan Architect* (March 1978).

"On Formalism." *The Japan Architect* (January 1979).

"Ma: Japanese Space/Time." *The Japan Architect* (February 1979).

"Gunma Prefectural Museum of Fine Arts." In *City Segments* (catalogue). Minneapolis, Minn.: Walker Art Center, 1980.

"House of Nine Squares." In *Houses for Sale* (catalogue). New York: Rizzoli, 1980.

"Façade" and "X." In *The Presence of the Past* (catalogue). Venice: Venice Biennale, 1980.

"When the King Was Killed." *GA Document Special Issue 1* (August 1980).

"N.E.G. Employees' Service Facilities, Civic Center of Tsukuba Academic New Town." *GA Document 2* (Fall 1980).

"Metamorphose: L'Autre Visage de Hiroshi Teshigahara." In *Hiroshi Teshigahara* (catalogue). Paris: 1981.

Essay in *Furniture by Architects* (catalogue). Cambridge, Mass.: M.I.T. Press, 1981.

"A Rethinking of Spaces of Darkness." *The Japan Architect* (March 1981).

"The Ledoux Connection." *Architectural Design* (January–February 1982).

"Hauserman Showroom at the Merchandise Mart, Chicago." *GA Document 5* (August 1982).

"Une Brise Rafraîchissante dans l'Architecture Japonaise." In *Tadao Ando.* Paris: Electa Moniteur, 1982.

"Katsura Villa: The Ambiguity of Its Space." In *Katsura Villa.* New York: Rizzoli, 1983.

"Prints by Architect ?" In *The Prints of Arata Isozaki 1977–83.* Tokyo: Gendai Hanga Center, 1983.

"Tsukuba Center Building." In *Ten New Buildings* (catalogue). London: Institute for Contemporary Arts, 1983.

"Thatched Hut Folly." In *Follies: Architecture for the Late-Twentieth-Century Landscape* (catalogue). New York: Rizzoli, 1983.

"K House, H House, AO House, N House." *GA Houses 14* (July 1983).

"Tsukuba Center Building." *GA Document 8* (October 1983).

"Twenty-three Works by Isozaki, with Notes by the Architect." In *Arata Isozaki 1976–84.* Tokyo: Kajima Institute, 1984.

Foreword to *Andrea Branzi: The Hot House.* London: Thames & Hudson, 1984.

"Drawings in a Constant Style." In *Michael Graves* (catalogue). Tokyo: GA Gallery, 1984.

"Of City, Nation, and Style." *The Japan Architect* (January 1984).

"The Metaphor of the Train." *GA Document 11* (September 1984).

"Architecture With or Without Irony." In *New Public Architecture: Recent Projects by Fumihiko Maki and Arata Isozaki* (catalogue). New York: Japan Society, 1985.

"To Envision a Living Space." In *Isamu Noguchi: Space of Akari and Stone.* San Francisco: Chronicle Books, 1985.

298 "The Paradox of Tradition." In *Kagu: Mobilier Japonais* (catalogue). Angers, France: Musée d'Angers, 1985.

"The Architecture of an Open-Port Japan." Foreword to *Contemporary Japanese Architecture,* by Botond Bognar. New York: Van Nostrand Reinhold, 1985.

"Floor = Furniture." In *Le Affinità Elettive* (catalogue). Milan: Milan Triennale, 1985.

"Breaking Out of the System." *The Japan Architect* (April 1985).

"The Palladium: Immaterial Building." *Domus* (November 1985).

"Gio Ponti from Today's Perspective." In *Gio Ponti, 1891–1979. From the Human Scale to the Postmodern.* Tokyo: Kajima Institute, 1986.

"Taking Part in the Contest: On the Design of the New Tokyo City Hall." *The Japan Architect* (July 1986).

"Buildings of Promise: Seven Japanese Architects Worth Watching." *House & Garden* (January 1987).

"A Chain of Subtle Changes (MOCA)." *The Japan Architect* (February 1987).

"Musashi-kyuryo Country Clubhouse." *GA Document 18* (April 1987).

"For the Barcelona Olympics." *L'Arca* (November 1987).

"The Current State of Design." In *International Design Yearbook 4.* New York: Abbeville, 1988.

"Ruins." In *Ryuji Miyamoto: Architectural Apocalypse.* Tokyo: Heibon-sha, 1988.

"An Architecture of Quotation and Metaphor." In *Il Polo Espositivo: Un Tema, Due Architetti* (catalogue). Florence: Electa Firenze, 1988.

"A Shakespearean Scholar Talks with the Architect of the Tokyo Globe: Minoru Fujita and Arata Isozaki." *The Globe* (April 1988).

"Hara Museum ARC." *GA Document 22* (June 1988).

"Björnson Studio." *GA Houses 24* (October 1988).

"Renzo Piano's ARCHI-TECTURE." In *Renzo Piano* (catalogue). Tokyo: Sunshine City Bunkukaikan, 1989.

"The Hans Hollein Question." In *Hans Hollein* (catalogue). Tokyo: Yuraku-cho Art Forum, 1989.

"Kitakyushu International Conference Center." *GA Document 23* (April 1989).

"To Ettore." In *Ettore Sottsass Advanced Studies 1986–90.* Tokyo: Yamagiwa Art Foundation, 1990.

"Daniel Buren: The Logic of Intervention." In *L'Art et la Ville, Art and the City.* Geneva: Skira, 1990.

"Stained Glass: Work of Art." In *Brian Clark: Into and Out of Architecture* (catalogue). London: Mayor Gallery, 1990.

"Sir John Soane's Museum: A Conversation Piece Without a Family." *Apollo* (April 1990).

Films
MA: Space/Time in the Garden of Ryoanji (with Taka Iimura). New York: Metropolitan Museum of Art, 1989.

Works on Arata Isozaki

Articles

Alhadeff, Gini. "The Palladium: Immaterial Building." *Domus* (November 1985).

Byron, Elizabeth S. "On the Björnson Studio." *House & Garden* (April 1988).

Castello, Aldo. "Il MOCA di Los Angeles." *L'Arca* (December 1986).

Chaitkin, Bill. "Zen and the Art of Arata Isozaki." *Architectural Design* (January 1977).

Cook, Peter. "Notes on Arata Isozaki." *A + U* (January 1972).

———. "On Arata Isozaki." *Architectural Design* (January 1977).

Davis, Douglas. "On Ochanomizu Square." *A + U* (January 1988).

Edelmann, Frederic. "Les Inventions Ludique d'Arata Isozaki." *Beaux Arts* (January 1989).

Estramps, Jean–Pierre. "Arata Isozaki." *Galerie* (October–November 1986).

Failing, Patricia. "MOCA." *Artnews* (October 1983).

Filler, Martin. "Eight Houses in Search of Their Owners." *House & Garden* (December 1980).

———. "Iso-morphisms." *Art in America* (February 1981).

———. "The Art of Isozaki." *House & Garden* (October 1983).

———. "The Recent Work of Arata Isozaki" (Parts 1 and 2). *Architectural Record* (October 1983 and May 1984).

———. "Evening Star." *House & Garden* (October 1985).

———. "Back on Track, Metaphorically Speaking." *Architectural Record* (May 1986).

———. "L.A. Elevation: Isozaki's Museum of Contemporary Art." *House & Garden* (January 1987).

Flacke, Christopher. "Isozaki's MOCA." *The New Criterion* (April 1987).

Fleming, Charles. "Isozaki." *California Magazine* (March 1986).

Frampton, Kenneth. "Modernism's Diffusion: Japan Diary" (Parts 1 and 2). *Skyline* (April and May 1982).

———. "Arata Isozaki's MOCA." *Domus* (November 1986).

Gandee, Charles K. "Heaven's Gate." *Architectural Record* (September 1985).

300

Giovannini, Joseph. "On Architecture: Museum Piece." *Artforum* (February 1987).

Goldberger, Paul. "Arata Isozaki." *Architectural Digest* (March 1989).

———. "Notes on the Work of Arata Isozaki." In *Arata Isozaki.* Tokyo: GA Gallery, 1983.

Herron, Ron. "Japan's Arata Isozaki." *Lotus 6* (1969).

Hollein, Hans. "Position and Move." *Space Design* (April 1974).

Huxtable, Ada Louise. "The Japanese New Wave." *The New York Times Magazine* (January 14, 1979).

Ishii, Kazuhiro. "A Guide to the World of Arata Isozaki." *Space Design* (April 1976).

———, and Hiroyuki Suzuki. "Post-Metabolism." *The Japan Architect* (October–November 1977).

Jencks, Charles. "Isozaki's Paradoxical Cube." *The Japan Architect* (March 1976).

———. "Arata Isozaki and Radical Eclecticism." *Architectural Design* (January 1977).

———, ed. "Post-Modern Classicism." *Architectural Design* (May–June 1980).

———. "The Presence of the Past." *Domus* (October 1980).

———, ed. "Free-Style Classicism." (AD Profiles) *Architectural Design* (January–February 1982).

———. "Phoenix Style and Free-Style Classicism." *Architectural Design* (September–October 1987).

Kaufman, Ann. "Comment on the Palladium." *The Japan Architect* (November–December 1985).

Koplos, Janet. "Two Giants of Japanese Architecture: Kenzo Tange and Arata Isozaki." *The World and I* (July 1987).

Miller, Nory. "Humanity and Architecture." *The Japan Architect* (October 1973).

———, and Heather Cass. "Arata Isozaki: Exploring Form and Experience." *The American Institute of Architects Journal* (November 1979).

Miyagawa, Atsushi. "In the Blank of the Theory of Maniera." *The Japan Architect* (March 1976).

Muschamp, Herbert. "The Museum of Contemporary Art: What's in a Name?" *Architectural Record* (May 1987).

Natalini, Adolfo. "Ready-Made Architecture." *Domus* (May 1980).

———. "The Metamorphosis of Isozaki." *Domus* (April 1984).

Nisewand, Nonier. "Genius or Sheer Folly?" *Vogue* (September 1990).

Otsuka, Takashi. "The Arts of MA." *Skyline* (May 1979).

Parent, Claude, Edith Giraud, Pierre Lajus, Fernando Montes, Philippe Robert, and Claude Vassari. *Crée* (Special Issue on Isozaki; October–November 1983).

Pastier, John. "L.A. Art: Dissimilar Duo." *Architecture* (February 1987).

Patton, Phil. "Japan's Best Architect Gives Los Angeles a New Museum." *Connoisseur* (November 1986).

Pawley, Martin. "Report on Osaka." *Architectural Design* (January 1970).

Pommer, Richard. "The New Architectural Supremacists." *Artforum* (October 1976).

Roe, Constance. "Cultural Infusions." *Designers West* (November 1983).

Ross, Michael Franklin. "Arata Isozaki." *L.A. Architect* (April 1981).

Smetana, Donatella. "A Poetics of Ambiguity." *Casa Vogue* (January 1985).

Stephens, Suzanne. "Iso's Club Act." *Vanity Fair* (June 1985).

Stewart, David B. "Through the Looking Glass." *Domus* (June 1981).

Sudjic, Deyan. "Tokyo's Lost City Hall." *Blueprint* (June 1986).

Taki, Koji. "World in a Mirror" (Parts 1 and 2). *The Japan Architect* (March and April 1976).

Taylor, Jennifer. "The Unreal Architecture of Arata Isozaki." *Progressive Architecture* (September 1976).

———. "A Visitation from Arata Isozaki." *Architecture Australia* (September 1977).

Tono, Yoshiaki. "Architecture for the Miniskirt Age." *The Japan Architect* (May 1968).

Treib, Marc. "Fragments on a Void: Tsukuba Center." *Landscape Architecture* (July–August 1985).

Viladas, Pilar. "On MOCA." *Progressive Architecture* (November 1986).

Watanabe, Hiroshi. "From Utopia to the Corner Drugstore: Japanese Architects." *Artnews* (February 1982).

———. "Friendly, Playful Art Museum." *Architecture* (September 1986).

Wild, David. "Sour Grapes." *Architectural Design* (January 1977).

Woodbridge, Sally. "Isozaki Originals." *Progressive Architecture* (June 1983).

Wundram, Edward C., and Gerald R. Plock. "The Phoenix Competition." *Architectural Design* (September–October 1987).

Yatsuka, Hajime. "Architecture in the Urban Desert." *Oppositions* 23 (Winter 1981).

———. "Architecture in the Creative Labyrinth: Arata Isozaki 1962–83." In *The Prints of Arata Isozaki 1977–83*. Tokyo: Gendai Hanga Center, 1983.

Books
Banham, Reyner. *Megastructure: Urban Futures of the Recent Past*. New York: Harper & Row, 1976.

Bohigas, Oriol, and Xavier Güell. *Barcelona Drawings*. Barcelona: Gustavo Gili, 1988.

Boyd, Robin. *New Directions in Japanese Architecture*. New York: George Braziller, 1962.

Benevolo, Leonardo. *History of Modern Architecture, Volume 2: The Modern Movement*. Cambridge, Mass.: M.I.T. Press, 1971.

Bognar, Botond. *Contemporary Japanese Architecture*. New York: Van Nostrand Reinhold, 1985.

Borras, Maria Lluisa. *Arquitectura Contemporanea Japonesa*. New York: Tudor Publishing, 1971.

Brawne, Michael. *Libraries: Architecture and Equipment*. New York: Praeger, 1970.

Capella, Juli, and Quim Larrea. *Diseo de Arquitectos en los 80*. Barcelona: Gustavo Gili, 1987.

Darragh, Joan, ed. *A New Brooklyn Museum: The Master Plan Competition*. New York: Rizzoli, 1988.

Di Russo, Bianca, and Brunilde Barattucci. *Arata Isozaki Architecture 1959–1982*. Rome: Officina Edizioni, 1983.

Drew, Philip. *The Architecture of Arata Isozaki*. New York: Harper & Row, 1982.

———. *Third Generation: The Changing Meaning of Architecture*. London: Pall Mall Press, 1962.

Hiroyuki, Suzuki, David B. Stewart, and Hajime Yatsuka. *Arata Isozaki 1976–84*. Tokyo: Kajima Institute, 1984.

Hollingsworth, Mary. *Architecture of the Twentieth Century*. London: Bison Books, 1988.

Jencks, Charles. *The Language of Post-Modern Architecture*. New York: Rizzoli, 1977.

———. *Late Modern Architecture*. London: Academy Editions, 1980.

———. *The Modern Movement in Architecture*. New York: Penguin Books, 1968.

———. *Post-Modernism: The New Classicism in Art and Architecture*. New York: Rizzoli, 1987.

Joedicke, Jurge. *Architecture Since 1945*. New York: Praeger, 1969.

Kawazoe, Noboru. *Contemporary Japanese Architecture*. Tokyo: Kokusai Bunka Shinkokai, 1968.

Kraft, Anthony, ed. *Architecture Contemporaine, Vol. 9*. Paris and Lausanne: Bibliothèque des Arts, 1987.

Kultermann, Udo. *The New Japanese Architecture*. London: Thames & Hudson, 1963.

Matsuoka, Seigow, and Hajime Yatsuka. *The Prints of Arata Isozaki 1977–83*. Tokyo: Gendai Hanga Center, 1983.

Miyoshi, Masao, and H. D. Harootunian, eds. *Postmodernism and Japan*. Durham, N.C.: Duke University Press, 1989.

Radice, Barbara. *Gioielli di Architetti*. Milan: Edizioni Electa, 1987.

———. *Memphis*. Milan: Edizioni Electa, 1984.

Ross, Michael Franklin. *Beyond Metabolism: The New Japanese Architecture*. New York: Architectural Record Books, 1978.

Salat, Serge, and Françoise Labbe. *Créateurs du Japon*. Paris: Hermann, 1986.

Stewart, David B. *The Making of a Modern Japanese Architecture: 1868 to the Present*. Tokyo and New York: Kodansha, 1987.

Tempel, Egon. *New Japanese Architecture*. New York: Praeger, 1969.

Films
Arata Isozaki. New York: Michael Blackwood Productions, 1985.

Japan: Three Generations of Avant-Garde Architects. New York: Michael Blackwood Productions, 1988.

Arata Isozaki

Biography

1931   Born in Oita City, Kyushu

1954   Received Bachelor of Architecture, University of Tokyo

1954–63 Member of Kenzo Tange's Team and URTEC

1963   Established Arata Isozaki Atelier (now Arata Isozaki & Associates) in Tokyo

Professional Affiliations and Awards

1967   Annual Prize, Architectural Institute of Japan (Oita Prefectural Library)

1968   Annual Prize, Architectural Year Book (Oita Prefectural Library)

1969   Artist's Newcomer Prize, Ministry of Culture (Oita Branch, Fukuoka City Bank)

1970   Special Prize of Expo '70, Architectural Institute of Japan (mechanics and electronics of Festival Plaza)

1975   Annual Prize, Architectural Institute of Japan (Gunma Prefectural Museum of Fine Arts)

      Annual Prize, Building Contractors Society (Kitakyushu Central Library)

1978   Honorary Fellow of Accademia Tiberina, Rome

1979–84 Juror, Pritzker Architecture Prize

1982   Juror, international competition for Parc de la Villette, Paris

1983   Interiors Magazine Award (Hauserman Showroom)

      Mainichi Art Award (Tsukuba Center Building)

      Honorary Fellow of the American Institute of Architects

      Honorary Member of the Bund Deutscher Architekten

      Juror, international competition for The Peak, Hong Kong

1984   Chevalier de l'Ordre des Arts et des Lettres, French Ministry of Culture

1985   Juror, R.S. Reynolds Memorial Award

1986   Gold Medal, Royal Institute of British Architects

      Juror, international competition for Information City proposal

      Juror, competition for Hawaii Loa College Media Arts Center

      Juror, competition for New National Theater of Japan (Ministry of Construction)

1988   Asahi Award, Asahi Shimbun

      Arnold W. Brunner Memorial Prize, American Academy and Institute of Arts and Letters

      Chairman of the Jury, competition for Sakamoto Ryoma Memorial Hall conceptual design

      Juror, competition for Passenger Terminal Building, Kansai International Airport

1988–89 Juror, "Triangle de la Folie" competition Saga-Défense, Paris

1988–90 General producer, International Garden and Greenery Exposition, Osaka, 1990

1988–   Commissioner, Kumamoto Artpolis Project

      Member of the Building Council, Japan

1990   Chicago Architecture Award

1990–   Juror, international competition for Expo '95, Vienna

Visiting Professor

Columbia University, New York
Harvard University, Cambridge, Mass.
Rhode Island School of Design, Providence, R.I.
University of California, Los Angeles
University of Hawaii, Honolulu
Yale University, New Haven, Conn.

Visiting Critic and Lecturer

The Architectural Association, London
The Architectural League, New York
Arte-Tekta, Frankfurt
Cambridge University, Cambridge, England
Carleton College, Northfield, Minn.
Centre Georges Pompidou, Paris
Hochschule für Angewandte Kunst, Vienna
Institute for Architecture and Urban Studies, New York
Istituto Universitario di Architettura di Venezia, Venice
Japan Society, New York
Kulturhuset, Stockholm
McGill University, Montreal
Pratt Institute, New York
San Francisco Museum of Modern Art
Technische Hochschule, Aachen, Germany
Tulane University, New Orleans, La.
University of Adelaide, Australia
University of Houston, Texas
University of Pennsylvania, Philadelphia
University of Sydney, Australia
University of Tokyo
University of Toronto
Werkbund, Darmstadt, Germany

Photograph Credits

304 Cooper-Hewitt Museum: 281, 284(1), 285

Katsuaki Furudate: 22(left), 136(3), 137(4), 139–41, 195

Yukio Futagawa: 115–17, 279(4)

Yasuhiro Ishimoto: 19, 20, 22(right), 23(right), 37, 40–42, 45–51, 57, 60–63, 65, 68–71, 74, 75, 77, 80–87, 89, 92, 93, 95–97, 105, 108, 109, 112, 113, 119–21, 152–53, 156, 157, 160–63, 164(1), 165, 168–71, 192–94, 205, 210–12, 217, 219, 225, 228–31, 233, 239–45, 248–49

The Japan Architect: 27, 30, 31, 43, 99, 102–3, 122(3), 123, 125–27

Osamu Murai: 36(1)

Tomio Ohashi: 72, 73, 129–31, 134(3), 135(4), 208–9, 213

Seiji Otsuji: 42

Shokoku-sha: 52, 53, 143

Hisao Suzuki: 215

Yoshio Takase: 21, 23(left), 34(1), 175, 178, 179, 198, 199(5), 203, 216(1), 221, 250(1), 251, 253, 259, 269, 273, 274(1), 275, 276(1), 277(4)

Shuji Yamada: 133, 282(1), 283

Tadahisa Yoshikawa: 302

Model Credits

Shoji Ishiguro: 34(1), 175, 178, 179, 203, 269

Arata Isozaki & Associates: 36(1), 42, 52, 53, 143, 215, 259, 275, 276(1), 277(4)

Inoue Kogyo Co., Ltd.: 216(1)

Watanabe Modeling: 250(1), 251